LIVING LANGUAGE®

COMPLETE
GERMAN
THE BASICS

Written by
Helga Schier

Edited by
Suzanne McQuade

Copyright © 2008 by Living Language, an imprint of Random House, Inc.

Living Language is a member of the Random House Information Group

Living Language and colophon are registered trademarks of Random House, Inc.

Published in the United States by Living Language, an imprint of Random House, Inc.

www.livinglanguage.com

Editor: Suzanne McQuade
Production Editor: Carolyn Roth
Production Manager: Tom Marshall
Interior Design: Sophie Chin

First Edition

ISBN: 978-1-4000-2411-7

Library of Congress Cataloging-in-Publication Data available upon request.

This book is available at special discounts for bulk purchases for sales promotions or
premiums. Special editions, including personalized covers, excerpts of existing books,
and corporate imprints, can be created in large quantities for special needs. For more
information, write to Special Markets/Premium Sales, 1745 Broadway, MD 6-2, New York,
New York 10019 or e-mail specialmarkets@randomhouse.com.

PRINTED IN THE UNITED STATES OF AMERICA

10 9 8 7 6 5 4 3 2 1

ACKNOWLEDGMENTS

Thanks to the Living Language team: Tom Russell, Nicole Benhabib, Christopher Warnasch, Zviezdana Verzich, Suzanne McQuade, Shaina Malkin, Elham Shabahat, Sophie Chin, Denise De Gennaro, Linda Schmidt, Alison Skrabek, Lisbeth Dyer, and Tom Marshall. Special thanks to Rita Wuebbeler.

DEDICATION

I wish to thank my editor, Suzanne McQuade, who kept me on my toes; my children, Gabriel and Sebastian, who quietly walked on theirs outside my office; and my husband, whose steady stride helped move us all along.

COURSE OUTLINE

Welcome to *Living Language Complete German: The Basics!* We know you're ready to jump right in and start learning German, but before you do, you may want to spend some time familiarizing yourself with the structure of this course. It will make it easier for you to find your way around and will really help you get the most out of your studies.

UNITS AND LESSONS

Living Language Complete German: The Basics includes ten *Units*, each of which focuses on a certain practical topic, from talking about yourself and making introductions to asking directions and going shopping. Each unit is divided into *Lessons* that follow four simple steps:

1. *Words*, featuring the essential vocabulary you need to talk about the topic of the unit;

2. *Phrases*, bringing words together into more complex structures and introducing a few idiomatic expressions;

3. *Sentences*, expanding on the vocabulary and phrases from previous lessons, using the grammar you've learned to form complete sentences; and,

4. *Conversations*, highlighting how everything works together in realistic conversational dialogues that bring all of the lessons in the unit together.

The lessons each comprise the following sections:

WORD LIST/PHRASE LIST/SENTENCE LIST/CONVERSATION
Every lesson begins with a list of words, phrases, or sentences, or a dialogue. The grammar and exercises will be based on these components, so it's important to spend as much time reading and rereading them as possible before getting into the heart of the lesson.

NOTES

A brief section may appear after the list or dialogue to highlight any points of interest in the language or culture.

NUTS & BOLTS

This is the nitty-gritty of each lesson, where you'll learn the grammar of the language, the nuts and bolts that hold the pieces together. Pay close attention to these sections; this is where you'll get the most out of the language and learn what you need to know to become truly proficient in German.

PRACTICE

It's important to practice what you've learned on a regular basis. You'll find practice sections throughout each lesson; take your time to complete these exercises before moving on to the next section. How well you do on each practice will determine whether or not you need to review a particular grammar point before you move on.

TIP!

In order to enhance your experience, you'll find several tips for learning German throughout the course. This could be a tip on a specific grammar point, additional vocabulary related to the lesson topic, or a tip on language learning in general. For more practical advice, you can also refer to the *Language learning tips* section that follows this introduction.

CULTURE NOTES AND LANGUAGE LINKS

Becoming familiar with the culture of German-speaking countries is nearly as essential to language learning as grammar. These sections allow you to get to know these cultures better through facts about German-speaking countries and other bits of cultural information. You'll also find the links to various websites you can visit on the internet to learn more about a particular country or custom or to find a language learning tool that may come in handy.

DISCOVERY ACTIVITY

Discovery activities are another chance for you to put your new language to use. They will often require you to go out into the world and interact with other German speakers, or simply to use the resources around your own home to practice your German.

UNIT ESSENTIALS

Finally, each unit ends with a review of the most essential vocabulary and phrases. Make sure you're familiar with these phrases, as well as their structure, before moving on to the next unit.

FURTHER REFERENCE

The coursebook also includes additional reference material to help you enhance your German studies. *German in action* offers more examples of German in everyday use, from resumes to recipes, using the vocabulary and grammar from all ten units. *Supplemental vocabulary* lists essential vocabulary by category, while the *Summary of German grammar* can be used for thorough review of key grammar points. Finally, the book contains a list of *Internet resources* where you can seek out more exposure to the language and information on German-speaking countries.

LEARNER'S DICTIONARY

If you've purchased this book as a part of the complete audio package, you also received a Learner's Dictionary with more than 15,000 of the most frequently used German words, phrases, and idiomatic expressions. Use it as a reference any time you're at a loss for words in the exercises and discovery activities, or as a supplemental study aid. This dictionary is ideal for beginner- or intermediate-level learners of German.

AUDIO

This course works best when used along with the four audio CDs included in the complete course package. These CDs feature all the word lists, phrase lists, sentence lists, and conversations from each unit, as well as key examples from the *Nuts & bolts* sections.

This audio can be used along with the book, or on the go for hands-free practice.

And it's as easy as that! To get even more out of *Living Language Complete German: The Basics,* you may want to read the *Language learning tips* section that follows this introduction. If you're confident that you know all you need to know to get started and would prefer to head straight for Unit 1, you can always come back to this section for tips on getting more out of your learning experience.

Good luck!

If you're not sure about the best way to learn a new language, take a moment to read this section. It includes lots of helpful tips and practical advice on studying languages in general, improving vocabulary, mastering grammar, using audio, doing exercises, and expanding your learning experience. All of this will make learning more effective and more fun.

GENERAL TIPS

Let's start with some general points to keep in mind when learning a new language.

1. FIND YOUR PACE

The most important thing to keep in mind is that you should always proceed at your own pace. Don't feel pressured into thinking that you only have one chance to digest information before moving on to new material. Read and listen to parts of lessons or entire lessons as many times as it takes to make you feel comfortable with the material. Regular repetition is the key to learning any new language, so don't be afraid to cover material again, and again, and again!

2. TAKE NOTES

Use a notebook or start a language journal so you can have something to take with you. Each lesson contains material that you'll learn much more quickly and effectively if you write it down or rephrase it in your own words once you've understood it. That includes vocabulary, grammar points and examples, expressions from conversations, and anything else that you find noteworthy. Take your notes with you to review wherever you have time to kill—on the bus or train, waiting at the airport, while dinner is cooking, or whenever you can find the time. Remember—practice (and lots of review!) makes perfect when it comes to learning languages.

3. Make a regular commitment

Make time for your new language. The concept of "hours of exposure" is key to learning a language. When you expose yourself to a new language frequently, you'll pick it up more easily. On the other hand, the longer the intervals between your exposure to a language, the more you'll forget. It's best to set time aside regularly for yourself. Imagine that you're enrolled in a class that takes place at certain regular times during the week, and set that time aside. Or use your lunch break. It's better to spend less time several days a week than a large chunk of time once or twice a week. In other words, spending thirty or forty minutes on Monday, Tuesday, Wednesday, Friday, and Sunday will be better than spending two and a half or three hours just on Saturday.

4. Don't have unrealistic expectations

Don't expect to start speaking a new language as if it were your native language. It's certainly possible for adults to learn new languages with amazing fluency, but that's not a realistic immediate goal for most people. Instead, make a commitment to become "functional" in a new language, and start to set small goals: getting by in most daily activities, talking about yourself and asking about others, following TV and movies, reading a newspaper, expressing your ideas in basic language, and learning creative strategies for getting the most out of the language you know. Functional doesn't mean perfectly native fluent, but it's a great accomplishment!

5. Don't get hung up on pronunciation

"Losing the accent" is one of the most challenging parts of learning a language. If you think about celebrities, scientists, or political figures whose native language isn't English, they probably have a pretty recognizable accent. But that hasn't kept them from becoming celebrities, scientists, or political figures. Really young children are able to learn the sounds of any language in the world, and they can reproduce them perfectly. That's part of the process of learning a native language. In an adult, or even in an older child, this ability has diminished, so if you agonize over sounding like a native speaker in your new language, you're just setting yourself up for disappointment. That's not to say that you can't learn pronunciation well. Even adults can get pretty far through mimicking the sounds that they hear. So listen carefully to the audio several times. Listening is a very important part of this process: you can't reproduce a sound until you learn to distinguish the sound. Then mimic what you hear. Don't be afraid of sounding strange. Just keep at it, and soon enough you'll develop good pronunciation. .

6. Don't be shy
Learning a new language inevitably involves speaking out loud, and it involves making mistakes before you get better. Don't be afraid of sounding strange, or awkward, or silly. You won't: you'll impress people with your attempts. The more you speak, and the more you interact, the faster you'll learn to correct the mistakes you do make.

TIPS ON LEARNING VOCABULARY
You obviously need to learn new words in order to speak a new language. Even though that may seem straightforward compared with learning how to actually put those words together in sentences, it's really not as simple as it appears. Memorizing words is difficult, even just in the short term. But long-term memorization takes a lot of practice and repetition. You won't learn vocabulary simply by reading through the vocabulary lists once or twice. You need to practice.

There are a few different ways to lodge a word in your memory, and some methods may work better for you than others. The best thing to do is to try a few different methods until you feel that one is right for you. Here are a few suggestions and pointers:

1. Audio repetition
Fix your eye on the written form of a word, and listen to the audio several times. Remind yourself of the English translation as you do this.

2. Spoken repetition

Say a word several times aloud, keeping your eye on the written word as you hear yourself speak it. It's not a race—don't rush to blurt out the word over and over again so fast that you're distorting its pronunciation. Just repeat it, slowly and naturally, being careful to pronounce it as well as you can. And run your eye over the shape of the word each time you say it. You'll be stimulating two of your senses at once that way—hearing and sight—so you'll double the impact on your memory.

3. Written repetition

Write a word over and over again across a page, speaking it slowly and carefully each time you write it. Don't be afraid to fill up entire sheets of paper with your new vocabulary words.

4. Flash cards

They may seem elementary, but they're effective. Cut out small pieces of paper (no need to spend a lot of money on index cards) and write the English word on one side and the new word on the other. Just this act alone will put a few words in your mind. Then read through your "deck" of cards. First go from the target (new) language into English—that's easier. Turn the target-language side face-up, read each card, and guess at its meaning. Once you've guessed, turn the card over to see if you're right. If you are, set the card aside in your "learned" pile. If you're wrong, repeat the word and its meaning, and then put it at the bottom of your "to learn" pile. Continue through until you've moved all of the cards into your "learned" pile.

Once you've completed the whole deck from your target language into English, turn the deck over and try to go from English into your target language. You'll see that this is harder, but also a better test of whether or not you've really mastered a word.

5. Mnemonics

A mnemonic is a device or a trick to trigger your memory, like "King Phillip Came Over From Great Spain," which you may have learned in high school biology to remember that species are classified into kingdom, phylum, class, order, family, genus, and species. Mnemonics work well for vocabulary, too. When you hear and read a new word, look to see if it sounds like anything— a place, a name, a nonsense phrase. Then form an image of that place or person or even nonsense scenario in your head. Imagine it as you say and read the new word. Remember that the more sense triggers you have—hearing, reading, writing, speaking, imagining a crazy image—the better you'll remember.

6. GROUPS

Vocabulary should be learned in small and logically connected groups whenever possible. Most of the vocabulary lists in this course are already organized this way. Don't try to tackle a whole list at once. Choose your method—repeating a word out loud, writing it across a page, etc.—and practice with a small group.

7. PRACTICE

Don't just learn a word out of context and leave it hanging there. Go back and practice it in the context provided in this course. If the word appears in a dialogue, read it in the full sentence and call to mind an image of that sentence. If possible, substitute other vocabulary words into the same sentence structure ("John goes to the *library*" instead of "John goes to the *store*"). As you advance through the course, try writing your own simple examples of words in context.

8. COME BACK TO IT

This is the key to learning vocabulary—not just holding it temporarily in your short-term memory, but making it stick in your long-term memory. Go back over old lists, old decks of flashcards you made, or old example sentences. Listen to vocabulary audio from previous lessons. Pull up crazy mnemonic devices you created at some point earlier in your studies. And always be on the lookout for old words appearing again throughout the course.

TIPS ON USING AUDIO

The audio in this course not only lets you hear how native speakers pronounce the words you're learning, but it also serves as a second kind of input to your learning experience. The printed words serve as visual input, and the audio serves as *auditory* input. There are a few different strategies that you can use to get the most out of the audio. First, use the audio while you're looking at a word or sentence. Listen to it a few times along with the visual input of seeing the material. Then, look away and just listen to the audio on its own. You can also use the audio from previously studied lessons as a way to review. Put the audio on your computer or an MP3 player and take it along with you in your car, on the train, while you walk, while you jog, or anywhere you spend your free time. Remember that the more exposure you have to and contact you have with your target language, the better you'll learn.

TIPS ON USING CONVERSATIONS

Conversations are a great way to see language in action—as it's really used by people in realistic situations. To get the most out of each of the conversations in this book as a language student, think of it as a cycle rather than a linear passage. First, read through the conversation once in the target language to get the gist. Don't agonize over the details just yet. Then, go back and read through a second time, but focus on individual sentences. Look for new words or new constructions. Challenge yourself to figure out what they mean from the context of the conversation. After all, that's something you'll be doing a lot of in the real world, so it's a good skill to develop! Once you've worked out the details, read the dialogue again from start to finish. Now that you're very familiar with the conversation, turn on the audio and listen to it as you read. Don't try to repeat yet; just listen and read along. This will build your listening comprehension. Then, go back and listen again, but this time, pause to repeat the phrases or sentences that you're hearing and reading. This will build your spoken proficiency and pronunciation. Now listen again without the aid of the printed dialogue. By now you'll know many of the lines inside out, and any new vocabulary or constructions will be very familiar.

TIPS ON DOING EXERCISES

The exercises are meant to give you a chance to practice the vocabulary and structures that you learn in each lesson, and, of course, to test yourself on retention. Take the time to write out the entire sentences to get the most out of the practice. Don't limit yourself to just reading and writing. Read the sentences and answers aloud, so you'll also be practicing pronunciation and spoken proficiency. As you gain more confidence, try to adapt the practice sentences by substituting different vocabulary or grammatical constructions. Be creative and push the practices as far as you can to get the most out of them.

TIPS ON LEARNING GRAMMAR

Each grammar point is designed to be as small and digestible as possible, while at the same time comprehensive enough to teach you what you need to know. The explanations are intended to be simple and straightforward, but one of the best things you can do is to take notes on each grammar section, putting the explanations into your own words, and then copying the example sentences or tables slowly and carefully. This will do two things. It will give you a nice, clear notebook that you can take with you so you can review and practice, and it will also force you to take enough time with each section so that it's really driven home. Of course, a lot of grammar is memorization—verb endings, irregular forms, pronouns, and so on. So a lot of the vocabulary learning tips will come in handy for learning grammar, too:

1. AUDIO REPETITION

Listen to the audio several times while you're looking at the words or sentences. For example, for a verb conjugation, listen to all of the forms several times, reading along to activate your visual memory as well.

2. SPOKEN REPETITION

Listen to the audio and repeat several times for practice. For example, to learn the conjugation of an irregular verb, repeat all of the forms of the verb until you're able to produce them without looking at the screen. It's a little bit like memorizing lines for a play—practice until you can make it sound natural. Practice the example sentences that way as well, focusing, of course, on the grammar section at hand.

3. WRITTEN REPETITION

Write the new forms again and again, saying them slowly and carefully, as well. Do this until you're able to produce all of the forms without any help.

4. FLASH CARDS

Copy the grammar point, whether it's a list of pronouns, a conjugation, or a list of irregular forms, on a flashcard. Stick the cards in your pocket so you can review them when you have time to kill. Glance over the cards, saying the forms to yourself several times, and when you're ready to test yourself, flip the cards over and see if you can produce all of the information.

5. GRAMMAR IN THE WILD

Do you want to see an amazing number of example sentences that use some particular grammatical form? Well, just type that form into a search engine. Pick a few of the examples you find at random, and copy them down into your notebook or language journal. Pick them apart, look up words you don't know, and try to figure out the other grammatical constructions. You may not get everything 100 percent correct, but you'll definitely learn and practice in the process.

6. COME BACK TO IT

Just like vocabulary, grammar is best learned through repetition and review. Go back over your notes, go back to previous lessons and read over the grammar sections, listen to the audio, or check out the relevant section in the grammar summary. Even after you've completed lessons, it's never a bad idea to go back and keep the "old" grammar fresh.

HOW TO EXPAND YOUR LEARNING EXPERIENCE

Your experience with your new language should not be limited to this course alone. Like anything, learning a language will be more enjoyable if you're able to make it a part of your life in some way. And you'd be surprised to know how easily you can do that these days!

1. USE THE INTERNET

The internet is an absolutely amazing resource for people learning new languages. You're never more than a few clicks away from online newspapers, magazines, reference material, cultural sites, travel and tourism sites, images, sounds, and so much more. Develop your own list of favorite sites that match your needs and interests, whether business, cooking, fashion, film, kayaking, rock climbing, or . . . well, you get the picture. Use search engines creatively to find examples of vocabulary or grammar "in the wild." Find a favorite blog or periodical and take the time to work your way through an article or entry. Think of what you use the internet for in English, and look for similar sites in your target language.

2. CHECK OUT COMMUNITY RESOURCES

Depending on where you live, there may be plenty of practice opportunities in your own community. There may be a cultural organization or social club where people meet. There may be a local college or university with a department that hosts cultural events such as films or discussion groups. There may be a restaurant where you can go for a good meal and a chance to practice a bit of your target language. Of course, you can find a lot of this information online, and there are sites that allow groups of people to get organized and meet to pursue their interests.

3. Foreign films

Films are a wonderful way to practice hearing and understanding a new language. With English subtitles and the pause and rewind functions, foreign films are practically really long dialogues with pictures, not to mention the cultural insight and experience they provide! And nowadays it's simple to rent foreign DVDs online or even access films online. So, if you're starting to learn a new language today, go online and rent yourself some movies that you can watch over the next few weeks or months.

4. Music

Even if you have a horrible singing voice, music is a great way to learn new vocabulary. After hearing a song just a few times, the lyrics somehow manage to plant themselves in the mind. And with the internet, it's often very easy to find the lyrics of a song online, print them out, and have them ready for whenever you're alone and feel like singing . . .

5. Television

If you have access to television programming in the language you're studying, including of course anything you can find on the Internet, take advantage of that! You'll most likely hear very natural and colloquial language, including idiomatic expressions and rapid speech, all of which will be a healthy challenge for your comprehension skills. But the visual cues, including body language and gestures, will help. Plus, you'll get to see how the language interacts with the culture, which is also a very important part of learning a language.

6. Food

A great way to learn a language is through the cuisine. What could be better than going out and trying new dishes at a restaurant with the intention of practicing your newly acquired language? Go to a restaurant, and if the names of the dishes are printed in the target language, try to decipher them. Then try to order in the target language, provided of course that your server speaks the language! At the very least, you'll learn a few new vocabulary items, not to mention sample some wonderful new food.

German spelling and pronunciation

Many German sounds are like English sounds, though the differences are significant enough that you will need to familiarize yourself with them in order to make yourself understood properly in the German language. Some key things to remember:

1. Each sound is pronounced clearly and distinctly; sounds are not slurred over or reduced as they often are in English.

2. Simple words have one stressed syllable (the part of the word that receives the most emphasis), generally the first one.

3. The **umlaut** (¨) changes the pronunciation of **a, o,** and **u,** when it appears above them.

4. All nouns are capitalized.

The rest is a matter of listening and repeating, which you should do with each word in this section as you start to learn how the German language sounds.

1. COGNATES

Let's begin with a few cognates. These are words that are similar in both German and English and descend from the same root. Notice how German spelling and pronunciation differ from English.

Adresse	*address*
Alkohol	*alcohol*
Amerikaner	*American*
Bank	*bank*
Bad	*bath*
Bett	*bed*
Bier	*beer*
Butter	*butter*
Charakter	*character*

Direktor	*director*
Doktor	*doctor*
Drama	*drama*
Ende	*end*
Export	*export*
Film	*film*
Garage	*garage*
Gas	*gas*
hier	*here*
Hotel	*hotel*
Hunger	*hunger*
Lampe	*lamp*
lang	*long*
Linie	*line*
Maschine	*machine*
Nation	*nation*
national	*national*
Oper	*opera*
Papier	*paper*
Person	*person*
parken	*to park*
Prinz	*prince*
Problem	*problem*
Publikum	*public*
Radio	*radio*
Restaurant	*restaurant*
Signal	*signal*
Station	*station*
Telefon	*telephone*
Tee	*tea*
Theater	*theater*
Tempel	*temple*

Triumph	*triumph*
Tunnel	*tunnel*
Wolf	*wolf*
Zone	*zone*

2. VOWELS

Now that you've looked at the difference between German and English on a broad scale, let's get down to the specifics by looking at individual sounds, beginning with German vowels.

Remember one of our rules: the **umlaut** may appear in German above an **a, o,** or **u** and change the nature of its sound. Another rule to remember: each sound is pronounced distinctly, including all vowel sounds.

Letter	Pronunciation	Examples
a	(long) *ah* in *father*	sagen, Datum, Laden, Tafel
	(short) *o* in *hot*	kann, Mann, Pfanne, was?
ä	(long) *ai* in *fair*	spät, Erklärung, Währung, Ernährung
	(short) *e* in *bet*	Männer
e	(long) *ay* in *may*	geben, stehen
	(short) *e* in *bent*	Adresse, Moment, wetten, rennen
	at the end of a word, *e* in *pocket*	beide, heute, Karte, seine
	followed by another **e** or **h**, *a* in *care*	Heer, mehr

Letter	Pronunciation	Examples
i	(long) *ee* in *see*	**Miete, dienen, Liebe, Dieb**
	(short) *i* in *ship*	**mit, Sitte, Witz, mittags**
o	(long) *o* in *lone*	**oben, Obst, Boden, holen**
	(short) *o* in *off*	**oft, kommen, Stoff, Loch**
ö	(long) like the German **e** in **geben**, pronounced by rounding the lips and saying the long **e**	**König, Löwe, hören, böse**
	(short) like a short **u** with rounded lips, as in *pup*, similar to the first vowel sound in *colonel*	**können, Töchter, möchte, Röcke**
u	(long) *oo* in *noon*	**Blume, Huhn, Hut, gut**
	(short) *u* in *bush*	**muss, dumm, bummeln, Russland**
ü	(long) *ee* in *see* but with rounded lips	**über, drüben, früher, Frühstück**
	(short) like short **i** but with rounded lips	**Stück, Brücke, dünn, müssen**
y	same as short **ü**	**typisch, Lyrik**

Letter	Pronunciation	Examples
ai	*y* in *by*	Mai
ei	*y* in *by*	Ei, Heimat
au	*ou* in *house*	Haus, Maus, Baum, Pflaume
äu	*oy* in *boy*	Häuser, träumen
eu	*oy* in *boy*	Leute, heute

3. CONSONANTS

Next, let's take a look at German consonants.

Letter	Pronunciation	Examples
b	*b* in *before*	Bett, Gabe
	at the end of a word, *p* in *trap*	Grab, Trab
c	before **a, o,** and **u,** *k* in *kilt*	Cato
	before e, i, ä, ö, **and** y, *ts* in *cats*	Cäsar
d	*d* in *date*	Datum, Norden
	at the end of a word, *t* in *but*	Bad, Hund
f	*f* in *fuss*	Fliege, Fluss
g	*g* in *garden*	Garten
	in foreign words, *g* in *general*	Genie

Letter	Pronunciation	Examples
h	*h* in *help*	hundert, Heimat, Geheimnis, behalten
	silent	Schuh, fröhlich
j	*y* in *your*	Jahr, jemand
k	*c* in *canal*	Katze, Kind, Keller, Kunde
l	*l* in *land*	Land, Wolf, Leben
m	*m* in *mother*	Meile, Maler
n	*n* in *never*	nur, Neffe
p	*p* in *park*	Preis, Papier
	in the combination **pf**, silent	Pfanne, Pferd
q	*q* in *quiet*	Quelle, Qualität
r	*r* in *risk*, but rolled and more strongly pronounced	Rede, rein
s	before a vowel, *z* in *zoo*	süß, Sahne
	at the end of a word or syllable, *s* in *son*	Maus, Eis
ß	*ss* in *less*	süß, Straße
t	*t* in *tea*, even when followed by **h**	Tanz, Tasse, Theater, Thron

Letter	Pronunciation	Examples
v	*f* in *fair*	**Vogel, Vater**
	when used in a word with Latin roots, *v* in *victory*	**Vase, Vulkan**
w	*v* in *vain*	**Wein, Waffe**
x	*x* in *next*	**Axt, Hexe**
z	*ts* in *cats*	**Zahn, Zauber**

4. SPECIAL GERMAN SOUNDS

There are several sound combinations in German that appear quite often as exceptions to the above rules, so study them carefully.

Cluster	Pronunciation	Examples
ch	*ch* in *character*	**Christ, Chor, Charakter**
	when followed by **s,** *x* in *next*	**Fuchs, Wachs**
	h in *hue*	**China, Kirche, mich, sicher**
ig	at the end of a word, like **ch** in **ich**	**ewig, König**
	when followed by **lich** or **e,** like a hard **g** or **k**	**wenigstens, richtige, königlich**
sch	*sh* in *shoe*	**Kirsche, Schuh, amerikanisch**

Letter	Pronunciation	Examples
sp	*sh* + *p*	**Spanien, Spiegel**
st	*sh* + *t*	**stehen, Stahl**
ng	*ng* in *sing*	**bringen, anfangen**
tz	*ts* in *cats*	**Mütze, Blitz**
er	at the end of a word, *a* in *father*	**kleiner, schöner, Vater, Wetter**

UNIT 1
Talking about yourself and making introductions

Guten Tag! *(Good day!)* In Unit 1, you'll learn how to introduce yourself and others, how to say **Hallo!** *(Hello!)*, how to explain where you're from and what you do, and how to ask other people for basic information about themselves. Naturally, you'll learn greetings and other essential courtesy expressions, along with important rules on how to put German sentences together. But don't worry; German grammar is not that tough. We'll lead you through it step-by-step, and before you know it, you'll be able to have simple conversations in German.

—————————— Lesson 1 (words) ——————————

WORD LIST 1

Guten Tag! *(fml.)*	*Good day!*
Hallo! *(infml.)*	*Hello!*
Auf Wiedersehen! *(fml.)*	*Good-bye!*
Tschüss! *(infml.)*	*Bye!*
Herr Schneider	*Mr. Schneider*
Frau Schneider	*Ms./Mrs. Schneider*
der Lehrer	*teacher (male)*
die Lehrerin	*teacher (female)*
der Student	*student (male)*
die Studentin	*student (female)*
der Rechtsanwalt	*lawyer (male)*
die Rechtsanwältin	*lawyer (female)*

NOTE
The following abbreviations will be used in this course: *(m.)* = masculine, *(f.)* = feminine, *(sg.)* = singular, *(pl.)* = plural, *(fml.)* = formal/polite, and *(infml.)* = informal.

NUTS & BOLTS 1
Gender

As you begin to acquire a vocabulary in German, you'll notice that all German words have gender. This applies to general vocabulary words, as well as to words describing people. Let's start by looking at some words that describe people. You may have noticed in the word list above that there is a male and a female version of the German word for *lawyer:* **der Rechtsanwalt** and **die Rechtsanwältin.** Most professions have two words, one for a man and one for a woman, and it is quite important to use the gender-appropriate form. Let's take a look at a few more professions showing gender.

der Chef	boss (male)
die Chefin	boss (female)
der Schauspieler	actor
die Schauspielerin	actress

The word that comes before each profession, **der** for a male and **die** for a female, is called an article. We'll learn about articles next. The female version of the profession often takes the ending **-in.**

There are a few words that have additional changes. The female version may change a vowel to an umlaut—i.e., **a** becomes **ä.**

der Rechtsanwalt	lawyer (male)
die Rechtsanwältin	lawyer (female)
der Arzt	doctor (male)
die Ärztin	doctor (female)

PRACTICE 1

Decide which vocabulary word best describes the person below.

1. Frau Schneider, *lawyer*
2. Peter, *student*
3. Herr Berger, *teacher*
4. Marilyn Monroe, *actress*
5. Frau Schmidt, *doctor*

WORD LIST 2

der Mann	*man*
die Frau	*woman*
das Kind	*child*
das Haus	*house*
das Büro	*office*
der Bus	*bus*
die Welt	*world*
der Amerikaner	*American (male)*
die Amerikanerin	*American (female)*
und	*and*
heißen	*to be called*
arbeiten	*to work*
bei	*at*
aus	*from*
in	*in*

NUTS & BOLTS 2

THE DEFINITE ARTICLE

As we said above, in German every noun has a gender—either masculine, feminine, or neuter—and this gender can be seen in many ways, including the form that *the* takes: **der** for masculine, **die** for feminine, and **das** for neuter words. For nouns with natural gender, this is easy—**der Mann** *(man)* and **der Lehrer** *(male* *teacher)* are all masculine, while **die Frau** *(woman)* and **die Lehrerin** *(female teacher)* are feminine, and **das Büro** *(office)* and **das Haus** *(house)* are neuter.

Masculine	Feminine	Neuter
der Mann	**die Frau**	**das Kind**
man	*woman*	*child*
der Lehrer	**die Lehrerin**	**das Haus**
teacher (male)	*teacher (female)*	*house*
der Bus	**die Haltestelle**	**das Auto**
bus	*stop*	*car*
der Beruf	**die Uhr**	**das Büro**
profession	*watch, clock*	*office*
der Zufall	**die Welt**	**das Jahr**
coincidence	*world*	*year*

But not all nouns have a natural gender. Just look at **die Welt** *(world)* or **der Bus** *(bus)* or **das Kind** *(child)*. There is no natural reason for the world to be considered feminine, the bus to be considered masculine, or the child to be considered neuter. So the best thing to do is simply to learn the definite article–**der, die,** or **das** (the equivalent of the English *the*)–along with the word. The vocabulary lists will always list the article **der, die,** or **das** as well. Let's look at the genders of some of the nouns you've learned so far, along with some new nouns.

You will also often see the article **das** used to mean *that* in German.

PRACTICE 2

Insert the correct definite article—**der, die,** or **das.**

1. _____ Welt

2. _____ Haus

3. _____ Rechtsanwalt

4. _____ Büro

5. _____ Zufall

6. _____ Chefin

Tip!

There are quite a few different ways to memorize new vocabulary, so it's a good idea to try a few out to see what works for you. Simply reading a word in a list isn't going to make you remember it. Write down your new vocabulary in a notebook, and then try to write it or say it out loud a few times so it'll sink in. You can use the recordings that go with this course for that, too. Make flash cards, with the German on one side and the English on the other. Start out translating from German into English, and once you've mastered that, go from English into German. Label things in your home or office with pieces of paper or sticky notes, so you'll see the German word every time you come into contact with an object. Experiment and explore, but whatever you do, pace yourself. Ideally you'll spend a little bit of time on your German every day—sometimes twenty minutes a day over the course of a week will go much further than a two-hour sitting in one day. If you can't find the time to practice some German every day, don't despair. Just work regularly, and grab a free moment here or there to remind yourself of what you've learned.

ANSWERS

PRACTICE 1: 1. die Rechtsanwältin; **2.** der Student; **3.** der Lehrer; **4.** die Schauspielerin; **5.** die Ärztin

PRACTICE 2: 1. die; **2.** das; **3.** der; **4.** das; **5.** der; **6.** die

Wie geht's? *(How are you?)* Are you ready to build on the words you've learned so far?

PHRASE LIST 1

Wie geht's? *(infml.)*	*How are you?*
Wie geht es Ihnen? *(fml.)*	*How are you?*
Gut, danke.	*Good, thanks.*
Ich bin Amerikaner.	*I'm American. (male)*
Ich bin Amerikanerin.	*I'm American. (female)*
Ich bin Deutscher.	*I'm German. (male)*
Ich bin Deutsche.	*I'm German. (female)*
aus Dresden	*from Dresden*
aus Chicago	*from Chicago*
in München	*in Munich*
in Deutschland	*in Germany*
Ich bin Rechtsanwalt.	*I'm a lawyer. (male)*
Ich bin Rechtsanwältin.	*I'm a lawyer. (female)*
. . . , nicht wahr?	*. . . , right?*

NUTS & BOLTS 1

PERSONAL PRONOUNS IN THE SINGULAR

The first words you'll need to become familiar with in German are the pronouns. Pronouns are used to talk about yourself and other people without using their names: *I, you, he, she,* etc. In German, the singular pronouns (pronouns referring to one person) are:

ich	*I*
du *(infml.)*	*you*
Sie *(fml.)*	*you*

er	he
sie	she
es	it

Notice that there are two different words for *you*. When speaking German, you have to distinguish between talking to strangers, business associates, people older than you, and anyone you want to show respect to *(formal)*, and talking to family, friends, children, and people you know better and are very familiar with *(informal)*. German has different forms of the pronoun *you* to show this distinction: the formal form **Sie,** and the informal form **du.**

PRACTICE 1
Which German pronoun would you use in the following situations?

1. *talking to your best friend Andreas*

2. *asking directions from an older gentleman you see on the street*

3. *talking about your brother*

4. *talking about yourself*

5. *talking about your boss, Frau Berger*

PHRASE LIST 2

Guten Morgen.	*Good morning.*
Guten Abend.	*Good evening.*
Gute Nacht.	*Good night.*
Bis bald.	*See you soon.*
Bis morgen.	*See you tomorrow.*
beruflich hier	*here on business*
von Beruf	*by profession*

Arzt von Beruf	*doctor by profession*
Lehrer von Beruf	*teacher by profession*
Wie peinlich!	*How embarrassing!*
Ganz und gar nicht.	*Not at all.*
pünktlich	*punctual, on time*

NUTS & BOLTS 2
THE VERB SEIN *(TO BE)* IN THE SINGULAR

Now let's look at one of the most important verbs in German, **sein** *(to be)*. The form **sein** is called the infinitive, and it corresponds to the basic *to*-form in English, *to be*. When you change the forms of a verb to match different subjects, as in the English *I speak* but *she speaks*, it's called conjugation. Here's the singular conjugation of **sein** *(to be)*:

ich bin	*I am*
du bist *(infml.)*	*you are*
Sie sind *(fml.)*	*you are*
er/sie/es ist	*he/she/it is*

Ich bin Amerikaner.
I'm American.

Er ist aus Dresden.
He is from Dresden.

Martina, du bist Rechtsanwältin, nicht wahr?
Martina, you are a lawyer, right?

Sind Sie aus Chicago?
Are you from Chicago?

Note in the last example that the first two words in the sentence are inverted to form a question, just as you would do in

English. We'll discuss question formation a bit more in a later unit.

PRACTICE 2
Follow the instructions below.

1. *Tell us that Klaus is from Munich.*
2. *Tell us that Susanne is from Dresden.*
3. *Talk to your best friend Horst and ask if he is a lawyer.*
4. *Ask your boss, Frau Schneider, if she is from Chicago.*
5. *Tell us which city you are from.*

Language link

Who'd have thought that you can surf the web and learn German at the same time? It's important to keep in contact with the culture of the language you're learning, so why not check out a few websites? For the official and independent portal to all things German, visit **www.deutschland.de**. For information on Switzerland, visit **www.schweiz.ch**. You can learn more about Austria at **www.oesterreich.at,** and **www.dw-world.de** offers news and general information on all three countries in English.

ANSWERS
PRACTICE 1: 1. du; **2.** Sie; **3.** er; **4.** ich; **5.** sie

PRACTICE 2: 1. Klaus ist aus München. **2.** Susanne ist aus Dresden. **3.** Horst, du bist Rechtsanwalt, nicht wahr? **4.** Frau Schneider, Sie sind aus Chicago, nicht wahr? **5.** Ich bin aus . . .

———————— Lesson 3 (sentences) ————————

You already began to learn a few sentences in German in the last lesson; let's expand on those phrases you learned in Lesson 2 with sentences such as **Wie heißen Sie?** *(What's your name?)*

SENTENCE LIST 1

Wie heißen Sie? *(fml.)*	*What's your name?*
Wie heißt du? *(infml.)*	*What's your name?*
Ich heiße . . .	*My name is . . .*
Wie war Ihr Name? *(fml.)*	*What was your name again?*
Wie war dein Name? *(infml.)*	*What was your name again?*
Mein Name ist . . .	*My name is . . .*
Woher kommen Sie? *(fml.)*	*Where are you from?*
Woher kommst du? *(infml.)*	*Where are you from?*
Ich bin aus Los Angeles.	*I'm from Los Angeles.*
Ich bin aus Chicago.	*I am from Chicago.*
Ich bin Amerikaner.	*I'm American. (male)*
Ich bin Amerikanerin.	*I'm American. (female)*

NUTS & BOLTS 1
NUMBERS 0–10

Let's look at the numbers 0 through 10 in German.

null	*zero*
eins	*one*
zwei	*two*
drei	*three*
vier	*four*
fünf	*five*
sechs	*six*
sieben	*seven*
acht	*eight*

neun	*nine*
zehn	*ten*

Eins und eins ist zwei.
One and one is two.

Fünf und drei ist acht.
Five and three is eight.

Sechs und vier ist zehn.
Six and four is ten.

PRACTICE 1
Complete the sentences.

1. Zwei und zwei ist . . . ?

2. Zwei und fünf ist . . . ?

3. Fünf und vier ist . . . ?

4. Drei und sieben ist . . . ?

5. Neun und eins ist . . . ?

SENTENCE LIST 2

Wie spät ist es?	*What time is it?*
Es ist sieben Uhr.	*It's seven A.M.*
Wir sind pünktlich um zehn Uhr hier.	*We are here at ten A.M. sharp.*
Ich bin um neun Uhr im Büro.	*I'll be in the office at nine A.M.*
Wie lange sind Sie schon bei InterCorp?	*How long have you been with InterCorp?*
Seit fünf Jahren.	*For five years.*
Das ist mein Bus.	*That's my bus.*
Das ist meine Haltestelle.	*That's my stop.*
Das ist unglaublich.	*That's unbelievable.*
Das ist ja geradezu unheimlich.	*That's truly uncanny.*

NUTS & BOLTS 2
Numbers 11–20

Now let's look at the numbers 11 through 20 in German.

elf	*eleven*
zwölf	*twelve*
dreizehn	*thirteen*
vierzehn	*fourteen*
fünfzehn	*fifteen*
sechzehn	*sixteen*
siebzehn	*seventeen*
achtzehn	*eighteen*
neunzehn	*nineteen*
zwanzig	*twenty*

Note that **sechs** loses the **-s** and **sieben** looses the **-en** when combined with **zehn**.

PRACTICE 2
Answer in German.

1. *How many months are in a year?*
2. *How much is a baker's dozen?*
3. *At what age are you allowed to vote in the USA?*
4. *How many fingers are there on your hands?*
5. *Now add up all your fingers and toes.*

Discovery activity

Learning the numbers in German can be a lot of fun. Memorize your telephone number in German. Go through your dresser and count all your socks in German—not the pairs, but the individual socks. Go through your kitchen drawers and count all your spoons, knives, and forks. How many chairs do you have in your house? And what about windows? How many people are in your immediate family, including spouses and children? How many in your family of origin, including parents and siblings? How many in your extended family, including grandparents, aunts, and uncles? How many years did you go to school, including college? The things you could count are endless—trees on your street, tables in your favorite restaurant, cups of coffee you drink every day. Make a point to find at least **drei** things to count per day for the next **sieben** days. Enjoy!

ANSWERS

PRACTICE 1: 1. vier; **2.** sieben; **3.** neun; **4.** zehn; **5.** zehn

PRACTICE 2: 1. zwölf; **2.** dreizehn; **3.** achtzehn; **4.** zehn; **5.** zwanzig

---
Lesson 4 (conversations)

Words, phrases, and sentences put together make up a conversation. Let's listen in.

CONVERSATION 1

Sabine Schmidt and Klaus Huber are waiting for the bus. Klaus is bored, so he decides to speak to the woman sitting next to him.

    Klaus: Guten Abend. Ich heiße Klaus Huber.
    Sabine: Guten Abend.

Sabine is reluctant to continue the conversation. After all, it is late at night, and Klaus is a stranger.

Klaus: Ich bin aus Dresden. Ich bin beruflich in München. Ich arbeite bei InterCorp.

Sabine: Na so was! Ich auch.

Klaus: Sie sind auch aus Dresden?

Sabine: Nein, ich arbeite auch bei InterCorp.

Klaus: Das ist ja ein Zufall.

Sabine: Ja, ich bin dort Rechtsanwältin. Ich heiße Sabine Schmidt.

Now Klaus is a bit reluctant to continue the conversation.

Sabine: Wie war noch Ihr Name? Klaus . . . ?

Klaus: . . . Huber. Ich bin auch . . .

Suddenly Sabine remembers.

Sabine: Moment mal . . . Sie sind auch Rechtsanwalt, nicht wahr?

Klaus: Ja.

Sabine: Dann bin ich ja . . .

Klaus: . . . meine Chefin. Ja.

Klaus: Good evening. My name is Klaus Huber.

Sabine: Good evening.

Klaus: I am from Dresden. I am in Munich on business. I work for InterCorp.

Sabine: Really? Me, too.

Klaus: You are from Dresden as well?

Sabine: No, I also work for InterCorp.

Klaus: What a coincidence.

Sabine: Yes, I am a lawyer there. My name is Sabine Schmidt.

Sabine: What was your name again? Klaus . . . ?

Klaus: . . . Huber. I am . . .

Sabine: Wait a minute . . . You are also a lawyer, right?

Klaus: Yes.

Sabine: Well, that means I am . . .

Klaus: . . . my boss. Yes.

Note that Klaus and Sabine are using the formal form **Sie** when addressing each other. From this we can gather that they are probably over twenty years old and don't know each other, at least not very well. Also note that they introduce themselves with their first and last names. Generally, adults won't be on a first-name basis until they've known each other for a little while.

NUTS & BOLTS 1
PERSONAL PRONOUNS IN THE PLURAL

Now let's look at the personal pronouns that refer to more than one person.

wir	*we*
ihr *(infml.)*	*you, you all*
Sie *(fml.)*	*you, you all*
sie	*they*

Even in the plural, German distinguishes between the informal **ihr** and the formal **Sie.** Please note that formal forms are always capitalized.

PRACTICE 1

In this exercise, replace each of the following nouns with the correct pronoun.

1. Heinz und Isabella *(they)*

2. die Chefin und ihr Mann *(you)*

3. ich, Peter, und Michael

4. der Chef

5. Susanne und Claudia *(you)*

CONVERSATION 2

Remember Sabine and Klaus? In the brief conversation they had while waiting for the bus, we discovered that Sabine is Klaus's boss. Let's see what happens next.

Klaus: Wie peinlich!

Sabine: Ganz und gar nicht. Die Welt ist klein. Wie lange sind Sie schon bei InterCorp?

Klaus: Seit vier Jahren. Und Sie?

Sabine: Auch seit vier Jahren.

Klaus: Was für ein Zufall.

Sabine: Ah, da ist der Bus. Die Nummer 13.

Klaus: Noch ein Zufall. Das ist auch mein Bus.

Sabine: Das ist meine Haltestelle.

Klaus: Das ist unglaublich. Schon wieder ein Zufall. Das ist auch meine Haltestelle.

Sabine: Ja, das ist ja geradezu unheimlich. Dann bis morgen, Herr Huber. Ich bin um acht Uhr im Büro.

Klaus: Ja, bis morgen, Frau Schmidt. Pünktlich um acht Uhr. Auf Wiedersehen.

Sabine: Auf Wiedersehen.

Klaus: *How embarrassing.*

Sabine: *Not at all. It's a small world. (lit., The world is small.) How long have you been with InterCorp?*

Klaus: *Four years. And you?*

Sabine: *Four years as well.*

Klaus: *What a coincidence.*

Sabine: *Ah, there's the bus. Number 13.*

Klaus: *Yet another coincidence. That is my bus, too.*

Sabine: *That is my stop.*

Klaus: *This is unbelievable. Another coincidence. This is my stop, too.*

Sabine: *Yes, this is uncanny. See you tomorrow, Herr Huber. I'll be in the office at eight A.M.*

> Klaus: Yes, see you tomorrow, Frau Schmidt. At eight A.M.
> sharp. Good-bye.
> Sabine: Good-bye.

NOTES

In most countries in Europe, parking is difficult in the city, so people tend to take public transportation rather than a personal car to get around town. And because people depend on public transportation that much, buses, trains, and streetcars adhere to their schedules and run on time. So make sure you are **pünktlich** *(punctual)!*

NUTS & BOLTS 2

THE VERB SEIN *(TO BE)* IN THE PLURAL

Now let's look at the plural conjugation of **sein** *(to be)*.

wir sind	*we are*
ihr seid *(infml.)*	*you (all) are*
Sie sind *(fml.)*	*you (all) are*
sie sind	*they are*

Wir sind aus Chicago.
We're from Chicago.

Sie sind Lehrer von Beruf.
They are teachers by profession.

Herr und Frau Schneider, Sie sind beruflich hier, nicht wahr?
Mr. and Mrs. Schneider, you are here on business, right?

PRACTICE 2
Answer the questions based on the cue in parentheses.

1. *Where are you and your friend from? (New York)*

2. *What is Horst by profession? (doctor)*

3. *Who is here on business?* (Herr und Frau Rosen)

4. *Which greeting would you use in the evening?*

5. *What is your profession? (Please answer truthfully. Check your German–English dictionary to find the German word for your profession.)*

Language link

Train travel is one of the most preferred forms of public transportation, particularly in Europe. Who wouldn't want to take a trip on the fast **ICE (Inter City Express)**, connecting major cities in Germany and the rest of continental Europe, or the convenient **Regional-express** *(regional express train)*, allowing passengers to travel between smaller cities around a particular metropolitan area? Check out **www.bahn.de** to get timetables for the **Deutsche Bundesbahn** *(German Railway)*, purchase tickets, and make travel arrangements including hotel reservations and car rentals. **www.oebb.at** offers the same service for the Austrian railway, and **www.rail.ch** for the Swiss railroad.

ANSWERS
PRACTICE 1: 1. sie; **2.** Sie; **3.** wir; **4.** er; **5.** ihr

PRACTICE 2: 1. Wir sind aus New York. **2.** Er ist Arzt von Beruf. **3.** Herr und Frau Rosen sind beruflich hier. **4.** Guten Abend. **5.** Ich bin . . . von Beruf.

UNIT 1 ESSENTIALS

The following phrases have been introduced in Unit 1. This isn't a list of every sentence you learned in the first unit, but it covers the most essential phrases. Be sure to practice these phrases as much as possible until they become natural to you.

Guten Tag! *(fml.)*	*Good day!*
Guten Morgen.	*Good morning.*
Guten Abend.	*Good evening.*
Gute Nacht.	*Good night.*
Hallo! *(infml.)*	*Hello!*
Wie geht's? *(infml.)*	*How are you?*
Wie geht es Ihnen? *(fml.)*	*How are you?*
Gut, danke.	*Good, thanks.*
Auf Wiedersehen! *(fml.)*	*Good-bye!*
Tschüss! *(infml.)*	*Bye!*
Bis bald.	*See you soon.*
Bis morgen.	*See you tomorrow.*
Wie heißen Sie? *(fml.)*	*What's your name?*
Wie heißt du? *(infml.)*	*What's your name?*
Ich heiße . . .	*My name is . . .*
Wie war Ihr Name? *(fml.)*	*What was your name again?*
Wie war dein Name? *(infml.)*	*What was your name again?*

Mein Name ist . . .	*My name is . . .*
Woher kommen Sie? *(fml.)*	*Where are you from?*
Woher kommst du? *(infml.)*	*Where are you from?*
Ich bin aus . . .	*I'm from . . .*

UNIT 2
Talking about family

We all have one. Some of us even have two. And even though some of us might rather have a different one, we're all stuck with the one we've got: our family. In this unit, you'll learn how to talk about **die Familie** *(family)* in German— **Brüder** *(brothers)*, **Schwestern** *(sisters)*, **Töchter** *(daughters)*, **und Söhne** *(sons)*, and all of the lovable quirks that come with them.

———————— Lesson 5 (words) ————————

First, let's learn the vocabulary for family members.

WORD LIST 1

die Mutter	*mother*
der Vater	*father*
die Eltern	*parents*
der Sohn	*son*
die Tochter	*daughter*
die Schwester	*sister*
der Bruder	*brother*
die Geschwister	*siblings*
die Familie	*family*
die Tante	*aunt*
der Onkel	*uncle*
die Großmutter	*grandmother*
der Großvater	*grandfather*
der Enkel	*grandson*
die Enkelin	*granddaughter*

die Hochzeit	wedding
der Ehemann	husband
der Mann	husband
die Ehefrau	wife
die Frau	wife
der Schwiegervater	father-in-law
die Schwiegermutter	mother-in-law
der Schwager	brother-in-law
die Schwägerin	sister-in-law

NOTES

Just as in English, the German words for *mother, father, grandmother,* and *grandfather* mentioned above are somewhat formal. And just like in English, there are many more personable German words to address these family members.

Mama	mom
Papa	dad(dy)
Oma	grandma
Opa	grandpa

Note that when speaking, most people will use the short forms **mein Mann** *(my husband)* and **meine Frau** *(my wife)* when referring to their husbands and wives.

Mein Mann ist Pianist.
My husband is a pianist.

Meine Frau hat drei Häuser.
My wife has three houses.

NUTS & BOLTS 1
THE VERB HABEN (*TO HAVE*)

The verb **haben** *(to have)*—just like the verb **sein** *(to be)*, which we looked at in Unit 1—changes depending on the pronoun you use with it. Let's look at the singular and plural conjugations of **haben** *(to have)*.

ich habe	*I have*
du hast	*you have*
Sie haben *(sg. fml.)*	*you have*
er/sie/es hat	*he/she/it has*
wir haben	*we have*
ihr habt	*you have*
Sie haben *(pl. fml.)*	*you have*
sie haben	*they have*

Ich habe zwei Schwestern.
I have two sisters.

Mein Vater hat drei Brüder.
My father has three brothers.

Meine Eltern haben ein Haus.
My parents have a house.

Herr Heinrich, Sie haben eine Schwester?
Mr. Heinrich, you have a sister?

Ich habe einen Sohn. Mein Sohn heißt Sebastian.
I have a son. My son's name is Sebastian.

Sebastian hat eine Schwester. Sie heißt Susanne.
Sebastian has a sister. Her name is Susanne.

PRACTICE 1

Answer the questions with the appropriate German word and article.

1. *Who is my father's father?* _____.

2. *Who is my mother's daughter, if she is not me?* _____.

3. *Who is my child's grandmother?* _____.

4. *Who is my husband's brother?* _____.

5. *Who is my wife's father?* _____.

6. *Who are my mother and my father?* _____.

WORD LIST 2

die Wohnung	*apartment*
das Zimmer	*room*
das Wohnzimmer	*living room*
das Esszimmer	*dining room*
das Schlafzimmer	*bedroom*
das Kinderzimmer	*children's room*
die Küche	*kitchen*
das Badezimmer (das Bad)	*bathroom*
die Toilette	*bathroom, toilet*
der Tisch	*table*
das Bett	*bed*
der Stuhl	*chair*
das Sofa	*couch*
der Schreibtisch	*desk*
der Schrank	*closet*
die Möbel	*furniture*

NUTS & BOLTS 2
REGULAR VERBS

Every German verb consists of a stem and an ending. The ending reveals who is performing the action described by the verb. For example, the verb **machen** *(to make, to do)* consists of the stem **mach-** and the infinitive ending **-en.** When conjugated, the endings you add to the stem **mach-** change. Here is the full conjugation.

ich mach<u>e</u>	*I make*
du mach<u>st</u> *(sg. infml.)*	*you make*
Sie mach<u>en</u> *(sg. fml.)*	*you make*
er/sie/es mach<u>t</u>	*he/she/it makes*
wir mach<u>en</u>	*we make*
ihr mach<u>t</u> *(pl. infml.)*	*you make*
Sie mach<u>en</u> *(pl. fml.)*	*you make*
sie mach<u>en</u>	*they make*

There are many other German verbs that take the same endings in the present tense, so it's worthwhile to get to know these endings well.

ich	-e	wir	-en
du *(sg. infml.)*	-st	**ihr** *(pl. infml.)*	-t
Sie *(sg. fml.)*	-en	**Sie** *(pl. fml.)*	-en
er/sie/es	-t	**sie**	-en

The chart below shows some of the verbs that take these endings.

arbeiten	*to work*
bezahlen	*to pay*
heiraten	*to get married*
kaufen	*to buy*
kochen	*to cook*
lernen	*to learn*
lieben	*to love*
sagen	*to say*
tanzen	*to dance*
wohnen	*to live, to reside*

Ich liebe dich.
I love you.

Wir heiraten.
We are getting married.

Er kauft ein Haus.
He buys a house.

Du kochst gut.
You cook well.

Sie arbeiten bei InterCorp.
They work for InterCorp.

PRACTICE 2
Fill in the correct verb form.

1. Wir _____ Deutsch. (lernen)

2. Meine Schwester _____ bei Acme. (arbeiten)

3. Mein Schwager und meine Schwägerin _____ in Hamburg. (leben)

4. Du _____ ein Haus. (kaufen)

5. Frau Sommer, Sie _____ gut, nicht wahr? (kochen)

6. Ich _____ dich. (lieben)

Discovery activity

Go through your address book and write down the name of everyone who is related to you. Then write down how they are related to you using the German terms for family relations. Once you're done with that, do the same for your husband's family, your wife's, your boyfriend's, your girlfriend's, the family of a friend, or even the relatives of an ex. You'll be surprised how many people you can come up with that are related to you. And if you feel like it, give them a call and teach them a few German words.

ANSWERS
PRACTICE 1: 1. der Großvater/der Opa; **2.** die Schwester; **3.** die Mutter/die Mama; **4.** der Schwager; **5.** der Schwiegervater; **6.** die Eltern

PRACTICE 2: 1. lernen; **2.** arbeitet; **3.** leben; **4.** kaufst; **5.** kochen; **6.** liebe

—————— Lesson 6 (phrases) ——————

Now let's learn a few phrases to describe our family members.

PHRASE LIST 1

ledig sein	*to be single*
verlobt sein	*to be engaged*

verheiratet sein	*to be married*
geschieden werden	*to get divorced*
schwanger sein	*to be pregnant*
ein Kind bekommen	*to have a baby*
unterwegs sein	*to be on the way (baby)*
na ja . . .	*well . . .*
Wie bitte?	*Excuse me?, I'm sorry?*
Was sagst du?	*What are you saying?*

NUTS & BOLTS 1
INDEFINITE ARTICLES

Just as the English definite article *the* has the German equivalents **der, die,** and **das,** the indefinite *a/an* has the equivalents **ein** and **eine.** The indefinite article **ein** precedes masculine and neuter nouns **(ein Mann, ein Kind),** whereas the indefinite article **eine** precedes feminine nouns **(eine Frau).**

Masculine	Feminine	Neuter
ein Vater	**eine Mutter**	**ein Kind**
a father	*a mother*	*a child*
ein Tisch	**eine Küche**	**ein Zimmer**
a table	*a kitchen*	*a room*
ein Onkel	**eine Schwester**	**ein Paar**
an uncle	*a sister*	*a couple*
ein Garten	**eine Adresse**	**ein Haus**
a garden	*an address*	*a house*

Hier wohnt ein Mann.
A man lives here.

Das Haus hat eine Küche.
The house has a kitchen.

Sie bekommt ein Kind.
She is having a baby.

PRACTICE 1
Insert the correct indefinite article.

1. _____ Tante

2. _____ Tisch

3. _____ Küche

4. _____ Esszimmer

5. _____ Garten

6. _____ Kind

PHRASE LIST 2

gut passen	*to fit well*
gut kochen	*to cook well*
so groß wie	*as big as*
groß genug	*large enough*
ganz neu	*completely new*
sehr schön	*very nice*
sehr gut	*very good*
Bestimmt!	*Sure!*
Das stimmt!	*That's true!*
Keine Sorge.	*No worries., Don't worry.*

NUTS & BOLTS 2
POSSESSIVE ADJECTIVES
The words that tell us who owns what are called possessive adjectives.

mein	*my*
dein *(sg. infml.)*	*your*
Ihr *(sg. fml.)*	*your*
sein	*his*
ihr	*her*
sein	*its*
unser	*our*
euer *(pl. infml.)*	*your*
Ihr *(pl. fml.)*	*your*
ihr	*their*

Possessive adjectives change depending on the gender and number of the noun they precede. Singular possessive adjectives work just like the indefinite article, so the masculine and neuter forms have no ending, while the feminine form ends in **-e.**

Masculine	Feminine	Neuter
mein Vater	**mein<u>e</u> Mutter**	**mein Kind**
my father	*my mother*	*my child*

Unlike the indefinite article, possessive adjectives have a plural form. The plural form in masculine, feminine, and neuter ends in an **-e.**

Masculine	Feminine	Neuter
meine Onkel	**meine Tanten**	**meine Häuser**
my uncles	*my aunts*	*my houses*

Heute ist unsere Hochzeit.
Today is our wedding.

Das ist mein Mann.
That's my husband.

Das ist seine Frau.
That's his wife.

Das sind unsere Kinder.
Those are our children.

Deine Küche ist groß.
Your kitchen is big.

PRACTICE 2
Insert the correct possessive adjective.

1. _____ Eltern *(her)*

2. _____ Kinder *(my)*

3. _____ Haus *(his)*

4. _____ Möbel *(our)*

5. _____ Tisch *(your, fml.)*

6. _____ Küche *(your, infml.)*

Tip!
Learning German can be easier than you think once you realize that English and German have a lot of words in common: **Arm, Bank, blind, blond, Finger, Hand, Hotel, Name, Problem, Radio, Restaurant, Rose, Sport, Taxi, Wind.** These are all German words, and they all have the same spellings and meanings as their English

counterparts. These words with similar meanings are called cognates. Just remember that all German nouns start with a capital letter and that German has different pronunciation rules than English. In addition to these cognates, German has borrowed many words from English that are spelled and pronounced just like their English counterparts: **Babysitter, Boss, Design, E-Mail, Fashion, Feeling, Jogging, Manager, Party, Shopping, Show, Steak, Thriller.** Finally, there are a few words that are almost the same in English and German, from which you can probably guess the meaning: **Adresse** *(address),* **Bett** *(bed),* **Bruder** *(brother),* **Doktor** *(doctor),* **Familie** *(family),* **Garten** *(garden),* **gut** *(good),* **Haus** *(house),* **Kaffee** *(coffee),* **kochen** *(to cook),* **Onkel** *(uncle),* **Paar** *(pair),* **Salz** *(salt),* **Wetter** *(weather).* So if you hear or see a German word that sounds or looks familiar, chances are that you already know what it means. As a bit of an experiment, visit one of the German websites mentioned in the previous unit and look for five or more German words that are the same as or similar to their English counterparts.

ANSWERS
PRACTICE 1: 1. eine; **2.** ein; **3.** eine; **4.** ein; **5.** ein; **6.** ein

PRACTICE 2: 1. ihre; **2.** meine; **3.** sein; **4.** unsere; **5.** Ihr; **6.** deine

--- Lesson 7 (sentences) ---

Ever wonder how to court somebody in a different language? Here are a few sentences that might help you.

SENTENCE LIST 1

Ich liebe dich.	*I love you.*
Willst du meine Frau werden?	*Will you marry me? (lit., Will you be my wife?)*
Willst du mein Mann werden?	*Will you marry me? (lit., Will you be my husband?)*

Heirate mich!	*Marry me!*
Sind Sie verheiratet?	*Are you married?*
Wir sind verlobt.	*We are engaged.*
Wir sind nicht verheiratet.	*We are not married.*
Wie alt sind Sie?	*How old are you?*
Ich bin zwanzig Jahre alt.	*I am twenty years old.*
Wo wohnen Sie?	*Where do you live?*

NUTS & BOLTS 1
NEGATION WITH NICHT (*NOT*)

Negation in German is rather easy. Just place the word **nicht** *(not)* after the verb, or after the verb + direct object pair.

Sie ist verheiratet.	**Sie ist nicht verheiratet.**
She is married.	*She is not married.*
Ich liebe dich.	**Ich liebe dich nicht.**
I love you.	*I don't love you.*
Mein Mann kocht gut.	**Mein Mann kocht nicht gut.**
My husband cooks well.	*My husband does not cook well.*

PRACTICE 1

Rewrite the following sentences in the negative.

1. Ich bin ledig.

2. Meine Tochter arbeitet bei InterCorp.

3. Mein Onkel wohnt in Berlin.

4. Die Kinder tanzen.

5. Das stimmt!

6. Meine Tochter kocht gut.

SENTENCE LIST 2

So viele Gäste.	*So many guests.*
Das ist aber teuer.	*That will be expensive.*
Mein Vater bezahlt die Hochzeit.	*My father pays for the wedding.*
Die Gäste tanzen auf der Hochzeit.	*The guests are dancing at the wedding party.*
Wir kaufen ein Haus.	*We are buying a house.*
Das Haus ist groß.	*The house is big.*
Unsere Möbel passen gut.	*Our furniture fits well.*
Wer wohnt hier?	*Who lives here?*
Unsere Kinder wohnen hier.	*Our children live here.*

NUTS & BOLTS 2

NEGATION WITH KEIN (*NO*)

As we learned above, verbs are negated by placing **nicht** after the verb. While **nicht** is roughly equivalent to *not* in English, **kein** is roughly equivalent to the English *no*. **Kein** is used to negate a noun with the indefinite article, such as **ein Kind,** or nouns with no article at all, such as **Kinder.**

Sie hat ein Kind.	**Sie hat kein Kind.**
She has a child.	*She has no children. (lit., She has no child.)*
Ich habe Kinder.	**Ich habe keine Kinder.**
I have children.	*I have no children.*
Meine Frau hat ein Haus.	**Meine Frau hat kein Haus.**
My wife has a house.	*My wife has no house.*

PRACTICE 2

Change the following sentences into the negative using **kein.**

1. Mein Vater hat eine Schwester.

2. Unser Boss hat zwei Söhne.

3. Du hast ein Esszimmer.

4. Da ist ein Garten.

5. Das Haus kostet Geld.

6. Wir haben Geld.

Tip!

When learning a foreign language, just listening to its sounds can help a great deal. Make sure as you're studying German to listen to German music, watch German movies, or tune in to a German talk radio station. Many American universities offer German radio programming on a weekly, or even daily, basis. And of course, you can always listen to the audio that goes with this program. Put it on while you take a shower, drive to work, work out, cook dinner . . . In fact, why not put it on right now?

ANSWERS

PRACTICE 1: 1. Ich bin nicht ledig. **2.** Meine Tochter arbeitet nicht bei InterCorp. **3.** Mein Onkel wohnt nicht in Berlin. **4.** Die Kinder tanzen nicht. **5.** Das stimmt nicht! **6.** Meine Tochter kocht nicht gut.

PRACTICE 2: 1. Mein Vater hat keine Schwester. **2.** Unser Boss hat keine Söhne. **3.** Du hast kein Esszimmer. **4.** Da ist kein Garten. **5.** Das Haus kostet kein Geld. **6.** Wir haben kein Geld.

CONVERSATION 1

Stefan and Andrea have been going out for a while. They want to move in together and are shopping for a house.

Andrea: Das Haus ist sehr schön.
Stefan: Ja. Und sehr teuer. Und die Diele ist sehr klein.
Andrea: Die Küche ist ganz neu.
Stefan: Na und? Du kochst doch nicht.
Andrea: Nein, aber du kochst. Sehr gut sogar.
Stefan: Danke. Das Schlafzimmer ist aber klein. Unser Bett passt hier nicht rein.
Andrea: Das ist doch nicht das Schlafzimmer. Das ist das Esszimmer. Und mein Esstisch passt gut.
Stefan: Dein Esstisch? Und was ist mit meinem Esstisch?
Andrea: *(Ignoring him)* Das Wohnzimmer ist so groß wie meine ganze Wohnung.
Stefan: Groß genug für ein Hochzeitsfest?
Andrea: Oh, bestimmt ... Wie bitte? Was sagst du da? Wer heiratet denn?
Stefan: Ich liebe dich, Andrea. Willst du meine Frau werden?

Andrea: *The house is very beautiful.*
Stefan: *Yes. And very expensive. And the foyer is very small.*
Andrea: *The kitchen is all new.*
Stefan: *So what? You don't even cook.*
Andrea: *No, but you cook. Very well.*
Stefan: *Thanks. The bedroom is really small. Our bed won't fit in here.*
Andrea: *That's not the bedroom. That's the dining room. And my dining table will fit well.*
Stefan: *Your dining table? And what about my dining table?*

> Andrea: The living room is as big as my entire apartment.
>
> Stefan: Big enough for a wedding party?
>
> Andrea: Oh, I'm sure . . . What was that? What did you say? Who is getting married?
>
> Stefan: I love you, Andrea. Will you marry me?

NOTES

Upon opening the door to an apartment or house in Germany, you will enter the **Diele,** a small vestibule for coats and shoes. The **Diele** is either a square room or a hallway, from which doors lead into the other rooms. You will very rarely step right into the living room.

NUTS & BOLTS 1
ASKING QUESTIONS

The usual word order in German sentences is subject-verb-object.

Sie haben Kinder.
You have children.

When asking questions, the word order changes: the subject and verb switch places.

Haben Sie Kinder?
Do you have children?

Wohnt sie in Berlin?
Does she live in Berlin?

Sind Sie verheiratet?
Are you married?

Sind Sie aus Deutschland?
Are you from Germany?

Subjects and verbs switch places in questions with question words, as well.

Er heißt Horst.
His name is Horst.

Wie heißt er?
What is his name?

Here are the most important question words you'll need to know in German.

Wer?	*Who?*
Was?	*What?*
Wann?	*When?*
Wie?	*How?*
Wo?	*Where?*
Woher?	*Where from?*

Wer ist das?
Who is this?

Was sagst du?
What did you say?

Wie alt sind Sie?
How old are you?

Was machen Sie beruflich?
What do you do professionally?

Wo wohnen Sie?
Where do you live?

Woher kommen Sie?
Where are you from?

PRACTICE 1

Form the appropriate questions. Use question words where possible.

1. Er ist 20 Jahre alt.

2. Sie sind verheiratet.

3. Du hast Kinder.

4. Ich wohne in Berlin.

5. Mein Vater ist Lehrer.

6. Wir kommen aus Deutschland.

CONVERSATION 2

Remember when Stefan popped the question? Andrea has agreed to marry him, and now they are discussing the list of wedding guests.

Stefan: So viele Gäste? Das ist aber teuer.

Andrea: Ich habe eine große Familie. Aber keine Sorge. Mein Vater bezahlt das Fest.

Stefan: Wer ist denn Andrea Bergner?

Andrea: Meine Großmutter. Klaus Schmidt ist ihr Freund.

Stefan: Deine Großmutter hat einen Freund?

Andrea: Ja.

Stefan: Wie alt ist deine Großmutter?

Andrea: Sie ist neunundsiebzig Jahre alt.

Stefan: Und ihr Freund?

Andrea: Ihr Freund ist fünfzig Jahre alt.

Stefan: Und wer ist Petra Gerten?

Andrea: Meine Schwägerin.

Stefan: Aber dein Bruder Thomas ist doch nicht verheiratet.

Andrea: Das stimmt, Thomas ist ledig. Aber Georg und Frank sind verheiratet.

Stefan: Georg und Frank?

Andrea: Ja, meine anderen Brüder.

Stefan: Und wer ist Hannelore Pietgen?
Andrea: Meine Schwester.
Stefan: Du hast auch eine Schwester?
Andrea: Ja.
Stefan: Du hast vier Geschwister?
Andrea: Ja.
Stefan: Deine Familie ist wirklich groß!
Andrea: Ich liebe große Familien. Ich will drei oder vier Kinder.
Stefan: Oh . . .
Andrea: Und eins ist schon unterwegs.
Stefan: Wie bitte? Was sagst du da?
Andrea: Ich bekomme ein Kind, Stefan.
Stefan: Das ist ja fantastisch!

Stefan: *So many guests? That's expensive.*
Andrea: *I have a big family. But don't worry. My father will pay for the party.*
Stefan: *Who is Andrea Bergner?*
Andrea: *My grandmother. Klaus Schmidt is her boyfriend.*
Stefan: *Your grandmother has a boyfriend?*
Andrea: *Yes.*
Stefan: *How old is your grandmother?*
Andrea: *She is seventy-nine years old.*
Stefan: *And her boyfriend?*
Andrea: *Her boyfriend is fifty years old.*
Stefan: *And who is Petra Gerten?*
Andrea: *My sister-in-law.*
Stefan: *But your brother Thomas is not married.*
Andrea: *That's true. Thomas is single. But Georg and Frank are married.*
Stefan: *Georg and Frank?*
Andrea: *Yes, my other brothers.*
Stefan: *And who is Hannelore Pietgen?*
Andrea: *My sister.*
Stefan: *You have a sister, too?*
Andrea: *Yes.*

Stefan:	You have four siblings?
Andrea:	Yes.
Stefan:	Your family is really big!
Andrea:	I love big families. I want to have three or four children.
Stefan:	Oh . . .
Andrea:	And one is on the way already.
Stefan:	What? What did you say?
Andrea:	I am having a baby.
Stefan:	That's fantastic!

NOTES

Families in German-speaking countries tend to be small. Most families have only one or two children. As a result, the birthrates in Germany, Austria, and Switzerland are lower than in many other industrialized countries. In fact, the birthrate in German-speaking countries is lower than the death rate, which means there is zero population growth. Obviously, this is not an ideal situation; in the hope of promoting family growth, the governments of these countries have instituted laws offering such incentives for parenthood as financial support for young families and paid maternity or paternity leave (called **Elternzeit**) for up to twelve months.

NUTS & BOLTS 2
NUMBERS 20–100

zwanzig	*twenty*
einundzwanzig	*twenty-one*
zweiundzwanzig	*twenty-two*
dreiundzwanzig	*twenty-three*
vierundzwanzig	*twenty-four*
fünfundzwanzig	*twenty-five*
sechsundzwanzig	*twenty-six*

siebenundzwanzig	*twenty-seven*
achtundzwanzig	*twenty-eight*
neunundzwanzig	*twenty-nine*
dreißig	*thirty*
einunddreißig	*thirty-one*
vierzig	*forty*
fünfzig	*fifty*
sechzig	*sixty*
siebzig	*seventy*
achtzig	*eighty*
neunzig	*ninety*
einhundert	*one hundred*

Note that **eins** becomes **ein** when followed by an **und,** as in **einundzwanzig,** and **dreißig** ends in **-ßig** rather than the usual **-zig.** All numbers in the twenties, thirties, and so on, follow the structure of the nursery rhyme "Sing a Song of Sixpence"–*four and twenty blackbirds.* In other words, the German word for forty-six, **sechsundvierzig,** literally translates to *six and forty.*

Zehn und zehn ist zwanzig.
Ten and ten is twenty.

Achtzig minus zwanzig ist sechzig.
Eighty minus twenty is sixty.

Ich bin siebenundvierzig Jahre alt.
I am forty-seven years old.

Mein Vater ist vierundachtzig Jahre alt.
My father is eighty-four years old.

PRACTICE 2
Write out the numbers in German as you do the math.

1. $25 + 74 =$
2. $49 - 12 =$
3. $100 - 67 =$
4. $59 + 1 =$
5. $77 + 23 =$
6. $86 - 22 =$

Language link

It's traditional in German-speaking countries for the bride, groom, and wedding guests to take part in the **Polterabend** the night before the wedding. At the **Polterabend,** guests break glass, porcelain, or ceramics, and the bride and groom have to clean up the mess to show that they can work together. Visit **www.weddix.de** and see if you can find more interesting German wedding customs. The website is in German, but don't get frustrated if you can't understand everything! Look for cognates to help you along. The more you are exposed to the language, the more you'll start to pick up.

ANSWERS
PRACTICE 1: 1. Wie alt ist er? **2.** Sind Sie verheiratet? **3.** Hast du Kinder? **4.** Wo wohnen Sie? **5.** Was ist Ihr Vater von Beruf? **6.** Woher kommt ihr?

PRACTICE 2: 1. neunundneunzig; **2.** siebenunddreißig; **3.** dreiunddreißig; **4.** sechzig; **5.** einhundert; **6.** vierundsechzig

die Mutter	*mother*
der Vater	*father*
die Eltern	*parents*
der Sohn	*son*
die Tochter	*daughter*
die Schwester	*sister*
der Bruder	*brother*
die Geschwister	*siblings*
die Familie	*family*
das Zimmer	*room*
die Küche	*kitchen*
die Toilette	*bathroom, toilet*
der Tisch	*table*
das Bett	*bed*
der Stuhl	*chair*
die Möbel	*furniture*
Ich liebe dich.	*I love you.*
Willst du meine Frau/mein Mann werden?	*Will you marry me?*
Heirate mich!	*Marry me!*
Wer?	*Who?*

Was?	*What?*
Wann?	*When?*
Wie?	*How?*
Wo?	*Where?*
Woher?	*Where from?*
Wie alt sind Sie?	*How old are you?*
Ich bin ____ Jahre alt.	*I am ____ years old.*
Ich bin ledig.	*I am single.*
Ich bin verheiratet.	*I am married.*
Ich bin geschieden.	*I am divorced.*
Ich bin schwanger.	*I am pregnant.*

UNIT 3
Everyday life

Wie die Zeit vergeht . . . *How quickly time passes.* And our daily routines help us pass that time. Let's learn how to talk about our daily lives in German.

————————— Lesson 9 (words) —————————

First, let's learn the vocabulary for the days of the week.

WORD LIST 1

der Tag	*day*
Montag	*Monday*
Dienstag	*Tuesday*
Mittwoch	*Wednesday*
Donnerstag	*Thursday*
Freitag	*Friday*
Samstag	*Saturday*
Sonntag	*Sunday*
die Woche	*week*
das Wochenende	*weekend*
der Morgen	*morning*
der Nachmittag	*afternoon*
der Abend	*evening*
die Nacht	*night*
morgens	*in the morning*
nachmittags	*in the afternoon*
abends	*in the evening*
nachts	*at night*

NUTS & BOLTS 1
TELLING TIME

There are two common ways to ask the time in German.

Wieviel Uhr ist es?

Wie spät ist es?

the full hour	**Es ist zehn Uhr.**	*It is ten o'clock.*
the half hour	**Es ist halb elf.**	*It is half past ten. (lit., It is half eleven.)*
the quarter hour	**Es ist Viertel vor acht.** **Es ist Viertel nach acht.**	*It is a quarter to eight.* *It is a quarter after eight.*
counting the minutes	**Es ist zehn vor zwölf.** **Es ist zehn nach zwölf.**	*It is ten to twelve.* *It is ten after twelve.*

If you use the twelve-hour clock, you need to specify whether you are talking about **zehn Uhr morgens** or **zehn Uhr abends** and **ein Uhr nachts** or **ein Uhr nachmittags.**

Es ist Viertel nach neun morgens.
It is 9:15 in the morning.

Es ist drei Uhr nachmittags.
It is 3:00 in the afternoon.

The twenty-four-hour clock is used in many European countries in official announcements and for bus, train, or plane schedules. But even in casual situations, people use it rather frequently.

the full hour	Es ist 14:00 Uhr. (Es ist vierzehn Uhr.)	*It is 2 P.M.*
	Es ist 2:00 Uhr. (Es ist zwei Uhr.)	*It is 2 A.M.*
the half hour	Es ist 16:30 Uhr. (Es ist sechzehn Uhr dreißig.*)	*It is 4:30 P.M.*
	Es ist 4:30 Uhr. (Es ist vier Uhr dreißig.)	*It is 4:30 A.M.*
the quarter hour	Es ist 18:15 Uhr. (Es ist achtzehn Uhr fünfzehn.)	*It is 6:15 P.M.*
	Es ist 6:15 Uhr. (Es ist sechs Uhr fünfzehn.)	*It is 6:15 A.M.*
counting the minutes	Es ist 19:13 Uhr. (Es ist neunzehn Uhr dreizehn.)	*It is 7:13 P.M.*
	Es ist 7:13 Uhr. (Es ist sieben Uhr dreizehn.)	*It is 7:13 A.M.*

*Notice that the word **Uhr** comes between the hour and the minutes when spoken but remains after the minutes in written German.

Midnight, by the way, is considered **00:00,** or **null Uhr.**

Ich bin um 7:30 Uhr im Büro.
I'll be in the office at 7:30 A.M.

Ich arbeite bis 16:30 Uhr.
I'll be working until 4:30 P.M.

PRACTICE 1
Wie spät ist es? Indicate what time it is in German.

1. It is 3:30. (Use the 12-hour clock.)

2. It is 12:00. (Use the 12-hour clock.)

3. It is 5:15 A.M. (Use the 24-hour clock.)

4. It is 4:45 P.M. (Use the 24-hour clock.)

5. It is 4:45. (Use the 12-hour clock.)

6. It is 12:25 P.M. (Use the 24-hour clock.)

7. It is 7:30. (Use the 12-hour clock.)

8. It is 8:50. (Use the 12-hour clock.)

WORD LIST 2

das Frühstück	*breakfast*
das Mittagessen	*lunch*
der Kaffee	*coffee*
das Abendessen	*dinner*
das Brötchen	*(breakfast) roll*
die Butter	*butter*
die Marmelade	*jam*
die Zeitung	*newspaper*
der Bäcker	*bakery*
frisch	*fresh*
schnell	*fast, quick*
langsam	*slow*
jetzt	*now*
gerade	*at the moment*

früh	*early*
spät	*late*
lang	*long*
frei	*vacant*

NUTS & BOLTS 2
NUMBERS ABOVE 100

einhundert(und)eins	*one hundred one*
einhundert(und)zehn	*one hundred ten*
einhundert(und)-einundzwanzig	*one hundred twenty-one*
einhundert(und)dreißig	*one hundred thirty*
eintausend	*one thousand*
eintausendeinhundert	*one thousand, one hundred*
zweitausend	*two thousand*
zehntausend	*ten thousand*
hunderttausend	*one hundred thousand*
eine Million	*one million*
eine Milliarde	*one billion*

PRACTICE 2
Write out the numbers.

1. Wir heiraten 2010.
2. $1\ 000 \times 1\ 000 = 1\ 000\ 000$
3. $3\ 987 + 9\ 705 = 13\ 692$
4. $894\ 563 - 765 = 893\ 798$
5. $100 \times 100 = 10\ 000$

Discovery activity

It's time to create a German log of your routines. Write down, **auf Deutsch,** when you get up in the mornings, what time you have breakfast, when you leave for work, when you have lunch, and when you get home in the evenings. And if you work out regularly, mention that, too. And what do you do **samstags und sonntags?**

ANSWERS

PRACTICE 1: 1. Es ist halb vier. **2.** Es ist 12:00 Uhr (zwölf Uhr). **3.** Es ist 5:15 Uhr (fünf Uhr fünfzehn). **4.** Es is 16:45 Uhr (sechzehn Uhr fünfundvierzig). **5.** Es ist viertel vor fünf. **6.** Es ist 12:25 Uhr (zwölf Uhr fünfundzwanzig). **7.** Es ist halb acht. **8.** Es ist zehn vor neun.

PRACTICE 2: 1. zweitausend(und)zehn; **2.** tausend × tausend = eine Million; **3.** dreitausendneunhundertsiebenundachtzig + neuntausendsiebenhundert(und)fünf = dreizehntausendsechshundertzweiundneunzig; **4.** achthundertvierundneunzigtausendfünfhundertdreiundsechzig – siebenhundertfünfundsechzig = achthundertdreiundneunzigtausendsiebenhundertachtundneunzig; **5.** (ein)hundert × (ein)hundert = zehntausend

————————— Lesson 10 (phrases) —————————

Now it's time to talk about the seasons.

PHRASE LIST 1

im Sommer	*in the summer*
im Winter	*in the winter*
schwimmen gehen	*to go swimming*
joggen (gehen)	*to jog*
Fahrrad fahren	*to ride a bicycle*
Ski fahren	*to go skiing*

Schlittschuh laufen	to go ice-skating
Urlaub machen	to go on vacation
Pläne machen	to make plans
eine (Ferien)wohnung mieten	to rent an apartment
pro Woche	per week
Es schneit.	It is snowing.
Es regnet.	It is raining.
Es ist kalt.	It is cold.
Es ist warm.	It is warm.
Es ist heiß.	It is hot.

NUTS & BOLTS 1
THE MONTHS AND SEASONS

Most of the German names of the months and seasons are cognates.

das Jahr	year		
der Winter	winter	Januar	January
		Februar	February
der Frühling	spring	März	March
		April	April
		Mai	May
der Sommer	summer	Juni	June
		Juli	July
		August	August

der Herbst	*fall*	September	*September*
		Oktober	*October*
		November	*November*
der Winter	*winter*	Dezember	*December*

Im Winter gehe ich Schlittschuh laufen.
I go ice-skating in winter.

Im Sommer ist es sehr heiß in Kalifornien.
In summer it is very hot in California.

Im August machen wir Urlaub.
In August we go on vacation.

PRACTICE 1
Answer the questions or fill in the blanks.

1. Wann ist es heiß, im Sommer oder im Herbst?

2. Wann gehen Sie Ski fahren, im Januar oder im August?

3. Wann schneit es, im Juli oder im Dezember?

4. Herbst ist von _____ bis _____.

5. Frühling ist von _____ bis _____.

PHRASE LIST 2

Brötchen holen	*to go get breakfast rolls*
zum Bäcker gehen	*to go to the bakery*
nur noch ein Viertelstündchen	*just another fifteen minutes (lit., quarter hour)*
früh aufstehen	*to get up early*
spät aufstehen	*to get up late*
gern schlafen	*to enjoy sleeping*

gern fern sehen	*to enjoy watching TV*
gern Ski fahren	*to enjoy skiing*
gern haben	*to like*
Geburtstag haben	*to have a birthday*
Aber gern!	*With pleasure!*
Gern geschehen!	*You're welcome!, My pleasure!*

NUTS & BOLTS 2
EXPRESSING LIKES AND DISLIKES WITH GERN + VERB

The word **gern** expresses enjoyment. It is used either in set expressions, such as **Aber gern!** *(With pleasure!)* or **Gern geschehen!** *(You're welcome!)*, or in combination with verbs. Note that **gern** follows the main verb.

Was machen Sie gern?
What do you enjoy doing?

Ich gehe gern schwimmen.
I enjoy swimming.

Ich schlafe gern.
I like sleeping.

Wir tanzen gern.
We enjoy dancing.

Wohnst du gern hier?
Do you like living here?

Gern + haben can be used to express likes and dislikes for people and things. Note that **gern** follows the object of like or dislike.

Ich habe Peter gern.
I like Peter.

Sie hat Horst sehr gern.
She likes Horst a lot.

Er hat Claudia nicht gern.
He doesn't like Claudia.

If you want to show a preference, use the word **lieber.**

Ich sehe nicht gern fern. Ich lese lieber.
I don't like watching TV. I'd rather read.

And to express your favorite activity, use **am liebsten.**

Ich gehe am liebsten schwimmen.
I like swimming best.

PRACTICE 2
Answer the questions in complete German sentences. Be truthful.

1. *Do you like swimming?*
2. *Do you like your mother?*
3. *Do you like working?*
4. *Do you like to read?*
5. *Do you prefer to dance?*

Discovery activity
What are some of the activities you enjoy in the summer? And what do you like doing in the winter? Do you ski in winter and jog in the summer? Take out your log of routines, and write down your thoughts on these activities. **Auf Deutsch, bitte!**

ANSWERS
PRACTICE 1: 1. im Sommer; **2.** im Januar; **3.** im Dezember; **4.** September (bis) Dezember **5.** März (bis) Juni

PRACTICE 2: 1. Ich schwimme (nicht) gern. **2.** Ich habe meine Mutter (nicht) gern. **3.** Ich arbeite (nicht) gern. **4.** Ich lese (nicht) gern. **5.** Ich tanze (nicht) lieber.

Let's now put some of these phrases together into sentences to talk about your day.

SENTENCE LIST 1

Wieviel Uhr ist es?	*What time is it?*
Ich stehe morgens gern früh auf.	*I like to get up early in the mornings.*
Meine Mutter geht lieber abends spät ins Bett.	*My mother prefers to go to bed late.*
Morgens schlafe ich gern noch ein Viertelstündchen.	*In the mornings I like to sleep just another fifteen minutes.*
Das Bad ist frei.	*The bathroom is vacant.*
Er geht schnell Brötchen holen.	*He'll go quickly and get breakfast rolls.*
Ich lese morgens gern Zeitung.	*I like reading the paper in the mornings.*
Nachmittags trinken wir Kaffee.	*In the afternoons, we have coffee.*
Mein Mann kocht das Abendessen.	*My husband cooks dinner.*

NUTS & BOLTS 1
THE PLURAL OF NOUNS I

If you are talking about more than one of a thing, English usually just adds -*s* or -*es* to the noun: *plan* becomes *plans*. But even English has a few plurals that are more complicated—for example, *child* becomes *children,* and *goose* becomes *geese.* In German, there are five different groups of plurals. Let's look at the first four groups.

The most common plurals add **-n** (if the noun ends in **-e, -el,** or **-er**) or **-en** (if the noun ends in **-g, -n,** or **-t**).

Singular	Plural	
die Schwester	**die Schwestern**	*sister(s)*
die Adresse	**die Adressen**	*address(es)*

Another group of nouns adds **-e** in the plural. Often, but not always, the vowels **a, o,** and **u** become the **Umlaute ä, ö,** and **ü.**

Singular	Plural	
der Tag	**die Tage**	*day(s)*
der Plan	**die Pläne**	*plan(s)*

A third group adds **-er.** The vowels **a, o,** and **u** become the **Umlaute ä, ö,** and **ü.**

Singular	Plural	
der Mann	**die Männer**	*man (men)*
das Haus	**die Häuser**	*house(s)*
das Kind	**die Kinder**	*child (children)*

Words that originate in English add the English plural **-s** or **-es,** and, as in English, plurals of words ending in **-y** are formed by dropping the **-y** and adding **-ies.**

Singular	Plural	
die Party	**die Parties**	*party (parties)*
das Steak	**die Steaks**	*steak(s)*

PRACTICE 1
What is the plural?

1. die Tante
2. das Bett
3. der Plan

4. das Haus
5. die Show
6. der Architekt

SENTENCE LIST 2

Ich mache Urlaubspläne.	*I'm making vacation plans.*
Im Winter fahre ich gern Ski.	*I like skiing in winter.*
Meine Ski sind neu.	*My skis are new.*
Die Hotels haben keine Zimmer frei.	*The hotels do not have any more vacant rooms.*
Es ist Hochsaison.	*It's peak season.*
Wir mieten eine Wohnung.	*We'll rent an apartment.*
Weihnachten ist im Dezember.	*Christmas is in December.*
Das Jahr beginnt im Januar.	*The year begins in January.*
Ich habe im August Geburtstag.	*My birthday is in August.*

NUTS & BOLTS 2
THE PLURAL OF NOUNS 2
Here is the last group of plurals. Nouns ending in **-er, -en,** and **-el** do not add an ending in the plural. Either they don't change at all, or the vowels **a, o,** and **u** become **ä, ö,** and **ü,** respectively.

Singular	Plural	
der Lehrer	**die Lehrer**	*teacher(s)*
der Garten	**die Gärten**	*garden(s)*

Please note that this group includes the words ending in **-chen** and **-lein,** endings that makes a German noun diminutive.

Singular	Diminutive	Plural	
das Brot	**das Brötchen**	**die Brötchen**	*(breakfast) roll(s)*
der Bruder	**das Brüderchen**	**die Brüderchen**	*(small) brother(s)*
die Schwester	**das Schwesterchen**	**die Schwesterchen**	*(small) sister(s)*

PRACTICE 2
Give the plural.

1. der Bruder
2. das Zimmer
3. der Vater

4. das Brötchen
5. die Mutter

Language link

Check out **www.donnerwetter.de** to stay abreast of the weather in Europe throughout the seasons. You'll find expressions like **es ist heiß** *(it is hot),* as well as tips on whether your travel plans will be ruined by **Regen** *(rain)* or **Schnee** *(snow),* or whether **die Sonne** *(the sun)* will be out for your day at the beach or in the park. **Donner,** by the way, is the German word for *thunder.* (**Blitz,** if you haven't already figured it out, means *lightning.*)

ANSWERS
PRACTICE 1: 1. die Tanten; **2.** die Betten; **3.** die Pläne; **4.** die Häuser; **5.** die Shows; **6.** die Architekten

PRACTICE 2: 1. die Brüder; **2.** die Zimmer; **3.** die Väter; **4.** die Brötchen; **5.** die Mütter

—————— Lesson 12 (conversations) ——————

CONVERSATION 1

It is Monday. Charlotte and Dieter are going through their daily morning routine. This routine involves Dieter's reluctance to get out of bed.

Charlotte: Dieter, aufstehen! Es ist schon sieben Uhr.

Dieter: Schon wieder Montag. Das Wochenende ist immer viel zu kurz.

Charlotte: Stimmt. Aber du arbeitest doch auch gern.

Dieter: Schon, aber nicht montags. Und schon gar nicht im Winter.

Charlotte: Pech. Das Bad ist frei. Steh bitte auf.

Dieter: Es ist viel zu kalt. Ich bleibe noch ein Viertelstündchen im Bett.

About fifteen minutes later.

Charlotte: Dieter. Raus jetzt! Es ist schon Viertel nach sieben. Ich gehe schnell Brötchen holen.

Another fifteen minutes later.

Charlotte: Es ist halb acht. Und wenn du jetzt nicht aufstehst . . .

Dieter: . . . dann verpasse ich das Frühstück. Ich weiß.

Yet another fifteen minutes later, Dieter sits down at the breakfast table.

Dieter: Mmmh . . . frische Brötchen. Sind die vom Bäcker?

Charlotte: Ja.

Dieter: Wo ist denn die Butter?

Charlotte: Hier.

Dieter: Und die gute Marmelade?

Charlotte: Hier.

Dieter: Und wo ist meine Zeitung?

Charlotte: Das ist unsere Zeitung, und ich lese sie gerade.

Charlotte:	*Dieter, get up! It is seven o'clock already.*
Dieter:	*Monday again. The weekend is much too short.*
Charlotte:	*True. But you enjoy working, too.*
Dieter:	*Yes, but not on Mondays. Particularly not in winter.*
Charlotte:	*Too bad. The bathroom is free. Please get up.*
Dieter:	*It is much too cold. I'll stay in bed for another fifteen minutes.*
Charlotte:	*Dieter. Quickly, now! It is a quarter past seven already. I'll go get breakfast rolls.*
Charlotte:	*It's seven thirty. And if you don't get up now . . .*
Dieter:	*. . . I'll miss breakfast. I know.*
Dieter:	*Mmmh . . . fresh breakfast rolls. Are they from the bakery?*
Charlotte:	*Yes.*
Dieter:	*Where is the butter?*
Charlotte:	*Here.*
Dieter:	*And the good jam?*
Charlotte:	*Here.*
Dieter:	*And where is my newspaper?*
Charlotte:	*It is our paper, and right now I'm reading it.*

Notes

Brötchen from the **Bäcker** are rather typical breakfast fare. Many people leave the house as early as six in the morning to go to a local bakery to get them fresh in time for breakfast. The variety of breakfast rolls available is seemingly endless, particularly in the south. Specialties in the south include the **Laugenbrötchen** and **Laugenbrezeln** (similar to our soft pretzels).

NUTS & BOLTS 1
DESCRIPTIVE WORDS 1

Adjectives describe nouns. When used with **sein** *(to be)*, their endings do not change.

Horst ist groß.

Horst is tall.

Susanne ist klein.
Susanne is small.

Das Haus ist teuer.
The house is expensive.

Die Wohnung ist billig.
The apartment is cheap.

If an adjective is used before a noun with a definite article, its ending does change. Note the difference between the two sentences below.

Die Tochter ist schön.
The daughter is beautiful.

Die schöne Tochter heiratet.
The beautiful daughter is getting married.

The singular ending is **-e;** the plural ending is **-en.**

	Masculine	Feminine	Neuter
Singular	**der junge Mann**	**die junge Frau**	**das junge Kind**
	the young man	*the young woman*	*the young child*
Plural	**die jungen Männer**	**die jungen Frauen**	**die jungen Kinder**
	the young men	*the young women*	*the young children*

Der junge Vater ist stolz.
The young father is proud.

Der stolze Vater ist jung.
The proud father is young.

Die kleinen Kinder weinen.
The small children are crying.

PRACTICE 1
Please complete the sentences.

1. Mein Vater ist _____. (alt)

2. Die _____ Häuser kosten viel. (groß)

3. Die _____ Mutter heißt Elisabeth. (jung)

4. Das Mittagessen ist _____. (kalt)

5. Der _____ Lehrer hat kein Geld. (gut)

CONVERSATION 2
It is evening. Charlotte is coming home from work and finds Dieter hunched over the dinner table.

Charlotte: Was machst du denn?

Dieter: Ich mache Pläne für unseren Urlaub.

Charlotte: Prima! Ich gehe gern schwimmen.

Dieter: Schwimmen? Es ist doch viel zu kalt. Ich fahre lieber Ski.

Charlotte: Im Sommer?

Dieter: Nein, im Winter. Ich mache Pläne für den Winterurlaub.

Charlotte: Ach so.

Dieter: Wann hast du Urlaub?

Charlotte: Im Januar.

Dieter: Das ist Hochsaison. Gute Hotels haben keine Zimmer frei.

Charlotte: Dann mieten wir eine kleine Wohnung.

Dieter: Das ist zu teuer. Auch die kleinen Wohnungen kosten achthundert Euro pro Woche.

Charlotte: Na, dann eben kein Winterurlaub.
Dieter: Gut, dann machen wir Pläne für den Sommerurlaub.
Charlotte: Ich habe im August Urlaub.
Dieter: Das ist Hochsaison. Gute Hotels haben . . .
Charlotte: . . . keine Zimmer frei.

Charlotte: *What are you doing?*
Dieter: *I'm making plans for our vacation.*
Charlotte: *Great! I enjoy swimming.*
Dieter: *Swimming? It is much too cold. I'd rather ski.*
Charlotte: *In summer?*
Dieter: *No, in winter. I'm making plans for our winter vacation.*
Charlotte: *Oh.*
Dieter: *When do you have time off?*
Charlotte: *In January.*
Dieter: *That's peak season. Good hotels have no more vacancies.*
Charlotte: *Then we'll rent a small apartment.*
Dieter: *That's too expensive. Even the small apartments cost eight hundred euros per week.*
Charlotte: *Well, no winter vacation, then.*
Dieter: *Good, then we'll make plans for our summer vacation.*
Charlotte: *I have vacation in August.*
Dieter: *That's peak season. Good hotels have . . .*
Charlotte: *. . . no more vacancies.*

NOTES

German employees have rather liberal vacation schedules. German companies offer the national minimum of twenty days of vacation; many of them offer thirty days or more. Hence it is rather typical for families to go on vacation frequently, particularly because schools offer shorter vacations at least three times a year.

NUTS & BOLTS 2
DESCRIPTIVE WORDS 2

If an adjective is used before the noun it modifies with an indefinite article or possessive pronoun, its ending changes. Please note this difference in the sentences below.

Ein Kind ist jung.

A child is young.

Das junge Kind tanzt.

The young child is dancing.

Ein junges Kind tanzt.

A young child is dancing.

The masculine ending is **-er**, the feminine ending is **-e**, and the neuter ending is **-es**.

Masculine	Feminine	Neuter
ein junger Mann	**eine junge Frau**	**ein junges Kind**
a young man	*a young woman*	*a young child*

There is no plural form of the indefinite article. The ending for plural nouns without articles in all three genders is **-e**.

Masculine	Feminine	Neuter
junge Männer	**junge Frauen**	**junge Kinder**
young men	*young women*	*young children*

Eine kleine Wohnung ist nicht teuer.

A small apartment is not expensive.

Ein gutes Hotel hat keine Zimmer frei.
Good hotels have no more rooms available.

Alte Hotels haben kalte Zimmer.
Old hotels have cold rooms.

PRACTICE 2
Please complete the sentences.

1. Ein _____ Haus ist teuer. (schön)

2. Das _____ Zimmer ist schön. (klein)

3. _____ Frauen machen gern Pläne. (Jung)

4. Ein _____ Winter hat Schnee. (kalt)

5. Der _____ Winter ist vorbei. (warm)

Culture note

Time is money, particularly in punctual Germany. Trains and buses run on schedule unless the weather takes its toll. Stores, restaurants, and offices open and close at the appointed time, and no argument any customer can come up with will keep them open any longer. The only exception may be **das akademische Viertel** *(lit., the academic quarter [hour])*: classes at the university start fifteen minutes after the hour even though they are scheduled on the hour. This rather old and ingrained custom has filtered through to other areas of life, and it is quite acceptable to arrive a few minutes late to a casual appointment. But don't show up late for a business appointment. If you want to close the deal, you must be **pünktlich** *(punctual)*.

ANSWERS
PRACTICE 1: 1. alt; **2.** großen; **3.** junge; **4.** kalt; **5.** gute

PRACTICE 2: 1. schönes; **2.** kleine; **3.** Junge; **4.** kalter; **5.** warme

Wieviel Uhr ist es?	*What time is it?*
Wie spät ist es?	*What time is it?*
Es ist neun Uhr.	*It is nine o'clock.*
der Tag	*day*
Montag	*Monday*
Dienstag	*Tuesday*
Mittwoch	*Wednesday*
Donnerstag	*Thursday*
Freitag	*Friday*
Samstag	*Saturday*
Sonntag	*Sunday*
die Woche	*week*
das Wochenende	*weekend*
der Morgen	*morning*
der Nachmittag	*afternoon*
der Abend	*evening*
die Nacht	*night*
morgens	*in the morning*
nachmittags	*in the afternoon*
abends	*in the evening*

nachts	*at night*
das Jahr	*year*
Januar	*January*
Februar	*February*
März	*March*
April	*April*
Mai	*May*
Juni	*June*
Juli	*July*
August	*August*
September	*September*
Oktober	*October*
November	*November*
Dezember	*December*
der Winter	*winter*
der Frühling	*spring*
der Sommer	*summer*
der Herbst	*fall*
das Frühstück	*breakfast*
das Mittagessen	*lunch*
der Kaffee	*coffee*

das Abendessen	*dinner*
frisch	*fresh*
schnell	*fast, quick*
langsam	*slow*
jetzt	*now*
früh	*early*
spät	*late*
kurz	*short*
lang	*long*
frei	*vacant*
früh aufstehen	*to get up early*
spät aufstehen	*to get up late*
gern Ski fahren	*to enjoy skiing*
gern haben	*to like*
Aber gern!	*With pleasure!*
Gern geschehen.	*You're welcome!, My pleasure!*

UNIT 4
Health and the human body

We hope it will never happen, but in case you do get sick while traveling in Germany, Austria, or Switzerland, this unit will teach you how to tell the **Arzt** or the **Ärztin** what hurts. And in case you have a toothache, you'll be able to talk to the **Zahnarzt** or **Zahnärztin.** Many of the body parts are cognates and will therefore be easy to remember.

—————————— Lesson 13 (words) ——————————

Let's learn the German words for body parts, from head to toe.

WORD LIST 1

der Kopf	*head*
das Haar	*hair*
das Auge	*eye*
die Nase	*nose*
der Mund	*mouth*
der Zahn	*tooth*
die Schulter	*shoulder*
der Arm	*arm*
der Ellbogen	*elbow*
die Hand	*hand*
der Finger	*finger*
der Bauch	*belly, stomach*
der Magen	*stomach*
das Bein	*leg*
das Knie	*knee*
der Fuß	*foot*

der Knöchel	ankle
die Zehe	toe

NUTS & BOLTS 1
THE PRESENT TENSE OF REGULAR VERBS
Let's review the present-tense endings.

ich	-e	wir	-en
du *(sg. infml.)*	-st	ihr *(pl. infml.)*	-t
Sie *(sg. fml.)*	-en	Sie *(pl. fml.)*	-en
er/sie/es	-t	sie	-en

Here is a list of more verbs that take these endings.

fragen	to ask
antworten	to answer
erklären	to explain
verstehen	to understand
hören	to hear
öffnen	to open
warten	to wait
suchen	to search, to look for
wechseln	to (ex)change
weinen	to cry (tears)
behandeln	to treat

Ich frage; du antwortest.
I ask; you answer.

Bitte, erklären Sie das noch einmal.
Please explain this again.

Verstehen Sie?
Do you understand?

PRACTICE 1
Please complete the sentences.

1. Was _____ du? *(to ask)*

2. Ich _____ nicht. *(to understand)*

3. Warum _____ er? *(to cry)*

4. Bitte, _____ Sie hier. *(to wait)*

5. Wir _____ Geld. *(to exchange)*

6. Der Arzt _____ das Kind. *(to treat)*

WORD LIST 2

die Praxis	*practice, doctor's office*
das Krankenhaus	*hospital*
die Notaufnahme	*emergency room*
die Krankenschwester	*nurse (female)*
der Krankenpfleger	*nurse (male)*
der Schmerz	*pain*
die Wunde	*wound*
das Medikament	*medicine, medication*
die Tropfen	*drops*
die Tablette	*pill*
die Spritze	*shot (medical), syringe*
der Verband	*bandage*
das Pflaster	*adhesive bandage*

NUTS & BOLTS 2
THE PRESENT TENSE OF STEM-CHANGING VERBS

In addition to the present-tense endings **-e, -st, -en, -t, -en, -t, -en,** and **-en** that are added to the stem, some verbs show a stem-vowel change in the **du**-form and the **er/sie/es**-form of the present tense—for example, **fahren** *(to drive)*, **du fährst, er fährt.** These verbs are called *strong verbs*.

Here's the full conjugation of **fahren** *(to drive)*.

fahren *(to drive)*	
ich fahre	*I drive*
du fährst *(sg. infml.)*	*you drive*
Sie fahren *(sg. fml.)*	*you drive*
er/sie/es fährt	*he/she/it drives*
wir fahren	*we drive*
ihr fahrt *(pl. infml.)*	*you drive*
Sie fahren *(pl. fml.)*	*you drive*
sie fahren	*they drive*

Here are the most common stem-changing verbs.

e to i			
brechen	*to break*	**ich breche**	**er bricht**
essen	*to eat*	**ich esse**	**er isst**
geben	*to give*	**ich gebe**	**er gibt**

e to i			
helfen	*to help*	ich helfe	er h<u>i</u>lft
messen	*to measure*	ich messe	er m<u>i</u>sst
nehmen	*to take*	ich nehme	er n<u>i</u>mmt
sprechen	*to speak*	ich spreche	er spricht

e to ie			
lesen	*to read*	ich lese	er l<u>ie</u>st
sehen	*to see*	ich sehe	er s<u>ie</u>ht

a to ä			
schlafen	*to sleep*	ich schlafe	er schl<u>ä</u>ft
fahren	*to drive*	ich fahre	er f<u>ä</u>hrt

Er nimmt seine Tabletten.
He is taking his pills.

Vorsicht, du brichst dir noch den Arm.
Careful, you'll break your arm.

Der Arzt gibt Tabletten.
The doctor gives out pills.

PRACTICE 2
Rewrite the sentences using the personal pronoun or name in parentheses.

1. Ich spreche gut Deutsch. (du)

2. Wir nehmen Medikamente. (sie, *sg.*)

3. Sie fahren ins Krankenhaus. (du)

4. Er liest gern Zeitung. (ich)

5. Ich schlafe gern lang. (Frau Schneider)

Discovery activity

Do you remember the children's song "Head, Shoulders, Knees, and Toes?" Go ahead and sing it in German—**Kopf, Schulter, Knie, und Fuß**—and then teach it to somebody: your children, friends, or colleagues. You'll be surprised at how much teaching the song will help you learn and remember the German words. It will be fun, too.

ANSWERS
PRACTICE 1: 1. fragst; **2.** verstehe; **3.** weint; **4.** warten; **5.** wechseln; **6.** behandelt

PRACTICE 2: 1. sprichst; **2.** nimmt; **3.** fährst; **4.** lese; **5.** schläft

---

Lesson 14 (phrases)

Wo tut's weh? Let's make sure you know how to say where it hurts. Here are a few common phrases.

PHRASE LIST 1

weh tun	*to hurt*
Schmerzen haben	*to be in pain*
Kopfweh haben	*to have a headache*
Zahnweh haben	*to have a toothache*
Grippe haben	*to have the flu*
(hohes) Fieber haben	*to run a (high) fever*
Fieber messen	*to take someone's temperature*
eine Erkältung bekommen	*to catch a cold*

Husten haben			to have a cough
Schnupfen haben			to have a runny nose, to have a cold
ansteckend sein			to be contagious

NUTS & BOLTS 1
SEPARABLE VERBS

Separable verbs have a prefix that separates from the main verb in the present tense. For example, in a sentence, the verb **zuhören** *(to listen)* splits: **Ich höre zu.** *(I listen.)*

Note that the separable prefix moves to the end of the sentence.

Many verbs can have a prefix added to them to form a separable verb. Here are a few typical separable prefixes: **mit, ein, aus, an, ab, auf, zu, vor.**

kommen	to come	mitkommen	to come along
kommen	to come	ankommen	to arrive
fahren	to drive	abfahren	to leave
sagen	to say	ansagen	to announce
sagen	to say	absagen	to cancel
schlafen	to sleep	einschlafen	to fall asleep
kaufen	to buy	einkaufen	to shop
machen	to do	aufmachen	to open
machen	to do	zumachen	to close
lesen	to read	vorlesen	to read to, to read out loud
sehen	to see	aussehen	to look, to appear

Ich schlafe ein.
I'm falling asleep.

Er kommt mit.
He is coming along.

Wir machen die Tür auf.
We'll open the door.

Er macht die Tür zu.
He closes the door.

Die Mutter liest vor.
The mother reads out loud.

Mein Freund sieht sehr gut aus.
My boyfriend looks very handsome.

PRACTICE 1
Form complete sentences using the separable verbs and the nouns or pronouns given in parentheses.

1. abfahren (ich)

2. mitkommen (wir)

3. die Praxis zumachen (der Arzt)

4. zuhören (die Kinder)

5. früh einschlafen (mein Mann)

6. gut aussehen (die Krankenschwester)

PHRASE LIST 2

gegen Katzen allergisch sein	*to be allergic to cats*
gegen Hunde allergisch sein	*to be allergic to dogs*
den Arzt rufen	*to call a doctor*
einen Termin machen	*to make an appointment*
ein Rezept schreiben	*to write a prescription*

die Tabletten verschreiben	*to prescribe pills*
die Wunde auswaschen	*to clean the wound*
eine Spritze geben	*to give a shot*
einen Verband anlegen	*to put on a bandage*
Vorsicht!	*Careful!*
Pass auf!	*Pay attention!*

NUTS & BOLTS 2
REFLEXIVE VERBS

There are a few verbs that always take a reflexive pronoun—such as *myself, yourself,* or *herself*—which refers back to the subject of the sentence.

Ich wasche mich.
I wash myself.

These verbs are called reflexive verbs.

sich waschen	*to wash oneself*
sich kämmen	*to comb one's hair*
sich verletzen	*to hurt oneself*
sich erkälten	*to catch a cold*
sich anstecken	*to catch something (somebody else's illness)*
sich schonen	*to take it easy*
sich beeilen	*to hurry*
sich kümmern	*to take care of*
sich ärgern	*to be annoyed*
sich fühlen	*to feel*

sich wohl fühlen	to feel well
sich krank fühlen	to feel sick
sich gesund fühlen	to feel healthy
sich setzen	to sit down

The reflexive pronouns change depending on the subject the pronoun refers to.

ich	mich	*myself*
du *(sg. infml.)*	dich	*yourself*
Sie *(sg. fml.)*	sich	*yourself*
er/sie/es	sich	*himself/herself/itself*
wir	uns	*ourselves*
ihr *(pl. infml.)*	euch	*yourselves*
Sie *(pl. fml.)*	sich	*yourself*
sie	sich	*themselves*

Der Arzt setzt sich.
The doctor sits down.

Wir waschen uns.
We are washing ourselves.

Es ist kalt. Du erkältest dich.
It's cold. You'll catch a cold.

Warum ärgern Sie sich?
Why are you annoyed?

Ich stecke mich an.

I am catching something.

Please note that **anstecken** is a reflexive verb with a separable prefix.

PRACTICE 2
Insert the correct possessive pronoun.

1. Ich kämme _____ morgens.

2. Meine Tochter kümmert _____ um ihre Kinder.

3. Warum ärgerst du _____?

4. Bitte, setzen Sie _____.

5. Wir beeilen _____.

6. Vorsicht! Ihr verletzt _____.

Culture note

Fieber *(fever)*, just like any temperature, is measured in centigrade in Germany, Austria, and Switzerland. 36.8 to 37 degrees is considered **Normaltemperatur** *(normal body temperature)*. 37.1 to 37.8 is considered **erhöhte Temperatur** *(elevated temperature)*. Anything above 37.8 is considered a **Fieber**. Make sure you consult a doctor immediately for **Fieber** of 40 degrees centigrade or over—this is considered a **hohes Fieber** *(high fever)*.

ANSWERS
PRACTICE 1: 1. Ich fahre ab. **2.** Wir kommen mit. **3.** Der Arzt macht die Praxis zu. **4.** Die Kinder hören zu. **5.** Mein Mann schläft früh ein. **6.** Die Krankenschwester sieht gut aus.

PRACTICE 2: 1. mich; **2.** sich; **3.** dich; **4.** sich; **5.** uns; **6.** euch

The sentences below will help you show compassion if someone is not feeling so well.

SENTENCE LIST 1

Was ist denn los?	*What's the matter?*
Wie fühlen Sie sich?	*How are you feeling?*
Er sieht nicht gut aus.	*He doesn't look good/well.*
Sie sehen schlecht aus.	*You look bad/sick.*
Ich fühle mich nicht wohl.	*I don't feel well.*
Ich bin krank.	*I am sick.*
Wir stecken uns an.	*We're catching it.*
Er kümmert sich um sie.	*He takes care of her.*
Das ist nicht nötig.	*It's not necessary., You don't have to.*

NUTS & BOLTS 1
THE ACCUSATIVE CASE OF NOUNS I

Just like in English, sentences in German consist of at least a subject and a verb.

The subject performs the action described by the verb. If a noun performs the action, it is in the nominative case. This is the case we've been dealing with so far. If a sentence adds a direct object—a person or thing the subject acts on—it is in the accusative case.

Nominative (subject case)	Accusative (direct object case)
<u>Der</u> Arzt arbeitet.	**Ich rufe <u>den</u> Arzt.**
The doctor works.	*I'm calling the doctor.*

In English, the direct object does not change its form. In German, the accusative case announces the role the noun plays in the sentence by changing the form of the article.

The good news is that only the masculine article **der** changes to **den**. The noun itself stays the same, as do the feminine, neuter, and the plural articles.

	Nominative (subject case)	Accusative (direct object case)
m. sg.	**Der** Arzt arbeitet viel.	Ich rufe **den** Arzt.
	The doctor works a lot.	*I'm calling the doctor.*
m. pl.	**Die** Ärzte arbeiten viel.	Ich rufe **die** Ärzte.
	The doctors work a lot.	*I'll call the doctors.*
f. sg.	**Die** Krankenschwester wohnt hier.	Ich sehe **die** Krankenschwester.
	The nurse lives here.	*I see the nurse.*
f. pl.	**Die** Frauen wohnen hier.	Ich sehe **die** Frauen.
	The women live here.	*I see the women.*
n. sg.	**Das** Rezept is teuer.	Ich habe **das** Rezept.
	The prescription is expensive.	*I have the prescription.*
n. pl.	**Die** Rezepte sind teuer.	Ich habe **die** Rezepte.
	The prescriptions are expensive.	*I have the prescriptions.*

Der Arzt verschreibt die Tabletten.

The doctor prescribes the pills.

Der Patient nimmt die Medikamente.
The patient takes the medication.

Meine Frau besucht den Arzt.
My wife is seeing the doctor.

Meine Kinder haben Grippe.
My children have the flu.

PRACTICE 1
Complete the sentences using the appropriate definite article.

1. Ich rufe _____ Arzt.

2. Die Schwester legt _____ Verband an.

3. Mein Arzt schreibt _____ Rezept.

4. Er verschreibt _____ Tropfen.

5. Mein Sohn hat _____ Grippe.

SENTENCE LIST 2

Sie hat eine Erkältung.	*She has a cold.*
Sie hat einen Husten.	*She has a cough.*
Sind Sie allergisch gegen Medikamente?	*Are you allergic to any medication?*
Nicht dass ich wüsste.	*Not that I know of.*
Ich bin allergisch gegen Penizillin.	*I am allergic to penicillin.*
Wir bleiben zu Hause.	*We're staying home.*
Die Grippe geht um.	*The flu is going around.*
Sie sind krank. Schonen Sie sich.	*You're sick. Take it easy.*
So war das nicht gemeint.	*That's not what this was supposed to mean., I didn't mean it that way.*

NUTS & BOLTS 2
THE ACCUSATIVE CASE OF NOUNS 2
The indefinite article also only changes in the masculine singular, taking the ending **-en**.

	Nominative (subject case)	Accusative (direct object case)
m.	**Ein Arzt arbeitet viel.**	**Ich rufe einen Arzt.**
	A doctor works a lot.	*I'm calling a doctor.*
f.	**Eine Frau wohnt hier.**	**Ich sehe eine Frau.**
	A woman lives here.	*I see a woman.*
n.	**Ein Rezept ist teuer.**	**Ich habe ein Rezept.**
	A prescription is expensive.	*I have a prescription.*

Haben Sie einen Husten?
Do you have a cough?

Ich habe eine Erkältung.
I have a cold.

Das Kind braucht ein Pflaster.
The child needs an adhesive bandage.

PRACTICE 2
Complete the sentences using the appropriate indefinite article.

1. Die Schwester gibt _____ Spritze.

2. Das Kind hat _____ Husten.

3. Haben Sie _____ Pflaster?

4. Brauche ich _____ Rezept für das Medikament?

5. Ich nehme _____ Kopfschmerztablette.

ANSWERS
PRACTICE 1: 1. den; 2. den; 3. das; 4. die; 5. die

PRACTICE 2: 1. eine; 2. einen; 3. ein; 4. ein; 5. eine

—————— Lesson 16 (conversations) ——————

Let's hear what happens if a colleague doesn't feel too well.

CONVERSATION 1
Herr Liedel and Frau Neumann are colleagues. Their offices are across from each other. One day Herr Liedel realizes that Frau Neumann is not her usual self.

Herr Liedel: Was ist denn los, Frau Neumann? Sie sehen gar nicht gut aus.

Frau Neumann: Hmmmm . . . das hört eine Frau aber gar nicht gern.

Herr Liedel: Nein, nein. So war das nicht gemeint. Fühlen Sie sich nicht wohl?

Frau Neumann: Nein, ich habe Kopfschmerzen.

Herr Liedel: Hier. Ich habe Kopfschmerztabletten. Ich hole schnell ein Glas Wasser.

Frau Neumann: Danke. Das ist sehr nett.

Herr Liedel: Gern geschehen.

About an hour later, Frau Neumann is not feeling better at all.

Herr Liedel: Frau Neumann, wie fühlen Sie sich jetzt?
Frau Neumann: Ich bekomme eine Erkältung.
Herr Liedel: Haben Sie Fieber?
Frau Neuman: Nein, ich habe kein Fieber.
Frau Neumann starts to cough.
Herr Liedel: Oh je, Sie haben auch Husten. Ich fahre Sie nach Hause.
Frau Neumann: Nein, nein. Das ist nicht nötig.
Herr Liedel: Aber ich kümmere mich gern um Sie.
Frau Neumann: Stecken Sie sich nur nicht an.

Herr Liedel: What's the matter, Frau Neumann? You don't look good at all.
Frau Neumann: Hmm . . . a woman sure doesn't like to hear that.
Herr Liedel: No, no. I didn't mean it that way. Don't you feel well?
Frau Neumann: No, I have a headache.
Herr Liedel: Here. I have headache pills. I'll get a glass of water.
Frau Neumann: Thanks. That's very nice.
Herr Liedel: My pleasure.
Herr Liedel: Frau Neumann, how are you feeling now?
Frau Neumann: I'm catching a cold.
Herr Liedel: Are you running a fever?
Frau Neuman: No, I don't have a fever.
Herr Liedel: Oh dear, you have a cough. I'll take you home.
Frau Neumann: No, no. That's not necessary.
Herr Liedel: But I like taking care of you.
Frau Neumann: Just don't catch my cold.

NOTES
Using the titles **Herr** and **Frau** is rather typical in offices, even among people who may have worked together for years.

NUTS & BOLTS 1

THE ACCUSATIVE OF KEIN

Kein *(not, none)* works just like the indefinite article in the accusative. In other words, only the masculine singular takes the ending **-en**.

	Accusative (direct object case)	Example
m. sg.	**keinen**	**Ich habe <u>keinen</u> Husten.**
		I don't have a cough.
m. pl.	**keine**	**Ich nehme <u>keine</u> Tropfen.**
		I don't take drops.
f. sg.	**keine**	**Der Arzt gibt <u>keine</u> Spritze.**
		The doctor doesn't give a shot.
f. pl.	**keine**	**Ich nehme <u>keine</u> Tabletten.**
		I don't take pills.
n. sg.	**kein**	**Das Kind braucht <u>kein</u> Pflaster.**
		The child doesn't need an adhesive bandage.
n. pl.	**keine**	**Wir nehmen <u>keine</u> Medikamente.**
		We don't take any medication.

Diese Wunde braucht keinen Verband.

This wound doesn't need a bandage.

Ich habe keinen Schnupfen.

I don't have a cold/runny nose.

PRACTICE 1

Rewrite the sentences in the negative, using the correct form of **kein.**

1. Ich habe einen Husten.
2. Wir brauchen ein Rezept.
3. Der Arzt verschreibt Tropfen.
4. Meine Tochter hat Fieber.
5. Wir haben einen Termin.

CONVERSATION 2

The morning after Herr Liedel took her home, Frau Neumann is still feeling rather ill, so she is calling the doctor's office to make an appointment.

Krankenpfleger: Ist das ein Notfall?

Frau Neumann: Nein, nein, ich habe nur eine Erkältung und Fieber.

Krankenpfleger: Wir haben erst um 16:30 Uhr (sechzehn Uhr dreißig) einen Termin frei.

Frau Neumann takes the afternoon appointment. When she arrives at the doctor's office, she has to answer a few questions first.

Krankenpfleger: Sind Sie allergisch gegen Medikamente?

Frau Neumann: Nicht dass ich wüsste.

Krankenpfleger: Warten Sie bitte einen Moment. Der Arzt kümmert sich sofort um Sie.

Frau Neumann: Danke.

Just moments later, the doctor enters the room.

Doktor Fischer: So Frau Neumann. Sie haben Kopfschmerzen und einen Husten?

Frau Neumann: Ja, und neununddreißig Grad Fieber.

Doktor Fischer: Machen Sie bitte den Mund auf. Jetzt sagen Sie bitte "Aah!" Oh je, Halsschmerzen haben Sie sicher auch.

Frau Neumann: Ja, stimmt.

Doktor Fischer: Die Grippe geht gerade um. Ich schreibe Ihnen ein Rezept. Nehmen Sie die Tabletten täglich morgens und abends ein. Und bleiben Sie zu Hause.

Frau Neumann: Aber ich habe morgen einen Termin.

Doktor Fischer: Sagen Sie den Termin ab. Schonen Sie sich ein paar Tage.

Nurse: *Is this an emergency?*

Frau Neumann: *No, no, I have a cold and a fever.*

Nurse: *We only have an appointment at 4:30 P.M.*

Nurse: *Are you allergic to any medication?*

Frau Neumann: *Not that I know of.*

Nurse: *Please wait a moment. The doctor will take care of you shortly.*

Frau Neumann: *Thanks.*

Dr. Fischer: *Well, Frau Neumann. You have a headache and a cough?*

Frau Neumann: *Yes, and 39-degree fever.*

Dr. Fischer: *Please open your mouth. Now say "Aah!" Oh dear, your throat probably hurts too.*

Frau Neumann: *Yes, that's right.*

Dr. Fischer: *The flu is going around. I'll write you a prescription. Take the pills daily in the mornings and the evenings. And stay home.*

Frau Neumann: *But I have an appointment tomorrow.*

Dr. Fischer: *Cancel the appointment. Take it easy for a few days.*

NOTES

While in English body parts are usually used with possessives, German mostly uses the definite article.

Machen Sie den Mund auf.

Open your mouth.

Machen Sie die Augen zu.

Close your eyes.

NUTS & BOLTS 2
THE ACCUSATIVE OF POSSESSIVE PRONOUNS

In the accusative, the possessive pronouns take the same endings as the indefinite article and **kein**. In other words, only the masculine singular possessive pronouns take an **-en** ending.

	masc.	fem.	neut.	pl.	
ich	meinen	meine	mein	meine	*my*
du *(pl. infml.)*	deinen	deine	dein	deine	*your*
Sie *(sg. fml.)*	Ihren	Ihre	Ihr	Ihre	*your*
er	seinen	seine	sein	seine	*his*
sie	ihren	ihre	ihr	ihre	*her*
es	seinen	seine	sein	seine	*its*
wir	unseren	unsere	unser	unsere	*our*
ihr *(pl. infml.)*	euren	eure	euer	eure	*your*
Sie *(pl. fml.)*	Ihren	Ihre	Ihr	Ihre	*your*
sie	Ihren	Ihre	Ihr	Ihre	*their*

Ich nehme meine Tablette.

I take my pill.

Er nimmt seine Tropfen.

He takes his drops.

Wir nehmen <u>unser</u> Medikament.

We take our medication.

Ihr seht <u>euren</u> Arzt.

You see your doctor.

PRACTICE 2

Complete the sentences using the correct possessive pronoun.

1. Herr Sommer, wann nehmen Sie _____ Tropfen?

2. Ich rufe _____ Arzt an.

3. Meine Tochter sagt _____ Termin ab.

4. Die Krankenschwester fragt _____ Patienten. *(one patient only)*

5. Die Krankenschwester fragt _____ Patienten. *(more than one patient)*

6. Du brauchst _____ Tabletten.

Language link

Body parts are often used in colloquial expressions. **Auf großem Fuß leben** (lit., *to live on the large foot*) means that you live above your means, **mit jemandem unter vier Augen sprechen** (lit., *to speak with someone under four eyes*) tells of your desire to speak privately with somebody, and **jemandem den Kopf waschen** (lit., *to wash someone's head*) does not refer to shampoo, but rather, to have a word with someone. Check out **www.german.about.com/library/blidioms_start.htm** to find more expressions just like these.

ANSWERS

PRACTICE 1: 1. keinen; **2.** kein; **3.** keine; **4.** kein; **5.** keinen

PRACTICE 2: 1. Ihre; **2.** meinen; **3.** ihren; **4.** ihren; **5.** ihre; **6.** deine

der Kopf	head
das Haar	hair
das Auge	eye
die Nase	nose
der Mund	mouth
der Zahn	tooth
die Schulter	shoulder
der Arm	arm
der Ellbogen	elbow
die Hand	hand
der Finger	finger
der Bauch	stomach
der Magen	stomach
das Bein	leg
das Knie	knee
der Fuß	foot
der Knöchel	ankle
die Zehe	toe
der Arzt	doctor
der Zahnarzt	dentist

der Augenarzt	*eye doctor*
das Krankenhaus	*hospital*
die Notaufnahme	*emergency room*
Mein Bein tut weh.	*My leg hurts.*
Mein Arm tut weh.	*My arm hurts.*
Schmerzen haben	*to be in pain*
Kopfweh haben	*to have a headache*
Zahnweh haben	*to have a toothache*
eine Erkältung haben	*to have a cold*
einen Husten haben	*to have a cough*
einen Schnupfen haben	*to have a runny nose*
eine Grippe haben	*to have the flu*
ein (hohes) Fieber haben	*to have a (high) fever*
ansteckend sein	*to be contagious*
den Arzt rufen	*to call a doctor*
einen Termin machen	*to make an appointment*
Wie fühlen Sie sich?	*How are you feeling?*
Ich fühle mich nicht wohl.	*I don't feel well.*
Ich bin krank.	*I am sick.*
Nehmen Sie Medikamente?	*Are you taking any medication?*
Sind Sie allergisch gegen Medikamente?	*Are you allergic to any medication?*

Nicht dass ich wüsste.	*Not that I know of.*
Ich bin allergisch gegen Penizillin.	*I am allergic to penicillin.*
Verstehen Sie?	*Do you understand?*

UNIT 5
Using the telephone and making appointments

Communication these days is no longer just face-to-face. **Das Telefon** *(telephone)* has become such an important part of our daily lives that you're bound to use it while in Germany, Austria, or Switzerland. But don't worry; here's how you deal with it.

———————— Lesson 17 (words) ————————

WORD LIST 1

das Telefon	*telephone*
das Handy	*cell phone*
die Telefonnummer	*phone number*
die Handynummer	*cell phone number*
der Anrufbeantworter	*answering machine*
die Nachricht	*message*
der Computer	*computer*
die E-Mail	*e-mail*
der Brief	*letter*
die Verabredung	*date, appointment*
der Termin	*appointment*
die Besprechung	*meeting*
telefonieren/anrufen	*to call*
zurückrufen	*to call back*
hinterlassen	*to leave (behind)*
schicken	*to send*
erreichen	*to reach*

NUTS & BOLTS 1

THE ACCUSATIVE CASE OF PERSONAL PRONOUNS

Just like the masculine articles, personal pronouns change their form depending on whether they are the subject or the object in a sentence.

Nominative (subject case)	Accusative (direct object case)
Er ruft an.	Ich rufe <u>ihn</u> an.
He calls.	*I call him.*

Here are the nominative and accusative forms of all personal pronouns.

Nominative (subject case)		Accusative (direct object case)	
ich	*I*	**mich**	*me*
du*	*you*	**dich**	*you*
Sie	*you*	**Sie**	*you*
er	*he*	**ihn**	*him*
sie	*she*	**sie**	*her*
es	*it*	**es**	*it*
wir	*we*	**uns**	*us*
ihr	*you*	**euch**	*you*
Sie	*you*	**Sie**	*you*
sie	*they*	**sie**	*them*

*Note: From now on, we won't be listing *sg. infml/sg. fml.* and *pl. infml./pl. fml.* for the different forms of *you*. We hope by now you've learned the difference. If you need to refresh your memory, however, please refer to Unit 1.

The personal pronoun is used to avoid repeating yourself.

Ich schreibe einen Brief. Ich schicke den Brief ab.
I am writing a letter. I send the letter.

Ich schreibe einen Brief. Ich schicke ihn ab.
I am writing a letter. I send it.

Let's look at a few more examples.

Der Arzt hilft bestimmt. Rufen Sie ihn an.
The doctor will surely help. Call him.

Du bist so schön. Ich liebe dich.
You are so beautiful. I love you.

Peter und Horst, das war sehr nett. Ich danke euch.
Peter and Horst, that was very nice. I thank you.

PRACTICE 1
Rewrite the sentences using the appropriate object pronoun to replace the underlined nouns.

1. Ich schicke <u>eine E-Mail</u>.

2. Der Arzt schreibt <u>ein Rezept</u>.

3. Mein Mann sucht <u>meinen Sohn</u>.

4. Meine Tochter liebt <u>ihre Großeltern</u>.

5. Der Zahnarzt behandelt <u>dich und mich</u>.

6. Ich habe Andreas sehr gern. Ich liebe <u>Andreas</u> sogar.

WORD LIST 2

sich treffen	*to meet*
leider	*unfortunately*
wichtig	*important*
eilig	*urgent*

lang	*long*
kurz	*short*
neu	*new*
nett	*nice*
erfolgreich	*successful*
wohlhabend	*wealthy*
reich	*rich*
arm	*poor*
gutaussehend	*handsome*
neugierig	*curious*
lästig	*annoying*
naseweis	*meddling, nosy*

NUTS & BOLTS 2
N-NOUNS

As we saw before, German nouns usually do not take any accusative case endings. But there is a small group of nouns, the *n-nouns*, to which **-n** or **-en** is added in order to form the accusative.

Nominative case (subject case)	Accusative case (direct object case)
Der Herr ruft an.	**Ich rufe den Herr̲n̲ an.**
The man calls.	*I call the man.*

These words are not easy to recognize, and so it is best to simply learn them. Note that they are all masculine nouns.

man	der Herr	den Herrn
patient	der Patient	den Patienten
name	der Name	den Namen
architect	der Architekt	den Architekten
assistant	der Assistent	den Assistenten
husband	der Gatte	den Gatten
Frenchman	der Franzose	den Franzosen
client	der Klient	den Klienten
colleague	der Kollege	den Kollegen
nephew	der Neffe	den Neffen
student	der Student	den Studenten
tourist	der Tourist	den Touristen

Der Arzt behandelt den Patienten.
The doctor treats the patient.

Der Lehrer ruft den Studenten an.
The teacher calls the student.

Die Frau liebt ihren Gatten.
The woman loves her husband.

PRACTICE 2

Form a sentence from these particles, keeping the word order intact.

1. Ich/besuchen/mein Neffe.

2. Der Chef/anrufen/sein Kollege.

3. Mein Mann/haben/ein Assistent.

4. Der Franzose/fahren/ein Tourist.

5. Wir/bezahlen/der Architekt.

Tip!

Sometimes it's a bit hard to know whether a noun is the subject or the direct object of a sentence. You can sometimes figure it out by asking the following questions: **Wer macht das?** *(Who* or *what is doing this?),* which asks for the subject, and **Wen oder was?** *(Whom or what?),* which asks for the direct object.

Ich sehe den Mann.
I see the man.

Wer sieht den Mann? Ich.
Who sees the man? I do.

Wen sehe ich? Den Mann.
Whom do I see? The man.

ANSWERS

PRACTICE 1: 1. Ich schicke sie. **2.** Der Arzt schreibt es. **3.** Mein Mann sucht ihn. **4.** Meine Tochter liebt sie. **5.** Der Zahnarzt behandelt uns. **6.** Ich habe Andreas sehr gern. Ich liebe ihn sogar.

PRACTICE 2: 1. Ich besuche meinen Neffen. **2.** Der Chef ruft seinen Kollegen an. **3.** Mein Mann hat einen Assistenten. **4.** Der Franzose fährt einen Touristen. **5.** Wir bezahlen den Architekten.

Here are the most important phrases you'll hear and use on the telephone.

PHRASE LIST 1

Schneider, guten Tag!	*Schneider, hello!*
Wer ist am Apparat?	*Who is speaking?*
Honberg am Apparat.	*Honberg speaking.*
Besetzt!	*Busy!*
eine Verabredung machen	*to make an appointment*
eine Nachricht hinterlassen	*to leave a message*
meine Nummer lautet . . .	*my number is . . .*
(den Hörer) auflegen	*to hang up (the receiver)*
auf der anderen Leitung (sprechen)	*(to speak) on the other line*
Es ist dringend.	*It's urgent.*
Ich verbinde.	*I'll connect you.*
Auf Wiederhören!	*Good-bye! (on the phone only)*

NUTS & BOLTS 1
THE ACCUSATIVE CASE OF ADJECTIVES I

As you know, adjectives change their form depending on the gender and number of the noun they describe. They also change their form depending on whether they describe the subject or the object of the sentence.

Note that the definite article and the adjective only change in the masculine singular.

	Nominative (subject case)	Accusative (direct object case)
m.	**Das ist <u>der lange</u> Brief.**	**Ich lese <u>den langen</u> Brief.**
	That's the long letter.	*I read the long letter.*
m. pl.	**Das sind <u>die langen</u> Briefe.**	**Ich lese <u>die langen</u> Briefe.**
	These are the long letters.	*I read the long letters.*
f.	**Das ist <u>die eilige</u> Nachricht.**	**Ich höre <u>die eilige</u> Nachricht.**
	That's the urgent message.	*I hear the urgent message.*
f. pl.	**Das sind <u>die eiligen</u> Nachrichten.**	**Ich höre <u>die eiligen</u> Nachrichten.**
	These are the urgent messages.	*I hear the urgent messages.*
n.	**Das ist <u>das neue</u> Handy.**	**Ich nehme <u>das neue</u> Handy.**
	That's the new cell phone.	*I take the new cell phone.*
n. pl.	**Das sind <u>die neuen</u> Handys.**	**Ich nehme <u>die neuen</u> Handys.**
	These are the new cell phones.	*I take the new cell phones.*

Ich rufe die gute Ärztin an.

I am calling the good (female) doctor.

Der neue Assistent hat den neuen Chef gern.

The new assistant likes the new boss.

Ich sehe die kleinen Kinder.
I see the small children.

PRACTICE 1

Form a sentence from these particles, keeping the word order intact.

1. Die schöne Frau/heiraten/der junge Mann.

2. Mein Sohn/essen/das frische Brötchen.

3. Ich/habe/die neue Telefonnummer.

4. Meine Tochter/gern haben/die langen Haare.

5. Ihr/schreiben/der lange Brief.

PHRASE LIST 2

Wer ist denn da?	*Who is speaking? (lit., Who is there?)*
Ich bin's.	*It's me.*
Na dann . . .	*Well, in that case . . .*
Aha!	*I see.*
Was gibt's Neues?	*What's new?*
Ist alles in Ordnung?	*Is everything okay?*
Pass gut auf dich auf!	*Take good care of yourself!, Be careful!*
Viel Glück!	*Good luck!*
Viel Spass!	*Have fun!*
Genehmigt!	*Accepted!*
Vielen Dank für die Blumen!	*Thanks for the compliment! (lit., Thanks for the flowers! [often used sarcastically])*

NUTS & BOLTS 2

THE ACCUSATIVE CASE OF ADJECTIVES 2

When used with the indefinite article, adjectives change their form depending on their case in the sentence as well.

Note that the indefinite article and the adjective only change in the masculine singular.

	Nominative (subject case)	Accusative (direct object case)
m.	**Das ist <u>ein</u> <u>wichtiger</u> Termin.**	**Ich habe <u>einen</u> <u>wichtigen</u> Termin.**
	That's an important appointment.	*I have an important appointment.*
f.	**Das ist <u>eine gute</u> Antwort.**	**Ich gebe <u>eine gute</u> Antwort.**
	That's a good answer.	*I give a good answer.*
n.	**Das ist <u>ein</u> <u>schönes</u> Büro.**	**Ich habe <u>ein</u> <u>schönes</u> Büro.**
	That's a nice office.	*I have a nice office.*

Ich habe einen neuen Computer.
I have a new computer.

Mein Sohn hat eine nette Frau.
My son has a nice wife.

Wir kennen einen guten Zahnarzt.
We know a good dentist.

PRACTICE 2
Form a sentence from these particles, keeping the word order intact.

1. Ich/haben/ein wichtiger Termin.

2. Ihr/kaufen/ein neues Haus.

3. Du/treffen/ein neuer Kollege.

4. Wir/essen/ein gutes Abendessen.

5. Sie/haben/ein neuer Anrufbeantworter.

Culture note

In Germany it is customary to answer the phone by announcing your name rather than with just a simple *hello*. An additional **Guten Tag** is optional. By the same token, it is a good idea to identify yourself when you are the one calling. It is considered rude if you ask to speak to someone, or ask for information, without stating your name first.

ANSWERS

PRACTICE 1: 1. Die schöne Frau heiratet den jungen Mann.
2. Mein Sohn isst das frische Brötchen. **3.** Ich habe die neue Telefonnummer. **4.** Meine Tochter hat die langen Haare gern.
5. Ihr schreibt den langen Brief.

PRACTICE 2: 1. Ich habe einen wichtigen Termin. **2.** Ihr kauft ein neues Haus. **3.** Du triffst einen neuen Kollegen. **4.** Wir essen ein gutes Abendessen. **5.** Sie haben einen neuen Anrufbeantworter.

Lesson 19 (sentences)

It is often more difficult to speak a foreign language on the telephone than in person, because you can't use the helpful clues provided by facial expressions and gestures to decipher what the other person is saying. So let's practice the sentences that are commonly used on the telephone. Once you're accustomed to these expressions, you'll have less trouble understanding someone on the phone in German.

SENTENCE LIST 1

Kann ich mit Frau Heinrich sprechen?   *Can I speak to Frau Heinrich?*

Es ist leider besetzt.	*Unfortunately, it is busy.*
Darf ich Sie jetzt verbinden?	*May I connect you now?*
Legen Sie (nicht) auf.	*(Don't) hang up.*
Kann ich eine Nachricht hinterlassen?	*Can I leave a message?*
Kann ich Ihre Nummer haben?	*Can I have your number?*
Ich muss ihn dringend sprechen.	*I have to speak to him urgently.*
Das ist eine gute Nachricht.	*That's good news.*

NUTS & BOLTS 1
MODAL VERBS

Modal verbs modify a verb, which means that they tell us how the speaker feels about the action described in the verb. They are rather irregular, so it is best to learn them separately. In a sentence, the modal verb is conjugated, while the verb that describes the action remains in the infinitive.

Ich kann tanzen.
I can dance.

Note that the modal verb takes the second position in the sentence, after the subject, and the infinitive moves to the end of the sentence.

dürfen *(to be allowed to)*			
ich	darf	wir	dürfen
du	darfst	ihr	dürft
Sie	dürfen	Sie	dürfen
er/sie/es	darf	sie	dürfen

können *(to be able to)*

ich	kann	wir	können
du	kannst	ihr	könnt
Sie	können	Sie	können
er/sie/es	kann	sie	können

möchten *(to like to)*

ich	möchte	wir	möchten
du	möchtest	ihr	möchtet
Sie	möchten	Sie	möchten
er/sie/es	möchte	sie	möchten

müssen *(to have to)*

ich	muss	wir	müssen
du	musst	ihr	müsst
Sie	müssen	Sie	müssen
er/sie/es	muss	sie	müssen

wollen *(to want to)*

ich	will	wir	wollen
du	willst	ihr	wollt
Sie	wollen	Sie	wollen
er/sie/es	will	sie	wollen

sollen (ought to)			
ich	soll	wir	sollen
du	sollst	ihr	sollt
Sie	sollen	Sie	sollen
er/sie/es	soll	sie	sollen

Was soll ich dazu sagen?
What am I supposed to say to that?

Können Sie mich hören?
Can you hear me?

Kann ich bitte mit Frau Schneider sprechen?
Can I speak to Frau Schneider, please?

Ich will alles wissen.
I want to know everything.

Wollen Sie eine Nachricht hinterlassen?
Do you want to leave a message?

Darf ich jemanden mitbringen?
May I bring somebody?

PRACTICE 1
Rewrite the sentences using the modal in parentheses.

1. Ich spreche mit Frau Tröger. (müssen)

2. Ruft er zurück? (können)

3. Kommst du mit? (wollen)

4. Ich höre Sie nicht. (können)

5. Was mache ich jetzt? (sollen)

SENTENCE LIST 2

Ich kann dich nicht hören.	*I can't hear you.*
Die Verbindung ist schlecht.	*The connection is bad.*
Wann kann ich Sie wiedersehen?	*When can I see you again?*
Wir geben nächste Woche eine Party.	*We'll throw a party next week.*
Kann ich jemanden mitbringen?	*Can I bring somebody?*
Kann ich etwas mitbringen?	*Can I bring anything?*
Ich glaube nicht.	*I don't think so.*
Kenne ich Sie?	*Do I know you?*
Ich weiss nicht.	*I don't know.*

NUTS & BOLTS 2
TALKING ABOUT THE FUTURE USING THE PRESENT TENSE

The present tense can be used to talk about things that are happening right now.

Ich lerne Deutsch.
I am learning German.

The present tense can also be used to speak about events in the near future.

Ich habe morgen Geburtstag.
My birthday is tomorrow.

Future events that are scheduled, such as the departure or arrival of trains, buses, and airplanes, for example, are usually expressed with the present tense.

Der Zug kommt um 18:13 Uhr (achtzehn Uhr dreizehn) an.
The train will arrive at 6:13 P.M. (The train arrives at 6:13 P.M.)

If you are using the present tense to talk about future events, you can use time expressions to clarify that you are talking about the future.

morgen	*tomorrow*
übermorgen	*the day after tomorrow*
bald	*soon*
nächsten Montag	*next Monday*
nächste Woche	*next week*
nächsten Monat	*next month*
nächstes Jahr	*next year*
in einer Stunde	*in an hour*
in zehn Minuten	*in ten minutes*

Ich habe übermorgen einen wichtigen Termin.
I have an important appointment the day after tomorrow.

Ich rufe Sie in zehn Minuten zurück.
I'll call you back in ten minutes.

PRACTICE 2
Answer the questions using the time expressions in parentheses.

1. Wann hat er einen Termin? *(tomorrow)*

2. Wann kann ich Sie zurückrufen? *(in an hour)*

3. Wann haben Sie Geburtstag? *(next Wednesday)*

4. Wann kann er sie wiedersehen? *(next week)*

5. Wann fährt der Zug ab? *(at 5:12 P.M.)*

Discovery activity

Practice makes perfect. So why don't you write this week's schedule, **auf Deutsch natürlich.**

Write down at least one activity you have planned for each day of next week. Use the present tense to express these future events, and use as many time expressions as you can think of. And if you can manage, throw in a few modal verbs as well. Here's an example: **Nächsten Dienstag will ich früh aufstehen.** *(Next Tuesday, I want to get up early.)* Revisit your German planner at least once a week to update it.

ANSWERS

PRACTICE 1: 1. Ich muss mit Frau Tröger sprechen. **2.** Kann er zurückrufen? **3.** Willst du mitkommen? **4.** Ich kann Sie nicht hören. **5.** Was soll ich jetzt machen?

PRACTICE 2: 1. Er hat morgen einen Termin. **2.** Sie können mich in einer Stunde zurückrufen. **3.** Ich habe nächsten Mittwoch Geburtstag. **4.** Er kann sie nächste Woche wiedersehen. **5.** Der Zug fährt um siebzehn Uhr zwölf ab.

––––––––––– Lesson 20 (conversations) –––––––––––

Now it's time to listen to a few phone conversations.

CONVERSATION 1
Ursula Marquardt is making an urgent phone call.

Michael Honberg: Möbel Schuch, Honberg am Apparat.
Ursula Marquardt: Marquardt, guten Tag. Kann ich bitte mit Herrn Marquardt sprechen?
Michael Honberg: Herr Marquardt ist gerade am anderen Apparat. Wollen Sie eine Nachricht hinterlassen?
Ursula Marquardt: Ja, gern. Mein Name ist Ursula Marquardt. Meine Nummer lautet 0711 311538 (null

sieben eins eins, drei eins eins fünf drei acht).
Er soll mich bitte gleich zurückrufen. Ich
muss ihn dringend sprechen.

Michael Honberg: Natürlich, Frau Marquardt.

Ursula Marquardt: Vielen Dank. Auf Wiederhören.

Michael Honberg: Moment, Frau Marquardt. Legen Sie nicht
auf. Ich kann Sie jetzt verbinden.

Peter Marquardt: Marquardt.

Ursula Marquardt: Hallo Peter. Ich bin's, Ursula.

Peter Marquardt: Hallo Ursula. Treffen wir uns heute abend?

Ursula Marquardt: Nein, leider muss ich unser Abendessen
absagen. Ich habe eine wichtige Verabredung.

Peter Marquardt: Ist unser Abendessen etwa nicht auch
wichtig?

Ursula Marquardt: Doch, natürlich, aber ich . . . nun . . .

Peter Marquardt: Aha! Du triffst einen anderen Mann!

Ursula Marquardt: Ja, ich . . .

Peter Marquardt: Kenne ich ihn?

Ursula Marquardt: Wen?

Peter Marquardt: Kenne ich meinen Rivalen?

Ursula Marquardt: Nein, ich glaube nicht.

Peter Marquardt: Was soll ich dazu sagen?

Ursula Marquardt: Ich weiss nicht . . . «Viel Glück!» oder «Viel
Spass!» oder so etwas.

Peter Marquardt: Wie wär's mit, «Pass gut auf dich auf,
Schwesterchen!»

Michael Honberg: *Furniture Schuch, Honberg speaking.*

Ursula Marquardt: *Marquardt, hello. Can I please speak with Mr.
Marquardt?*

Michael Honberg: *Mr. Marquardt is on the other line. Do you want to
leave a message?*

Ursula Marquardt: *Yes, please. My name is Ursula Marquardt. My
number is 0711 311538. He should call me right
back. I have to speak to him urgently.*

Michael Honberg: *Of course, Ms. Marquardt.*

Ursula Marquardt: *Thanks. Good-bye.*

Michael Honberg:	Just a minute, Ms. Marquardt. Don't hang up. I can transfer you now.
Peter Marquardt:	Marquardt.
Ursula Marquardt:	Hello, Peter. It's me, Ursula.
Peter Marquardt:	Hello, Ursula. Will we see each other tonight?
Ursula Marquardt:	No; unfortunately, I have to cancel our dinner tonight. I have an urgent appointment.
Peter Marquardt:	Isn't our dinner important as well?
Ursula Marquardt:	Yes, of course, but I . . . well . . .
Peter Marquardt:	I see! You are meeting with another man!
Ursula Marquardt:	Yes, I . . .
Peter Marquardt:	Do I know him?
Ursula Marquardt:	Who?
Peter Marquardt:	Do I know my rival?
Ursula Marquardt:	No, I don't think so.
Peter Marquardt:	What am I supposed to say to that?
Ursula Marquardt:	I don't know . . . "Good luck!" or "Have fun!" or something like that.
Peter Marquardt:	How about, "Take good care of yourself, little sister!"

NOTES

The verbs **kennen** and **wissen** both translate as *to know*. **Kennen** is used with people, animals, places, and things, whereas **wissen** is used with facts.

Ich kenne den Mann, aber ich weiß seinen Namen nicht.

I know this man, but I don't know his name.

NUTS & BOLTS 1
THE FUTURE TENSE

As we said above, you can often use the present tense to express future events and actions. But there is also a special future tense reserved for talking about things to come. It is formed with the present tense of the auxiliary verb **werden** *(to become)* and the infinitive of the main verb. The conjugated form of **werden** stands in the second position, and the infinitive of the main verb moves to the end of the sentence.

Ich werde zurückrufen.
I will call back.

Here is the present tense of **werden** *(to become)*.

werden *(to become)*			
ich	werde	wir	werden
du	wirst	ihr	werdet
Sie	werden	Sie	werden
er/sie/es	wird	sie	werden

Werde ich Sie wiedersehen?
Will I see you again?

Er wird Blumen mitbringen.
He will bring flowers.

If **sein** or **werden** is the main verb, its infinitive is optional.

Ich werde am Samstag vierzig Jahre alt (werden).
I'll be forty years old on Saturday.

PRACTICE 1
Rewrite the sentences below using the future tense.

1. Ich sehe ihn bald wieder.
2. Er ruft mich an.
3. Unser Chef hat viel Arbeit.
4. Wir laden Freunde ein.
5. Wie alt sind Sie?

CONVERSATION 2

When Ursula comes home from her date late that same night, the phone rings.

Ursula Marquardt: Marquardt.

Peter Marquardt: Hallo Schwesterchen. Ich bin's, Peter.

Ursula Marquardt: Hallo Peter. Du rufst aber spät an. Ist alles in Ordnung?

Peter Marquardt: Ja, natürlich. Du hast nur einen sehr neugierigen Bruder. Ich will alles wissen. Ist er nett? Reich? Gutaussehend? Erfolgreich?

Ursula Marquardt: Mein Bruder? *(teasing)* Nein, ich habe einen sehr lästigen Bruder.

Peter Marquardt: Vielen Dank für die Blumen! Ich meine natürlich deinen neuen Freund.

Ursula Marquardt: Ach so. Ja, der ist sehr nett, gutaussehend und ein wohlhabender Geschäftsmann.

Peter Marquardt: Na dann . . . Genehmigt! Wirst du ihn wiedersehen?

Ursula Marquardt: Ja, wir sehen uns am Wochenende wieder. Er hat am Samstag Geburtstag und er gibt eine Party.

Peter Marquardt: Eine Party?

Ursula Marquardt: Ja, und ich soll einen Freund oder eine Freundin einladen.

Peter Marquardt: Einen Freund?

Ursula Marquardt: Oder eine Freundin.

Peter Marquardt: Darfst du auch deine Familie einladen?

Ursula Marquardt: Nicht die ganze Familie. *(She pauses.)* Aber einen naseweisen Bruder werde ich wohl mitbringen können.

Ursula Marquardt: Marquardt.

Peter Marquardt: Hello, little sister. It's me, Peter.

Ursula Marquardt: Hello, Peter. You're calling late. Is everything okay?

Peter Marquardt: Yes, of course. You just have a very curious brother. I

	want to know everything. Is he nice? Rich? Handsome? Successful?
Ursula Marquardt:	My brother? No, I have a very annoying brother.
Peter Marquardt:	Thanks for the compliment! I mean your new boyfriend, of course.
Ursula Marquardt:	Oh. Yes, he is very nice, handsome, and a wealthy businessman.
Peter Marquardt:	Well, in that case . . . accepted! Will you see him again?
Ursula Marquardt:	Yes, we'll see each other on the weekend. His birthday is on Saturday, and he is having a party.
Peter Marquardt:	A party?
Ursula Marquardt:	Yes, and I am supposed to invite a friend or a girlfriend.
Peter Marquardt:	A friend?
Ursula Marquardt:	Or a girlfriend.
Peter Marquardt:	Are you also allowed to invite your family?
Ursula Marquardt:	Not the whole family. But I am sure I will be allowed to bring along a nosy brother.

NOTES

Note that in German the host is not *having a party*, but *giving it*.

Er gibt eine Party.

He is having a party. (lit., He is giving a party.)

NUTS & BOLTS 2

THE FUTURE TENSE WITH MODAL VERBS

If a sentence dealing with future events or actions uses a modal verb, both the modal verb (**können,** for example) and the main verb (**mitbringen,** for example) are in the infinitive. Both infinitives move to the end of the sentence, whereas the conjugated form of **werden** stays in the second position.

Ich werde einen Freund mitbringen können.

I will be able to bring a friend.

Er wird mich zurückrufen wollen.

He'll want to call me back.

Der Arzt wird einen neuen Termin machen müssen.

The doctor will have to make a new appointment.

PRACTICE 2

Rewrite the sentences using the verb in parentheses.

1. Ich werde meine Mutter anrufen. (müssen)

2. Ihr Mann kann einen Termin machen. (werden)

3. Auf der Party werde ich etwas trinken. (wollen)

4. Wir dürfen Freunde mitbringen. (werden)

5. Du kannst mich anrufen. (werden)

Culture note

Germans have fully embraced the **Handy** *(cell phone)*, so much so that by now a greater percentage of the population owns **Handys** than in the U.S. As a result, many private households and even some businesses or individual offices may not have an **Anrufbeantworter** *(answering machine)*, let alone an answering service. And even if they do, they may not check it frequently. So if it's urgent that you get your message across, make sure you keep calling back until you talk to a live person.

ANSWERS

PRACTICE 1: 1. Ich werde ihn bald wiedersehen. **2.** Er wird mich anrufen. **3.** Unser Chef wird viel Arbeit haben. **4.** Wir werden Freunde einladen. **5.** Wie alt werden Sie?

PRACTICE 2: 1. Ich werde meine Mutter anrufen müssen. **2.** Ihr Mann wird einen Termin machen können. **3.** Auf der Party werde ich etwas trinken wollen. **4.** Wir werden Freunde mitbringen dürfen. **5.** Du wirst mich anrufen können.

das Telefon	telephone
das Handy	cell phone
die Telefonnummer	phone number
die Handynummer	cell phone number
telefonieren	to call, to telephone
anrufen	to call
wichtig	important
nett	nice
erfolgreich	successful
wohlhabend	wealthy
gutaussehend	handsome
der Patient	patient
der Assistent	assistant
der Klient	client
der Kollege	colleague
der Tourist	tourist
Wer ist am Apparat?	Who is speaking?
Es ist dringend.	It's urgent.
Wer ist denn da?	Who is speaking?
Ich bin's.	It's me.

Ist alles in Ordnung?	*Is everything okay?*
Viel Glück!	*Good luck!*
Viel Spass!	*Have fun!*
Auf Wiederhören!	*Good-bye! (on the phone only)*
Legen Sie (nicht) auf.	*(Don't) hang up.*
Kann ich eine Nachricht hinterlassen?	*Can I leave a message?*
Kann er mich zurückrufen?	*Can he call me back?*
Kann ich Ihre Nummer haben?	*Can I have your number?*
Wann kann ich Sie wiedersehen?	*When can I see you again?*
Kann ich jemanden mitbringen?	*Can I bring somebody?*
Kann ich etwas mitbringen?	*Can I bring anything?*

UNIT 6
Getting around town

——————— Lesson 21 (words) ———————

Traveling in a foreign country will take you to many different cities. Let's look at the vocabulary for describing the sights you'll see.

WORD LIST 1

die Stadt	*city*
der Stadtplan	*(city) map*
die Strasse	*street*
die Einbahnstrasse	*one-way street*
die Ecke	*corner*
der Gehweg	*sidewalk*
der Fußgänger	*pedestrian*
der Fußgängerüberweg	*crosswalk*
die Fußgängerzone	*pedestrian zone*
der Verkehr	*traffic*
die Verkehrsdurchsage	*traffic announcement*
die Ampel	*traffic light*
die Kreuzung	*intersection*
der Stau	*traffic jam, stopped traffic*
die Autobahn	*highway (interstate)*
die Landstrasse	*(country) road (state highway)*
die Richtung	*direction*
die Karte	*map*
folgen	*to follow*

NUTS & BOLTS 1
THE DATIVE CASE OF NOUNS
We've learned that German sentences consist of a subject, a verb, and sometimes an object. The subject performs the action de-

scribed by the verb, and the direct object (accusative object) is acted upon.

Der Taxifahrer *(subject)* **fährt** *(verb)* **den Fahrgast** *(direct object)*.
The taxi driver drives the passenger.

Some sentences add another object, the indirect object (dative object), which receives the action.

Der Fahrgast *(subject)* **gibt** *(verb)* **dem Taxifahrer** *(indirect object)* **das Fahrgeld** *(direct object)*.
The passenger gives the fare to the taxi driver.

In English, the indirect object is often preceded by a preposition, such as *to* or *with*. In German, the noun and its article change form to show the role that the noun plays in the sentence. Let's take a look at the dative forms of the definite article.

	Nominative (subject case)	Dative (indirect object case)
m.	**<u>Der</u> Taxifahrer fährt viel.**	**Ich gebe <u>dem</u> Taxifahrer Geld.**
	The taxi driver drives a lot.	*I give money to the taxi driver.*
m. pl.	**<u>Die</u> Taxifahrer fahren viel.**	**Ich gebe <u>den</u> Taxifahrer<u>n</u> Geld.**
	The taxi drivers drive a lot.	*I give money to the taxi drivers.*
f.	**<u>Die</u> Frau ist fremd hier.**	**Ich zeige <u>der</u> Frau den Weg.**
	The woman is new in town.	*I show the woman the way.*

	Nominative (subject case)	Dative (indirect object case)
f. pl.	**<u>Die</u> Frauen sind fremd hier.**	**Ich zeige <u>den</u> Frauen den Weg.**
	The women are new in town.	*I show the women the way.*
n.	**<u>Das</u> Auto ist teuer.**	**Ich fahre mit <u>dem</u> Auto.**
	The car is expensive.	*I drive in/with the car.*
n. pl.	**<u>Die</u> Autos sind teuer.**	**Ich fahre mit <u>den</u> Autos.**
	The cars are expensive.	*I drive in/with the cars.*

Please note that in the dative case, the definite article changes in all three genders. The plural form of the definite article in the dative case is **den** in all three genders.

Let's take a look at the dative forms of the indefinite article.

	Nominative (subject case)	Dative (indirect object case)
m.	**<u>Ein</u> Taxifahrer fährt viel.**	**Ich gebe <u>einem</u> Taxifahrer Geld.**
	A taxi driver drives a lot.	*I give money to a taxi driver.*
f.	**<u>Eine</u> Frau ist fremd hier.**	**Ich zeige <u>einer</u> Frau den Weg.**
	A woman is new in town.	*I show a woman the way.*
n.	**<u>Ein</u> Auto ist teuer.**	**Ich fahre mit <u>einem</u> Auto.**
	A car is expensive.	*I drive in/with a car.*

Please note that in the dative case, the indefinite article also changes for all three genders. Let's look at more examples of the dative case in use.

Mein Bruder fährt mit einem Auto.
My brother is driving in/with a car.

Meine Frau gibt dem Gast einen Stadtplan.
My wife gives the guest a map.

Zeigen Sie bitte der Frau den Weg.
Please show the way to the woman.

PRACTICE 1
Please complete the sentences, using the words in parentheses in the dative case.

1. Bitte zeigen Sie _____ den Weg. (der Mann)

2. Ich fahre mit _____. (ein Taxi)

3. Bitte, folgen Sie _____. (das Auto)

4. Der Fußgänger steht an _____. (die Ampel)

5. Der Verkäufer gibt _____ die Rechnung. (eine Kundin)

6. Die Kundin gibt _____ das Geld. (ein Verkäufer)

7. Die Mutter gibt _____ die Geschenke. (das Kind)

WORD LIST 2

das Museum	*museum*
die Schule	*school*
das Rathaus	*town hall*
die Polizei	*police*
das Parkhaus	*parking garage*
die Tankstelle	*gas station*
der Tankwart	*gas station attendant*

rechts	right
links	left
geradeaus	straight (ahead)
abbiegen	to turn
dort	there
umdrehen	to make a U-turn, to turn around
umsteigen	to change (trains or buses)
weit	far
weiter	farther
der Meter	meter
der Kilometer	kilometer

NUTS & BOLTS 2
THE DATIVE CASE OF EIN-WORDS

The negation **kein** and the possessive pronouns **mein, dein, sein,** etc., work just like the indefinite article in all cases and numbers. That's why they are usually referred to as **ein**-words. Let's look at the dative case of these **ein**-words.

	Nominative (subject case)	Dative (indirect object case)
m.	**Sein** Taxifahrer biegt rechts ab.	Ich gebe **seinem** Taxifahrer Geld.
	His taxi driver takes a right turn.	*I give money to his taxi driver.*
f.	**Meine** Frau ist fremd hier.	Ich zeige **meiner** Frau den Weg.
	My wife is new in town.	*I show my wife the way.*
n.	**Ihr** Auto fährt schnell.	Ich fahre mit **ihrem** Auto.
	Her car goes fast.	*I drive in/with her car.*

In the plural, an **ein**-word takes the same ending as the definite article in the dative.

	Nominative (subject case)	Dative (indirect object case)
pl.	**<u>Unsere</u> Kinder haben die Telefonnummer.**	**Ich gebe <u>unseren</u> Kinder<u>n</u> die Telefonnummer.**
	Our children have the phone number.	*I give the phone number to our children.*

Können Sie meinem Mann Ihre Addresse geben?

Can you give my husband your address?

Ich helfe seiner Mutter.

I am helping his mother.

Der Arzt gibt den Patienten ein Rezept.

The doctor gives a prescription to the patients.

Please note that the same nouns that add **-n** or **-en** in the accusative add **-n** or **-en** in the dative as well. Some of the most common nouns are: **der Architekt** *(architect)*, **der Herr** *(mister)*, **der Patient** *(patient)*, **der Student** *(student)*, **der Gatte** *(husband)*, **der Kollege** *(colleague)*, **der Tourist** *(tourist)*. Some nouns only add **-n** in the plural dative: **die Kinder** *(children)*, **die Fahrer** *(drivers)*.

Ich zeige dem Touristen den Weg.

I show the way to the tourist.

PRACTICE 2

Please complete the sentences, using the words in parentheses in the dative case.

1. Ich gebe _____ ein Geschenk. (seine Kinder)

2. Wir zeigen _____ den richtigen Weg. (unser Gast)

3. Fahren Sie gern mit _____? (Ihr Taxi)

4. Bitte hören Sie _____ zu. (meine Frau)

5. Gibst du _____ Trinkgeld? (kein Kellner)

Tip!

Sometimes it's difficult to know whether an object is the direct object and should take the accusative case, or whether it is the indirect object and should take the dative case. If you're not sure, check whether, in the English sentence, a preposition such as *to* could be used with that object. If so, that's the dative object.

Ich gebe meinen Kindern Taschengeld.
I give my children an allowance.

or

I give an allowance <u>to</u> my children.

ANSWERS

PRACTICE 1: 1. Bitte zeigen Sie dem Mann den Weg. **2.** Ich fahre mit einem Taxi. **3.** Bitte, folgen Sie dem Auto. **4.** Der Fußgänger steht an der Ampel. **5.** Der Verkäufer gibt einer Kundin die Rechnung. **6.** Die Kundin gibt einem Verkäufer das Geld. **7.** Die Mutter gibt dem Kind die Geschenke.

PRACTICE 2: 1. Ich gebe seinen Kindern ein Geschenk. **2.** Wir zeigen unserem Gast den richtigen Weg. **3.** Fahren Sie gern mit Ihrem Taxi? **4.** Bitte hören Sie meiner Frau zu. **5.** Gibst du keinem Kellner Trinkgeld?

Here are a few important phrases that will help you to get around town.

PHRASE LIST 1

Wo . . . ?	*Where . . . ?*
Entschuldigung, wo ist . . . ?	*Excuse me, where is . . . ?*
Wie komme ich . . . ?	*How do I get to . . . ?*
Entschuldigung, wie komme ich . . . ?	*Excuse me, how do I get to . . . ?*
Wie weit . . . ?	*How far . . . ?*
Entschuldigung, wie weit ist . . . ?	*Excuse me, how far is . . . ?*
sich auskennen	*to know one's way around*
rechts abbiegen	*to turn right*
links abbiegen	*to turn left*
geradeaus gehen	*to continue straight ahead*
an der Ecke	*at the corner*
an der Ampel	*at the traffic light*
zwei Straßen weiter	*two blocks farther*
(etwa) 100 Meter weiter	*(about) 100 meters farther*
noch (etwa) ein Kilometer	*(about) one more kilometer*

NUTS & BOLTS 1

THE DATIVE CASE OF ADJECTIVES 1

As you know, adjectives change their form depending on the gender, number, and case of the noun they describe. Let's take a look at the dative forms of adjectives with definite articles.

	Nominative (subject case)	Dative (indirect object case)
m.	**Das ist <u>der nette</u> Gast.**	**Ich zeige <u>dem netten</u> Gast den Weg.**
	This is the nice guest.	*I show the way to the nice guest.*
m. pl.	**Das sind <u>die netten</u> Gäste.**	**Ich zeige <u>den netten</u> Gästen den Weg.**
	These are the nice guests.	*I show the way to the nice guests.*
f.	**Das ist <u>die schöne</u> Frau.**	**Ich gebe <u>der schönen</u> Frau meine Telefonnummer.**
	This is the beautiful woman.	*I give my phone number to the beautiful woman.*
f. pl.	**Das sind <u>die schönen</u> Frauen.**	**Ich gebe <u>den schönen</u> Frauen meine Telefonnummer.**
	These are the beautiful women.	*I give my phone number to the beautiful women.*
n.	**Das ist <u>das neue</u> Auto.**	**Ich fahre mit <u>dem neuen</u> Auto.**
	That's the new car.	*I drive in/with the new car.*
n. pl.	**Das sind <u>die neuen</u> Autos.**	**Ich fahre mit <u>den neuen</u> Autos.**
	These are the new cars.	*I drive in/with the new cars.*

Note that the plural dative is the same in all genders: the plural definite article **den** plus the ending **-en**.

Ich helfe den jungen Männern.
I help the young men.

Können Sie der schönen Frau den Weg zeigen?
Can you show the way to the beautiful woman?

Wir fahren mit dem nächsten Bus.
We take the next bus. (lit., We go with the next bus.)

PRACTICE 1
Please translate these sentences into German.

1. *Can you help the old man?*
2. *The father gives a present to his little children.*
3. *They take the next train. (use* fahren mit*)*
4. *The students listen to the new teacher.*
5. *The teacher gives books to the good students.*

PHRASE LIST 2

ein Taxi rufen	*to call a cab*
mit dem Taxi fahren	*to go by cab*
den Bus nehmen	*to take the bus*
das Auto nehmen	*to take the car*
die Straßenbahn nehmen	*to take the tram*
mit dem Bus fahren	*to go by bus*
mit dem Auto fahren	*to go by car*
mit der Straßenbahn fahren	*to go by tram*
zu Fuß gehen	*to go by foot, to walk*
im Parkhaus parken	*to park in a parking garage*
eine Stadtrundfahrt machen	*to take a city tour*
ein Museum besichtigen	*to visit a museum*
im Stau stehen	*to be stopped in traffic*
im Stau stecken	*to be stuck in traffic*

| Gute Fahrt! | Drive safely! (lit., Good drive!) |
| Keine Ursache! | Don't mention it! |

NUTS & BOLTS 2
THE DATIVE CASE OF ADJECTIVES 2

Now let's take a look at the dative forms of adjectives with the indefinite article.

	Nominative (subject case)	Dative (indirect object case)
m.	**Das ist <u>ein netter</u> Gast.**	**Ich zeige <u>einem netten</u> Gast den Weg.**
	This is a nice guest.	*I show the way to a nice guest.*
f.	**Das ist <u>eine schöne</u> Frau.**	**Ich gebe <u>einer schönen</u> Frau meine Telefonnummer.**
	This is a beautiful woman.	*I give my phone number to a beautiful woman.*
n.	**Das ist <u>ein neues</u> Auto.**	**Ich fahre mit <u>einem neuen</u> Auto.**
	That's a new car.	*I drive in/with a new car.*

Ich helfe einem alten Mann gern.

It's my pleasure to help an old man. (lit., I like to help an old man.)

Können Sie einer neuen Kollegin das Büro zeigen?

Can you show the office to a new (female) colleague?

Ich fahre mit einem anderen Taxi.

I take another cab. (lit., I drive with another cab.)

Please note that all **ein**-words follow this pattern.

Ich fahre mit meinem neuen Auto.

I drive my new car.

Ich gebe keiner fremden Frau meine Addresse.

I don't give my address to any strange woman. (lit., I give to no strange woman my address.)

PRACTICE 2

Please translate these sentences into German.

1. *Please give your young wife the credit card.*

2. *Please follow a long street.*

3. *The manager shows the big hotel room to a rich guest.*

4. *I follow no bad advice. (Use der Rat.)*

5. *Why don't you (sg. infml.) help my little sister?*

Tip!

There are a few verbs that are always followed by a dative object. Let's take a look. The underlined words are in the dative case.

geben	**Geben Sie mir bitte die Karte.**
to give to	*Please give me the map.*
helfen	**Ich helfe meiner Mutter.**
to help, to give help to	*I help my mother.*
schulden	**Sie schulden mir Geld.**
to owe	*You owe me money.*
folgen	**Bitte folgen Sie dem Taxi.**
to follow	*Please follow the cab.*
zeigen	**Ich zeige Ihnen den Weg.**
to show to	*I'll show you the way.*
zuhören	**Bitte hören Sie mir zu.**
to listen to	*Please listen to me.*

---

gehören	**Das Haus gehört <u>meinem Vater</u>.**
to belong to	*This house belongs to my father.*
gefallen	**Die Musik gefällt <u>mir</u>.**
to like (to be to one's liking)	*I like the music.*
schmecken	**Das Steak schmeckt <u>mir</u>.**
to like (to be to one's taste)	*I like the steak.*

ANSWERS

PRACTICE 1: 1. Können Sie dem alten Mann helfen? **2.** Der Vater gibt seinen kleinen Kindern ein Geschenk. **3.** Sie fahren mit dem nächsten Zug. **4.** Die Studenten hören dem neuen Lehrer zu. **5.** Der Lehrer gibt den guten Schülern Bücher.

PRACTICE 2: 1. Bitte geben Sie Ihrer jungen Frau die Kreditkarte. **2.** Bitte folgen Sie einer langen Straße. **3.** Der Manager zeigt einem reichen Gast das große Hotelzimmer. **4.** Ich folge keinem schlechten Rat. **5.** Warum hilfst du meiner kleinen Schwester nicht?

Lesson 23 (sentences)

And now we'll move on to the sentences you'll need just in case you have to get around in a strange town.

SENTENCE LIST 1

Können Sie mir helfen?	*Can you help me?*
Können Sie mir den Weg zeigen?	*Can you show me the way?, Can you give me directions?*
Wie komme ich in die Innenstadt?	*How do I get downtown?*
Muß ich den Bus nehmen?	*Do I have to take the bus?*
Nehmen Sie den Bus Linie 3.	*Take the number 3 bus.*
Wo fährt der Bus ab?	*Where does the bus leave from?*
Muß ich umsteigen?	*Do I have to change buses?*

Wie weit ist es bis zur Sonnenstrasse?	*How far is it to the Sonnenstrasse?*
Es ist noch etwa fünfhundert Meter.	*It is about five hundred meters farther.*
Noch zwei Haltestellen weiter.	*Two more stops.*
Kann ich zu Fuß gehen?	*Can I go on foot?, Can I walk?*
Nein, das ist zu weit.	*No, it is too far.*

NUTS & BOLTS 1
THE DATIVE CASE OF PERSONAL PRONOUNS

As you know, personal pronouns change their form depending on their function in the sentence, just like nouns, articles, and adjectives.

Ich zeige <u>der Frau</u> den Weg. → Ich zeige <u>ihr</u> den Weg.
I am showing the way to the woman. → I'm showing her the way.

Here are the dative forms of the personal pronouns.

Nominative (subject pronoun)		Dative (indirect object pronoun)	
ich	*I*	mir	*to me*
du	*you*	dir	*to you*
er	*he*	ihm	*to him*
sie	*she*	ihr	*to her*
es	*it*	ihm	*to it*
wir	*we*	uns	*to us*
ihr	*you*	euch	*to you*
Sie	*you*	Ihnen	*to you*
sie	*they*	ihnen	*to them*

Geben Sie mir bitte Ihre Adresse.
Please give me your address.

Können Sie ihm helfen?
Can you help him?

Ich zeige dir den Stadtplan.
I'll show you the map.

PRACTICE 1

Please translate these sentences from English into German.

1. *Can you show me the way?*
2. *Please give (sg. fml.) her the map.*
3. *Our children listen to us.*
4. *She follows him.*
5. *Can you help me?*

SENTENCE LIST 2

Wie komme ich zum Museum?	*How do I get to the museum?*
Gehen Sie geradeaus.	*Go straight.*
Biegen Sie hier links ab.	*Turn left here.*
Biegen Sie an der Ampel rechts ab.	*Turn right at the traffic light.*
Gehen Sie über den Fußgängerweg.	*Take the crosswalk.*
An der Ecke gehen Sie nach links.	*Turn left at the corner.*
Nach etwa zweihundert Metern biegen Sie rechts ab.	*After about two hundred meters, turn right.*
Wie komme ich nach Hannover?	*How do I get to Hannover?*
Sie müssen die Autobahn nehmen.	*You have to take the Autobahn.*

Nehmen Sie die A8 Richtung Karlsruhe.	*Take the A8 towards Karlsruhe.*
Fahren Sie in Richtung München.	*Drive towards/in the direction of Munich.*
Fahren Sie an der nächsten Ausfahrt ab.	*Get off at the next (highway) exit.*

NUTS & BOLTS 2
GERMAN WORD ORDER IN SENTENCES WITH TWO OBJECTS
If a German sentence has both a direct and an indirect object, the indirect object always comes first.

Thomas gibt dem Gast einen Stadtplan.
Thomas gives the guest a map.

This is also true if the indirect object is a personal pronoun.

Bitte zeigen Sie mir den Weg.
Please show me the way.

But if both objects are pronouns, the direct object comes first.

Ich gebe dir das Geld.
I give you the money.

but

Ich gebe es dir.
I give it to you.

PRACTICE 2
Please unscramble the sentences.

1. gibt/das Kind/das Spielzeug/dem Vater/.
2. helfen/Sie/uns/können/?

3. Geld/schulde/ich/Ihnen/.

4. gebe/es/Ihnen/ich.

5. den Touristen/wir/den Weg/zeigen/.

Discovery activity

Imagine that a friend is visiting from out of town. Give him or her directions from your place to a few sights in town: the museum, a park to stroll in, your place of work, your school, the best restaurant in town. Give directions first orally, and then write them down. **Auf Deutsch, bitte!**

ANSWERS
PRACTICE 1: 1. Können Sie mir den Weg zeigen? **2.** Bitte geben Sie ihr den Stadtplan. **3.** Unsere Kinder hören uns zu. **4.** Sie folgt ihm. **5.** Können Sie mir helfen?

PRACTICE 2: 1. Das Kind gibt dem Vater das Spielzeug. **2.** Können Sie uns helfen? **3.** Ich schulde Ihnen Geld. **4.** Ich gebe es Ihnen. **5.** Wir zeigen den Touristen den Weg.

——————— Lesson 24 (conversations) ———————

What happens if you get lost on a business tip?

CONVERSATION 1
Margit Brenner is on a business trip in München. She has rented a car and is on the **Autobahn** *on her way to an important appointment in nearby Augsburg. Unfortunately, she is stuck in traffic. Margit is listening to the radio while she is stopped in traffic.*

Margit: Die Musik gefällt mir. *(She hums softly.)*

Radiosprecher: Meine Damen und Herren, wir unterbrechen unser Programm für eine Verkehrsdurchsage. A 8 München Richtung Augsburg, vier Kilometer Stau bei Sulzemoos.

Margit: Vier Kilometer Stau! Das kann auch nur mir passieren. Ich bin so spät dran und stecke im Stau. Ich muß die nächste Ausfahrt nehmen. Es ist noch ein Kilometer bis zur nächsten Ausfahrt. Na endlich! *(She takes the exit.)* So, und was jetzt? Ich kenne mich hier nicht aus. Ich muß an der Tankstelle nach dem Weg fragen. *(She drives into the gas station, parks the car, and addresses the attendant.)* Entschuldigung, wie komme ich nach Augsburg?

Tankwart: Nehmen Sie die Autobahn, die A 8.

Margit: Ich komme gerade von der Autobahn. Vier Kilometer Stau.

Tankwart: Wie immer. Ja dann nehmen Sie einfach die Landstrasse Richtung Friedberg. Biegen Sie an der Ampel links ab, und folgen Sie der Landstrasse nach Friedberg. Das sind noch etwa zwanzig Kilometer. In Friedberg folgen Sie dann den Schildern nach Augsburg.

Margit: Vielen Dank.

Tankwart: Keine Ursache. Brauchen Sie eine Karte?

Margit: Nein danke.

Tankwart: Na dann, gute Fahrt!

Margit: *I like the music.*

Radio announcer: *Ladies and gentlemen, we are interrupting our program for our traffic watch. A 8 towards Augsburg, four kilometers of stopped traffic near Sulzemoos.*

Margit: *Four kilometers of stopped traffic! This could only happen to me. I am so late and I am stuck in traffic. I have to take the next exit. One more kilometer to the next exit. Finally! Now what? I don't know my way around here. I have to ask for directions at the gas station. Excuse me, how do I get to Augsburg?*

Attendant: *Take the Autobahn, the A 8.*

Margit: *I'm just coming from the Autobahn. Four kilometers of stopped traffic.*

Attendant:	As usual. Well, then, take the road towards Friedberg. Take a left turn at the traffic light, and follow the road to Friedberg. That's another twenty kilometers. In Friedberg, just follow the signs to Augsburg.
Margit:	Thanks a lot.
Attendant:	Don't mention it. Do you need a map?
Margit:	No thanks.
Attendant:	Well, then, drive safely.

NOTES

The **Autobahn** *(highway)* is probably one of the most famous characteristics of Germany. But the **Autobahn** is in fact many different **Autobahnen,** no different from the American highway system. And just like American highways, the German **Autobahnen** are numbered. The A 8 between München and Karlsruhe is among the busiest stretches of highway in Europe.

NUTS & BOLTS 1

PREPOSITIONS WITH THE DATIVE CASE

Such words as *to, with, after,* and *from* are called prepositions. They express the location or direction of the action described by the verb or the relationship of the objects in the sentence. In German, the noun that follows a preposition must be in a given case. There are a few prepositions that always introduce the dative case. Let's take a look. The underlined noun is in the dative case following the dative preposition.

mit	Ich fahre mit <u>dem Taxi</u>.
in/with	*I am taking a cab. (lit., I'm driving with a cab.)*
nach	Nach <u>der Ampel</u> biegen Sie links ab.
after	*After the traffic light, take a left.*

bei	**Es ist immer nett bei <u>dir</u>.**
with, by, at	*It is always nice at your house.*
zu	**Ich komme gern zu <u>dir</u>.**
to	*I like coming to your house.*
aus	**Er kommt aus <u>dem Hotel</u>.**
from	*He is coming from the hotel.*
von	**Ich komme von <u>der Autobahn</u>.**
from, of	*I am coming from the Autobahn.*
seit	**Ich warte seit <u>einer Woche</u>.**
since, for	*I've been waiting for a week.*
außer	**Außer <u>mir</u> fährt keiner mit <u>meinem Auto</u>.**
except for	*Except for me, nobody drives (in/with) my car.*
gegenüber	**Das Hotel ist gegenüber <u>dem Museum</u>.**
across from	*The hotel is across from the museum.*

Note that the prepositions **zu** and **von** contract with the masculine and neuter dative articles.

zu dem = zum	Ich fahre zum Hotel.
to the	*I am driving to the hotel.*
von dem = vom	Ich komme vom Hotel.
from the	*I am coming from the hotel.*

PRACTICE 1
Please complete the sentences.

1. Die Bank ist gegenüber _____. (das Rathaus)

2. Mein Vater kommt aus _____. (das Büro)

3. Es ist immer nett bei _____. (Sie)

4. Fahren Sie mit _____? (der Bus)

5. Nach _____ biegen Sie rechts ab. (die Tankstelle)

CONVERSATION 2
Margit has arrived safely in Augsburg. Now she must find the office where she is supposed to meet with a colleague.

Margit: Das Büro ist direkt neben der Augsburger Puppenkiste. Dann frage ich einfach nach dem Weg zur Augsburger Puppenkiste. Entschuldigung, wo ist die Augsburger Puppenkiste?

Fußgänger: Die Augsburger Puppenkiste ist in der Spitalstrasse.

Margit: Können Sie mir den Weg zur Spitalstrasse zeigen?

Fußgänger: Aber gern. Gehen Sie hier geradeaus. An der Ecke biegen Sie rechts ab. Dann gehen Sie zwei Straßen weiter bis zu einer Schule. Dort biegen Sie links ab. An der nächsten Ampel nehmen

Sie den Fußgängerüberweg. Der führt direkt
zum Rathaus. Die Spitalstrasse ist rechts neben
dem Rathaus.

Margit: Muß ich zu Fuß gehen?

Fußgänger: Nein, Sie müssen nicht zu Fuß gehen. Aber es
ist einfacher für Sie. In der Innenstadt werden
Sie keinen Parkplatz für Ihr Auto finden.

Margit: Kann ich hier parken?

Fußgänger: Ja, Sie können in dem Parkhaus parken. Die
Einfahrt in das Parkhaus ist gleich um die
Ecke.

Margit: Gut, dann drehe ich einfach um.

Fußgänger: Nein, das ist eine Einbahnstrasse. Sie dürfen
hier nicht umdrehen.

Margit: Oh, vielen Dank.

Fußgänger: Keine Ursache.

Margit: *The office is right next to the Augsburger Puppenkiste.
So I'll simply ask for directions to the Augsburger
Puppenkiste. Excuse me, where is the Augsburger
Puppenkiste?*

Pedestrian: *The Augsburger Puppenkiste is in the Spitalstrasse.*

Margit: *Can you give me directions to the Spitalstrasse?*

Pedestrian: *Of course. Go straight ahead. At the corner, turn right.
Then go two more blocks to a school. There, you turn
left. At the next traffic light, take the crosswalk. That
leads directly to the town hall. The Spitalstrasse is next
to the town hall, on the right.*

Margit: *Do I have to go by foot?*

Pedestrian: *No, you don't have to go by foot. But it will be easier
for you. Downtown, you will not find parking for your
car.*

Margit: *Can I park here?*

Pedestrian: *Yes, you can park in the parking garage. The entrance to
the parking garage is just around the corner.*

Margit: *Good. I'll turn around here.*

Pedestrian:	No, this is a one-way street. You are not allowed to turn here.
Margit:	Oh, thanks a lot.
Pedestrian:	Don't mention it.

NOTES

The **Augsburger Puppenkiste** is a famous marionette theater in Augsburg, which had its opening night on February 26, 1948, with *Der Gestiefelte Kater (Puss in Boots)*. Since then, the **Augsburger Puppenkiste** has had regular live performances in its original theater in the Spitalstrasse. In the 1970s, the **Puppenkiste** became famous well beyond Augsburg through numerous TV productions of fairy tales and modern plays for children.

NUTS & BOLTS 2
PREPOSITIONS WITH THE ACCUSATIVE CASE

There are also a few prepositions that are always followed by the accusative case.

für	**Es ist einfacher für mich.**
for	*It is easier for me.*
ohne	**Der Bus fährt ohne uns ab.**
without	*The bus is leaving without us.*
gegen	**Ich habe nichts gegen ein neues Auto.**
against	*I have nothing against a new car.*
durch	**Sie müssen durch die Stadt fahren.**
through	*You have to drive through town.*

um	Die Tankstelle ist gleich um die Ecke.
around	*The gas station is just around the corner.*

PRACTICE 2
Please complete the sentences.

1. Ich suche einen Parkplatz für _____. (mein Auto)

2. Ist das Museum um _____ oder neben _____. (die Ecke/die Tankstelle)

3. Kann ich mit _____ durch _____ fahren? (das Auto/die Stadt)

4. Ich habe ein Geschenk für _____. (du)

5. Er geht nicht ohne _____ aus _____. (seine Frau/das Haus)

Culture note
Germany, Switzerland, and Austria, like most European countries, use the decimal system. This means that distance is measured in meters and kilometers, and weight is measured in grams and kilograms. 1 **Kilometer** is about 0.62 miles, and 1 mile is about 1.61 **Kilometer**. 1 **Kilogramm** is about 2.2 pounds, and 1 pound is about 0.45 **Kilogramm.** You may not need to know how much you weigh in **Kilogramm,** but it is important to remember that the speed limit within city limits is 50 km/hr, and in residential neighborhoods, 30 km/hr. On most **Landstrassen,** you are not allowed to go any faster than 130 km/hr, and while it is true that there are parts of the **Autobahn** where you can go as fast as you wish, around towns and cities and near airports there are speed limits even on the **Autobahn.** The general trend—even on the **Autobahn**—goes toward a suggested speed limit of 130 km/hr.

ANSWERS

PRACTICE 1: 1. dem Rathaus; **2.** dem Büro; **3.** Ihnen; **4.** dem Bus; **5.** der Tankstelle

PRACTICE 2: 1. mein Auto; **2.** die Ecke/der Tankstelle; **3.** dem Auto/die Stadt; **4.** dich; **5.** seine Frau/dem Haus

UNIT 6 ESSENTIALS

Entschuldigung, wo ist . . . ?	*Excuse me, where is . . . ?*
Entschuldigung, wie komme ich . . . ?	*Excuse me, how do I get to . . . ?*
Entschuldigung, wie weit ist . . . ?	*Excuse me, how far is . . . ?*
Können Sie mir helfen?	*Can you help me?*
Können Sie mir den Weg zeigen?	*Can you show me the way?, Can you give me directions?*
Gehen Sie geradeaus.	*Go straight.*
Biegen Sie links ab.	*Turn left here.*
Biegen Sie rechts ab.	*Turn right here.*
Biegen Sie an der Ampel rechts ab.	*Turn right at the traffic light.*
Biegen Sie an der Ecke rechts ab.	*Turn right at the corner.*
Sie müssen die Autobahn nehmen.	*You have to take the Autobahn.*
Nehmen Sie die A 8 Richtung Karlsruhe.	*Take the A 8 towards Karlsruhe.*

Fahren Sie an der nächsten Ausfahrt ab.	*Get off at the next (highway) exit.*
Gute Fahrt!	*Drive safely! (lit., Good drive!)*
Keine Ursache!	*Don't mention it!*

UNIT 7
Shopping

Shopping in a foreign country can be quite a challenge. Let's take a look at the vocabulary you'll need if you'd like to update your wardrobe or fill your picnic basket.

WORD LIST 1

das Kaufhaus	*department store*
die Boutique	*boutique*
der Kunde	*customer (male)*
die Kundin	*customer (female)*
einkaufen	*to shop*
die Kleider	*clothes*
die Kleidung	*clothing*
das Hemd	*shirt*
die Bluse	*blouse*
der Pullover	*sweater*
die Hose	*pants*
die Jeans	*jeans*
der Rock	*skirt*
das Kleid	*dress*
der Anzug	*suit*
die Jacke	*jacket*
der Mantel	*coat*
die Schuhe	*shoes*
die Socken	*socks*
die Krawatte	*tie*
der Gürtel	*belt*

der Hut	*hat*
die Handschuhe	*gloves*
der Schal	*scarf*
der Schirm	*umbrella*
die Uhr	*watch*
das Regal	*shelf*
die Umkleidekabine	*fitting room*
der Spiegel	*mirror*

NUTS & BOLTS 1

TWO-WAY PREPOSITIONS

In the last lesson, you learned that there are prepositions that are always followed by the dative, and prepositions that are always followed by the accusative. There are nine prepositions that can be followed by the dative or the accusative. They are called two-way prepositions, and they all indicate location.

Two-way prepositions introduce the dative case when they indicate a position in space. In that case, they answer the question *where?*

Die Kundin kauft in der Boutique ein.

The client shops in the boutique.

Two-way prepositions are followed by the accusative case when they indicate a change of location or movement. In that case, they answer the question *where to?*

Die Kundin geht in die Boutique.

The client enters (goes into) the boutique.

Preposition	Accusative/ Direction	Dative/Location
in	**Ich packe das Hemd <u>in den</u> Koffer.**	**Das Hemd ist <u>im</u> Koffer.**
in, inside, into	*I am putting the shirt in the suitcase.*	*The shirt is in the suitcase.*
an	**Ich fahre <u>an die</u> Kreuzung heran.**	**Wir biegen <u>an der</u> nächsten Kreuzung rechts ab.**
at, to the side of, to, on	*I am approaching the intersection.*	*We turn right at the next intersection.*
auf	**Ich lege die Handschuhe <u>auf den</u> Tisch.**	**Die Handschuhe sind <u>auf dem</u> Tisch.**
on, on top of, onto	*I am putting the gloves on the table.*	*The gloves are on the table.*
über	**Der Verkäufer hängt den Pullover <u>über das</u> T-shirt.**	**Ich trage den Pullover <u>über dem</u> T-shirt.**
above, over, across	*The salesperson hangs the sweater above the T-shirt.*	*I am wearing the sweater over the T-shirt.*
unter	**Der Verkäufer hängt das T-shirt <u>unter den</u> Pullover.**	**Ich trage das T-shirt <u>unter dem</u> Pullover.**
under, beneath, among	*The salesperson hangs the T-shirt under the sweater.*	*I am wearing the T-shirt under the sweater.*

Preposition	Accusative/ Direction	Dative/Location
vor	**Ich stelle mich <u>vor den</u> Spiegel.**	**Ich stehe <u>vor dem</u> Spiegel.**
in front of, before, ago	*I am placing myself in front of the mirror.*	*I am standing in front of the mirror.*
hinter	**Ich stelle mich <u>hinter dich</u>.**	**Ich stehe <u>hinter dir</u>.**
in back of, behind	*I am placing myself behind you.*	*I am standing behind you.*
neben	**Ich stelle mich <u>neben dich</u>.**	**Ich stehe <u>neben dir</u>.**
beside, next to	*I am placing myself next to you.*	*I am standing next to you.*
zwischen	**Ich lege den Pullover <u>zwischen das</u> T-shirt und <u>das</u> Hemd.**	**Der Pullover liegt <u>zwischen dem</u> T-shirt und <u>dem</u> Hemd.**
between	*I am laying the sweater between the T-shirt and the shirt.*	*The sweater is lying between the T-shirt and the shirt.*

Please note that many prepositions followed by a definite article in the accusative form a contraction: **in das** contracts to **ins, an das** contracts to **ans, auf das** contracts to **aufs,** and so on. As you know, the same is true for many prepositions followed by a definite article in the dative case: **in dem** contracts to **im, an dem** contracts to **am,** and **zu dem** contracts to **zum.**

There are a few verb pairs that come up frequently with two-way prepositions. One, the transitive verb in the pair, usually refers to movement or action and needs an accusative object. The intransitive verb in the pair usually refers to location and does not need an accusative object.

Transitive (movement)		Intransitive (location)	
legen	*to place, to put*	**liegen**	*to lie (location)*
hängen	*to hang*	**hängen**	*to hang*
stellen	*to place, to put*	**stehen**	*to stand*
setzen	*to place, to put*	**sitzen**	*to sit*

PRACTICE 1
Please complete the sentences using the correct case.

1. Die Kundin steht _____. (vor/der Spiegel)

2. Die Verkäuferin geht _____. (in/die Umkleidekabine)

3. Mein Mann legt die Hose _____. (neben/die Schuhe)

4. Ich kaufe gern _____ ein. (in/das Kaufhaus)

5. Warum legst du das Hemd nicht _____. (auf/das Regal)

6. Die Pullover liegen schon _____. (auf/das Regal)

WORD LIST 2

der Supermarkt	*grocery store*
das Brot	*bread*
das Brötchen	*(breakfast) roll*
das Obst	*fruit*
der Apfel	*apple*
die Orange	*orange*
die Banane	*banana*
das Gemüse	*vegetables*

die Kartoffel	*potato*
die Tomate	*tomato*
die Zwiebel	*onion*
der Mais	*corn*
die Karotte	*carrot*
der Salat	*lettuce*
die Paprika	*pepper*
die Gurke	*cucumber*
der Spinat	*spinach*
der Wurstaufschnitt	*cold cuts*
der Schinken	*ham*
die Salami	*salami*
die Lyoner	*bologna*
das Fleisch	*meat*
das Rindfleisch	*beef*
das Kalbfleisch	*veal*
das Schweinefleisch	*pork*
das Lamm	*lamb*
das Huhn	*chicken*
das Hühnchen	*chicken (cooked)*
die Nudeln	*pasta*
der Reis	*rice*
das Gewürz	*spice*
der Zucker	*sugar*
das Salz	*salt*
der Pfeffer	*pepper*
der Paprika	*paprika*
die Milch	*milk*
der Joghurt	*yogurt*
der Käse	*cheese*
das Getränk	*drink*
das Wasser	*water*

das Mineralwasser	mineral water
der Saft	juice
der Orangensaft	orange juice
der Apfelsaft	apple juice
der Wein	wine
das Bier	beer
der Sekt	champagne, sparkling wine

NUTS & BOLTS 2
EXPRESSING MORE LIKES AND DISLIKES

German features a whole host of verbs to express the shades of emotion surrounding *love* and *hate*.

gefallen and schmecken

As we mentioned in the last unit, **gefallen** and **schmecken** always take the dative case: **gefallen** + dative *(to like someone/something; lit., to be pleasing [to someone])*; **schmecken** + dative *(to like [some food]; lit., to taste good [to someone])*.

Gefallen can be used with people and things. Preferences for food are expressed with **schmecken**.

Obst schmeckt mir.
I like fruit. (lit., Fruit tastes good to me.)

Der Rock gefällt mir.
I like the skirt. (lit., The skirt is pleasing to me.)

Du gefällst mir.
I like you. (lit., You are pleasing to me.)

Note that the subject in the English sentence *(I)* becomes the object in the German sentence **(mir)**. The object in the English sentence *(fruit/skirt/you)* is the subject in the German sentence **(Obst/Rock/du)**. Therefore, if the object of liking is in the plural, **gefallen** and **schmecken** need to be in the plural as well.

Die Schuhe gefallen mir.
I like the shoes. (lit., The shoes are pleasing to me.)

Bananen schmecken mir nicht.
I don't like bananas. (lit., Bananas are not pleasing to me.)

gern + verb *(to enjoy, to like)*

We talked about **gern** + verb in Unit 3 already. Remember that **gern** is always used in conjunction with a verb referring to the action enjoyed by the subject.

Ich kaufe gern ein.
I enjoy shopping.

Ich esse nicht gern Gemüse.
I don't like eating vegetables.

mögen *(to like)*

Ich mag dich.
I like you.

Ich mag Milch.
I like milk.

Mögen can be used to express likes and dislikes for people, things, and food or drinks.

lieb haben *(to like)*

Ich habe dich lieb.
I like you.

Lieb haben is usually used among family members. It can also be used for romantic overtones.

lieben _(to love)_

Ich liebe dich.
I love you.

Lieben is usually reserved for people, expressing romantic love and love within a family. The German language rarely uses this word to express enjoyment of a sport, a food, or an activity.

PRACTICE 2
Please translate the following sentences using the verb in parentheses.

1. _I like bananas._ (schmecken)

2. _Do you like this T-shirt?_ (gefallen)

3. _She doesn't like the shoes._ (gefallen)

4. _My mother loves me._ (lieben)

5. _I like to drink coffee._ (gern + _verb_)

6. _My father likes wine._ (mögen)

Culture note

The German language is rather picky with regard to expressing emotions toward people. Here are the verbs as they are used in ascending order of intensity.

1. **Er interessiert mich.** _(I'm interested in him.)_ This usually has romantic overtones.

2. **Sie gefällt mir.** _(I like her.)_ This does not necessarily have any romantic connotations.

3. **Ich habe ihn gern.** _(I like him.)_ This might be used in reference to a friend or a distant relative.

4. **Ich mag dich.** _(I like you.)_ This usually has romantic overtones or expresses deep devotion to a friend.

5. **Ich habe dich lieb.** (*I love you.*) This usually has romantic connotations or expresses love among family members.

6. **Ich liebe dich.** (*I love you.*) This is reserved for lovers and close family members.

ANSWERS

PRACTICE 1: 1. vor dem Spiegel; **2.** in die Umkleidekabine; **3.** neben die Schuhe; **4.** im Kaufhaus; **5.** auf das Regal; **6.** auf dem Regal

PRACTICE 2: 1. Bananen schmecken mir. **2.** Gefällt dir das T-Shirt? **3.** Die Schuhe gefallen ihr nicht. **4.** Meine Mutter liebt mich. **5.** Ich trinke gern Kaffee. **6.** Mein Vater mag Wein.

———————————— Lesson 26 (phrases) ————————————

The phrases in this lesson will help you get the right size and color for yourself, your sister, your brother, and all those friends for whom you promised to bring something back from your trip to Europe.

PHRASE LIST 1

Welche Größe . . . ?	*What size . . . ?*
in meiner Größe	*in my size*
in einer anderen Größe	*in a different size*
in einer kleineren Größe	*in a smaller size*
in einer größeren Größe	*in a larger size*
eine Nummer kleiner	*one size smaller*
eine Nummer größer	*one size larger*
in einer anderen Farbe	*in a different color*
in schwarz	*in black*
weiß	*white*
gelb	*yellow*
rot	*red*

blau	blue
grün	green
grau	gray
rosa	pink
violet	purple
kariert	checkered
gestreift	striped
passen	to fit
gut passen zu	to go well with
jemandem gut stehen	to look good on (lit., to suit someone well)
Kann ich . . . anprobieren?	Can I try on . . . ?
Kann ich . . . umtauschen?	Can I exchange . . . ?
Ich suche . . .	I am looking for . . .
als Geschenk für . . .	as a present for . . .

NUTS & BOLTS 1
THE PRESENT PERFECT WITH HABEN

The present perfect is the most commonly used tense to describe actions and events in the past. It is a compound tense, which means it consists of two parts: the conjugated form of the helping verbs **haben** or **sein** and the past participle of the main verb (the verb that describes the action).

Most verbs use the helping verb **haben** in the present perfect. Let's take a look at the forms with **haben.**

Ich <u>habe</u> ein neues Kleid <u>gekauft</u>.
I bought/have bought/did buy a new dress.

The main verb carries the meaning of the sentence, and the conjugated form of **haben** tells us that we are talking about the past. Note that the past participle is separated from the conjugated helping verb and moves to the end of the sentence.

Haben Sie auch die rote Hose gekauft?

Did you also buy the red pants?

In questions, the conjugated helping verb moves to the beginning of the question, whereas the past participle of the main verb remains at the end.

Nein, ich habe die rote Hose nicht gekauft.

No, I didn't buy the red pants.

In negative sentences, the conjugated helping verb is in the usual second position, and the past participle remains at the end of the sentence.

Let's review the conjugation of **haben: ich habe, du hast, Sie haben, er/sie/es hat, wir haben, ihr habt, Sie haben, sie haben.**

Next we need to look at the past participle, which in English would be a word such as *bought, gone, eaten*, etc. The past participle **gekauft,** for example, is equivalent to the English *bought*. The past participle of regular verbs is formed in German with the prefix **ge-** + stem + the ending **-(e)t**.

Infinitive		Past participle	
kaufen	*to buy*	**gekauft**	*bought*
sagen	*to say*	**gesagt**	*said*
kosten	*to cost*	**gekostet**	*cost*
suchen	*to search*	**gesucht**	*searched*
passen	*to fit*	**gepasst**	*fit*
zeigen	*to show*	**gezeigt**	*shown*
lernen	*to learn*	**gelernt**	*learned*

Regular verbs that end in **-d, -t,** or a consonant combination add **-et** to the stem to make pronunciation easier.

arbeiten	*to work*	gearbeitet	*worked*

PRACTICE 1
Please transform the following sentences into the present perfect.

1. Ich kaufe eine Hose.
2. Mein Freund sucht ein Geschenk für mich.
3. Lernen Sie Deutsch?
4. Die Verkäuferin arbeitet in einer Boutique.
5. Der Anzug passt Ihnen gut.
6. Wieviel kosten die Schuhe?

PHRASE LIST 2

wiegen	*to weigh*
auf die Waage legen	*to put on the scale*
Ich hätte gern . . .	*I'd like . . .*
Ich nehme . . .	*I'll take . . . , I'll have . . .*
Ich brauche . . .	*I need . . .*
eine Einkaufsliste machen	*to make a shopping list*
ein Laib Brot	*a loaf of bread*
ein Liter Milch	*a liter of milk*
einkaufen gehen	*to go (grocery) shopping*
bummeln gehen	*to go (window-)shopping*
an der Kasse	*at the cashier, at the cash register*

NUTS & BOLTS 2
THE PRESENT PERFECT WITH SEIN

There are many verbs that use the helper verb **sein** to form the present perfect tense.

Ich bin in den Supermarkt gegangen.

I went into the supermarket.

Let's review the forms of **sein: ich bin, du bist, Sie sind, er/sie/es ist, wir sind, ihr seid, Sie sind, sie sind.**

Most of the verbs using **sein** refer to movement or a change of position, such as **fahren** *(to drive)* or **kommen** *(to come)*, as well as the verbs **sein** itself and **bleiben** *(to stay)*. Most of the verbs using **sein** are intransitive, which means they do not take a direct object. Most of them are irregular (strong) verbs.

The past participle of irregular verbs is formed with the prefix **ge-** + stem + the ending **-(e)n.** Many irregular (strong) verbs show a stem-vowel change in the past participle. Here are a few common examples.

Infinitive		Past participle	
gehen	*to go*	**gegangen**	*gone*
stehen	*to stand*	**gestanden**	*stood*
finden	*to find*	**gefunden**	*found*

The following chart lists a few common examples of strong verbs with no stem-vowel change.

Infinitive		Past participle	
fahren	*to drive*	**gefahren**	*driven*
laufen	*to run*	**gelaufen**	*run*
kommen	*to come*	**gekommen**	*come*

Irregular (strong) verbs are rather unpredictable, so it is best to simply memorize their past participles.

Please note that most verbs that take **sein** in the present perfect are irregular, but not all irregular verbs take **sein** in the present perfect. The following are a few common irregular verbs that take **haben**.

helfen	*to help*	**geholfen**	*helped*
nehmen	*to take*	**genommen**	*taken*
geben	*to give*	**gegeben**	*given*
essen	*to eat*	**gegessen**	*eaten*
trinken	*to drink*	**getrunken**	*drunk*

PRACTICE 2
Please transform these sentences into the present perfect.

1. Ich trinke eine Tasse Kaffee.

2. Meine Schwester geht einkaufen.

3. Nehmen Sie ein Taxi?

4. Die Verkäuferin fährt zur Arbeit.

5. Die Kundin steht vor dem Spiegel.

6. Wir geben Ihnen das Geld.

ANSWERS

PRACTICE 1: 1. Ich habe eine Hose gekauft. **2.** Mein Freund hat ein Geschenk für mich gesucht. **3.** Haben Sie Deutsch gelernt? **4.** Die Verkäuferin hat in einer Boutique gearbeitet. **5.** Der Anzug hat Ihnen gut gepasst. **6.** Wieviel haben die Schuhe gekostet?

PRACTICE 2: 1. Ich habe eine Tasse Kaffee getrunken. **2.** Meine Schwester ist einkaufen gegangen. **3.** Haben Sie ein Taxi genommen? **4.** Die Verkäuferin ist zur Arbeit gefahren. **5.** Die Kundin ist vor dem Spiegel gestanden. **6.** Wir haben Ihnen das Geld gegeben.

--- Lesson 27 (sentences) ---

Let's move on to some sentences that will help you navigate shopping in a department store. Be sure to have your credit card ready!

SENTENCE LIST 1

Kann ich Ihnen helfen?	*Can I help you?*
Ich möchte die Hose anprobieren.	*I'd like to try on these pants.*
Kann ich das Kleid anprobieren?	*Can I try on the dress?*
Die Hose steht mir gut.	*The pants look good on me. (lit., The pants suit me well.)*
Kann ich die Krawatte umtauschen?	*Can I exchange the tie?*

Wo ist die Umkleidekabine?	*Where is the fitting room?*
Wo ist die Schuhabteilung?	*Where is the shoe department?*
Haben Sie den Anzug auch in einer anderen Größe/Farbe?	*Do you have this suit in a different size/color?*
Ich brauche eine kleinere Größe.	*I need a smaller size.*
Ich suche einen blauen Pullover.	*I am looking for a blue sweater.*
Ich brauche ein Geschenk für meinen Mann.	*I need a present for my husband.*
Wo ist die Kasse?	*Where is the cash register?*
Kann ich mit Kreditkarte bezahlen?	*Can I pay with a credit card?*

NUTS & BOLTS 1

THE PRESENT PERFECT OF SEPARABLE VERBS

The present perfect of separable verbs–verbs with a separable prefix–is made up of the conjugated form of **haben** or **sein** plus the past participle. To form the past participle, separable verbs place **-ge-** between the prefix and the stem. There are regular and irregular separable verbs. Here are a few examples of regular separable verbs. Their past participle pattern is: prefix + **-ge-** + stem + **-(e)t.**

einkaufen	*to shop*	**eingekauft**	*shopped*
absagen	*to cancel*	**abgesagt**	*cancelled*

Here are a few examples of irregular separable verbs. Their past participle pattern is: prefix + **-ge-** + stem (with/without stem-vowel change) + **-en.**

abfahren	*to leave*	**abgefahren**	*left*
mitnehmen	*to take along*	**mitgenommen**	*taken along*
anrufen	*to call*	**angerufen**	*called*

PRACTICE 1

Please rewrite the following sentences in the present perfect.

1. Der Zug fährt ab.

2. Ich rufe dich an.

3. Wir kommen gern mit in das Kaufhaus.

4. Meine Schwester kauft Gemüse ein.

5. Er sagt die Party ab.

SENTENCE LIST 2

Was darf's denn sein?	*What can I get you?*
Ich möchte gern dreihundert Gramm Lyoner.	*I'd like 300 grams of bologna.*
Geschnitten oder am Stück?	*(Would you like this) sliced or in one piece?*
Die Salami am Stück, bitte.	*The salami in one piece, please.*
Darf's sonst noch etwas sein?	*Anything else?*
Ich nehme zweihundertundfünfzig Gramm Wurstaufschnitt.	*I'll have 250 grams of cold cuts.*
Darf's etwas mehr/weniger sein?	*Can it be a little more/less?*
Es darf auch etwas mehr/ weniger sein.	*It can be a little more/less.*
Ich brauche einen Laib Brot.	*I need a loaf of bread.*
Haben Sie noch Laugenbrötchen?	*Do you still have pretzel rolls?*

Leider haben wir keine Butter mehr.	*Unfortunately we are out of butter.*

NUTS & BOLTS 2
The present perfect of modal verbs

All modal verbs form their present perfect with **haben**.

Das habe ich nicht gewollt.
I didn't want that.

The past participle is formed by the prefix **ge-** + stem + **-t**.

dürfen	*to be allowed to*	**gedurft**	*allowed to*
können	*to be able to*	**gekonnt**	*been able to*
möchten	*to like to*	**gemocht**	*liked to*
müssen	*to have to*	**gemusst**	*had to*
wollen	*to want to*	**gewollt**	*wanted to*
sollen	*to be supposed to*	**gesollt**	*been supposed to*

Modal verbs usually modify another verb in the sentence.

Ich will (dir) helfen.
I want to help (you).

When the modal verb describes another verb in the present perfect, both verbs—the modal and the main verb—remain in the infinitive and move to the end of the sentence.

Ich habe (dir) helfen wollen.
I have wanted to help (you).

Mein Vater hat gut singen können.
My father was able to sing well.

PRACTICE 2
Please rewrite the sentences using the modals in parentheses.

1. Der Verkäufer hat das Hemd in das Regal gelegt. (müssen)
2. Der Kunde ist vor dem Spiegel gestanden. (wollen)
3. Die Frau probiert das Kleid an. (dürfen)
4. Meine Mutter hat ein Geschenk gekauft. (sollen)
5. Ich habe Brot geschnitten. (müssen)

Tip!

Note that verbs ending in **-ieren** do not take the **ge-** prefix in the past participle.

Ich habe telefoniert.
I was on the phone.

Ich habe die Salami probiert.
I tried the salami.

This is also true for separable verbs that end in **-ieren**.

Haben Sie das Kleid anprobiert?
Did you try on the dress?

ANSWERS
PRACTICE 1: 1. Der Zug ist abgefahren. **2.** Ich habe dich angerufen. **3.** Wir sind gern mit in das Kaufhaus gekommen. **4.** Meine Schwester hat Gemüse eingekauft. **5.** Er hat die Party abgesagt.

PRACTICE 2: 1. Der Verkäufer hat das Hemd in das Regal legen müssen. **2.** Der Kunde hat vor dem Spiegel stehen wollen. **3.** Die Frau hat das Kleid anprobieren dürfen. **4.** Meine Mutter hat ein Geschenk kaufen sollen. **5.** Ich habe Brot schneiden müssen.

Let's go shopping!

CONVERSATION 1

Sibylle Wicker's husband has a birthday coming up, and she is out shopping for a present at a clothing boutique.

Verkäufer:	Guten Tag. Kann ich Ihnen helfen?
Sibylle:	Ja, ich suche ein Geschenk für meinen Mann.
Verkäufer:	Eine Krawatte vielleicht?
Sibylle:	Nein, ich habe an einen Pullover gedacht. Hier, der schwarze Pullover ist sehr schön.
Verkäufer:	Das ist ein Damenpullover. Möchten Sie ihn anprobieren?
Sibylle:	Ja, gern. Wo ist denn die Umkleidekabine?
Verkäufer:	Hier. *(Just a few minutes later, Sibylle emerges wearing the sweater.)* Oh, der Pullover steht Ihnen aber gut.
Sibylle:	Danke.
Verkäufer:	Ich habe inzwischen ein Geschenk für Ihren Mann gesucht. Gefällt Ihnen das Hemd?
Sibylle:	Das Hemd? Der Pullover gefällt mir sehr gut. Haben Sie eine passende Hose?
Verkäufer:	Für Sie oder für Ihren Mann?
Sibylle:	Für mich.
Verkäufer:	Wie wär's mit der grauen Hose hier?

Sibylle takes the pants and disappears into the fitting room.

Sibylle:	*(from the fitting room)* Ich brauche eine kleinere Größe. Und einen Gürtel.
Verkäufer:	Hier ist die Hose eine Nummer kleiner, und zwei passende Gürtel. Der schwarze Gürtel ist kürzer.
Sibylle:	Der längere Gürtel gefällt mir besser.

A few minutes later, Sibylle emerges from the fitting room.

Sibylle:	Ich nehme die Hose, den Pullover, und den längeren Gürtel.

Verkäufer:	Gute Wahl. Ich habe inzwischen auch eine Krawatte für das Hemd gefunden.
Sibylle:	Hemd? Ich brauche kein Hemd.
Verkäufer:	Aber Sie haben doch ein Geschenk für Ihren Mann kaufen wollen.
Sibylle:	Oh, das habe ich ganz vergessen. Aber das kann ich auch später machen.

Salesclerk:	Hello. Can I help you?
Sibylle:	Yes, I am looking for a present for my husband.
Salesclerk:	A tie, perhaps?
Sibylle:	No, I was thinking of a sweater. Here, this black sweater is very beautiful.
Salesclerk:	That's a woman's sweater. Would you like to try it on?
Sibylle:	Yes, please. Where is the fitting room?
Salesclerk:	Here. Oh, the sweater looks good on you.
Sibylle:	Thanks.
Salesclerk:	In the meantime, I've looked for a present for your husband. Do you like the shirt?
Sibylle:	The shirt? I like the sweater a lot. Do you have pants that would go with it?
Salesclerk:	For you or your husband?
Sibylle:	For me.
Salesclerk:	How about these gray pants?
Sibylle:	I need a smaller size. And a belt.
Salesclerk:	Here are the pants one size smaller, and two suitable belts. The black belt is shorter.
Sibylle:	I like the longer belt better.
Sibylle:	I'll take the pants, the sweater, and the longer belt.
Salesclerk:	Good choice. In the meantime, I've also found a tie to go with the shirt.
Sibylle:	Shirt? I don't need a shirt.
Salesclerk:	But you wanted to buy a present for your husband.
Sibylle:	Oh, I forgot all about that. But I might as well do that later.

NOTES

The verb **denken** *(to think)* is a mixed verb, which means that even though it forms the past participle with the prefix **ge-** plus the ending **-t**, just like regular (weak) verbs, it also has a stem-vowel change, just like irregular verbs.

Ich habe an einen Pullover gedacht.
I was thinking about a sweater.

Other such verbs are **bringen** *(to bring)*, **kennen** *(to know)*, **rennen** *(to run)*, and **wissen** *(to know)*.

NUTS & BOLTS 1
THE COMPARATIVE OF ADJECTIVES

There are three degrees of comparison—positive, comparative, and superlative. Let's look at how this works, using the adjective **groß** *(big)*.

Positive	Comparative	Superlative
groß	**größer**	**am größten**
big	*bigger*	*the biggest*

An adverb or adjective in the positive form simply describes a noun or a verb.

Das Kleid ist schön.
The dress is beautiful.

The construction **so . . . wie** compares similar persons and things and is equivalent to the English *as . . . as.*

Das T-shirt ist so teuer wie der Anzug.
The T-shirt is as expensive as the suit.

The comparative compares persons or things that are not alike.

Meine Schuhe sind größer als deine Schuhe.
My shoes are bigger than your shoes.

The comparative of an adjective or adverb is formed by adding **-er** to the positive.

Positive		Comparative	
schön	*beautiful*	**schöner**	*more beautiful*
klein	*small*	**kleiner**	*smaller*
teuer	*expensive*	**teurer**	*more expensive*
billig	*cheap*	**billiger**	*cheaper*
frisch	*fresh*	**frischer**	*fresher*
grün	*green*	**grüner**	*greener*
spät	*late*	**später**	*later*
früh	*early*	**früher**	*earlier*

Many one-syllable adjectives and adverbs with the stem-vowels **a, o,** or **u** add an umlaut in the comparative.

groß	*big*	**größer**	*bigger*
stark	*strong*	**stärker**	*stronger*
warm	*warm*	**wärmer**	*warmer*
kalt	*cold*	**kälter**	*colder*
jung	*young*	**jünger**	*younger*
alt	*old*	**älter**	*older*
lang	*long*	**länger**	*longer*
kurz	*short*	**kürzer**	*shorter*

Das Hemd ist größer als die anderen.
This shirt is bigger than the others.

If a comparative adjective precedes the noun, its ending changes depending on the gender, number, and case of the noun.

Wir können uns die teureren Schuhe nicht leisten.
We can't afford the more expensive shoes.

Lass uns doch die grüneren Bananen kaufen.
Let's buy the greener bananas.

Let's look at a few more important irregular comparative forms.

gut	*good*	**besser**	*better*
viel	*a lot, much*	**mehr**	*more*
gern	*like*	**lieber**	*rather*
hoch	*high*	**höher**	*higher*

Das blaue Kleid gefällt mir besser.
I like the blue dress better.

We'll look at the superlative in the next section.

PRACTICE 1
Please rewrite these sentences using the comparative.

1. Meine Schuhe sind teuer. (deine Schuhe)

2. Ich bin spät dran. (du)

3. Die lange Krawatte ist schön. (kurze Krawatte)

4. Das kurze Kleid gefällt mir gut. (das lange Kleid)

5. Mein Mantel ist warm. (dein Mantel)

CONVERSATION 2
Wilfried is out grocery shopping with his daughter. He is about to realize that perhaps it was not such a good idea to take her along.

Wilfried: Wir brauchen Orangen, Salat, und Tomaten.

Anna: Ich mag Äpfel lieber als Orangen. Orangen schmecken gut, Äpfel schmecken besser, aber Schokolade schmeckt am besten.

Wilfried: Mama hat gesagt, wir brauchen Orangen. Sie sind frischer als Äpfel. Und wir brauchen auch Wurstaufschnitt. Wie wär's mit Salami und Schinken?

Anna: Ich mag Lyoner lieber. Salami schmeckt gut, Lyoner schmeckt besser, aber Schokolade schmeckt am besten.

Wilfried: Mama hat gesagt, wir brauchen Salami und Schinken. Und wir brauchen noch Brot.

Anna: Ich mag Brötchen lieber. Brot schmeckt gut, Brötchen schmecken besser, aber Schokolade schmeckt am besten.

Wilfried: Mama hat gesagt, wir brauchen Brot. Das ist

billiger als Brötchen. Und wir brauchen
Rindfleisch für das Abendessen.

Anna: Ich mag Huhn lieber als Rindfleisch.
Rindfleisch schmeckt gut, Huhn schmeckt
besser, aber Schokolade schmeckt am besten.

Wilfried: Mama hat gesagt, wir brauchen Rindfleisch.
Und wir brauchen auch noch Milch und Wein.

Anna: Ich mag Apfelsaft lieber als Milch. Und
Apfelsaft ist gesünder als Wein. Milch
schmeckt gut, Apfelsaft schmeckt besser, aber
Schokolade schmeckt am besten.

Wilfried: Mama hat gesagt, wir brauchen Milch und
Wein.

About twenty minutes later, Wilfried and his daughter are at the cash register.

Wilfried: Haben wir auch alles? Äpfel, Lyoner, Brot,
Huhn und Apfelsaft. Ja, wir haben alles.

Anna: Nein, das wichtigste haben wir ganz vergessen.

Wilfried: Was denn?

Anna: Na, die Schokolade.

Wilfried: We need oranges, lettuce, and tomatoes.

Anna: I like apples better than oranges. Oranges taste good,
apples taste better, but chocolate tastes best.

Wilfried: Mama said we need oranges. They are fresher than
apples. And we need cold cuts. What about salami and
ham?

Anna: I like bologna better. Salami tastes good, bologna tastes
better, but chocolate tastes best.

Wilfried: Mama said we need salami and ham. And we need
bread.

Anna: I like breakfast rolls better. Bread tastes good, breakfast
rolls taste better, but chocolate tastes best.

Wilfried: Mama said we need bread. That's cheaper than
breakfast rolls. And we need beef for dinner.

Anna: I like chicken better than beef. Beef tastes good, chicken
tastes better, but chocolate tastes best.

Wilfried:	Mama said we need beef. And we need milk and wine.
Anna:	I like apple juice better than milk. And apple juice is healthier than wine. Milk tastes good, apple juice tastes better, but chocolate tastes best.
Wilfried:	Mama said we need milk and wine.
Wilfried:	Do we have everything? Apples, bologna, bread, chicken, and apple juice. Yes, we have everything.
Anna:	No, we forgot all about the most important thing.
Wilfried:	What's that?
Anna:	Well, the chocolate.

NOTES

The German word **ganz** *(whole, complete)* can be used for emphasis.

Das habe ich ganz vergessen.

I forgot all about that.

Bist du ganz sicher?

Are you absolutely sure?

Du bist schon ganz groß.

You're all grown up. (lit., You're already completely big.)

NUTS & BOLTS 2
THE SUPERLATIVE

A superlative adjective describes a person, thing, or action that cannot be surpassed.

Das ist die schönste Jacke.

That's the most beautiful jacket.

The superlative adjective is formed by adding **-st-** plus the ending denoting the gender, number, and case of the noun it describes.

schön	schönst- -er, -e, -es

The one-syllable adjectives that add an umlaut in the comparative do so as well in the superlative.

warm	wärmst- -er, -e, -es

Das ist die wärmste Hose.
Those are the warmest pants.

If the positive of the adjective ends in **-d, -t, -s, -ß,** or **-z, e-** is usually added to the stem to facilitate pronunciation.

alt *(old)*	ältest-
naß *(wet)*	näßest-

Note that the adjective **groß** is an exception to this rule.

groß *(big)*	größt-

The adjectives with irregular comparatives have irregular superlatives as well.

gut *(good)*	best-
viel *(much)*	meist-
gern *(like)*	liebst-
hoch *(high)*	höchst-

Das sind die besten Schuhe.
These are the best shoes.

As with the comparative, if the superlative form of the adjective precedes the noun, the appropriate endings reflecting gender, number, and case have to be added.

Das ist mein schönster Pullover.

That is my most beautiful sweater.

The superlative of adverbs is formed by adding the suffix **-en** to the superlative and inserting **am** before the word.

Der Pullover passt am besten zu meiner Hose.

This sweater goes best with my pants.

PRACTICE 2
Please complete the sentences.

1. Der schwarze Pullover steht mir gut, der blaue Pullover steht mir _____, und der grüne Pullover steht mir _____. *(good)*

2. Es ist kalt draußen. Ich ziehe den _____ Mantel an. *(the warmest)*

3. Welches Kleid ist _____, das blaue oder das gelbe? *(more beautiful)*

4. Die weißen Schuhe sind teuer, die schwarzen Schuhe sind _____, und die braunen Schuhe sind _____. *(expensive)*

5. Der blaue Rock ist kurz, der gelbe Rock ist _____, und der rosa Rock ist _____. *(short)*

Culture note

WOMEN'S CLOTHING SIZES (*Frauengrößen*)

COATS, DRESSES, SKIRTS, SLACKS (*Mäntel, Kleider, Röcke, Hosen*)

U.S.	4	6	8	10	12	14	16
GERMANY	36	38	40	42	44	46	48

BLOUSES, SWEATERS (*Blusen, Pullover*)

U.S.	32/6	34/8	36/10	38/12	40/14	42/16
GERMANY	38/2	40/3	42/4	44/5	46/6	48/7

SHOES (*Schuhe*)

U.S.	4-4½	5-5½	6-6½	7-7½	8-8½	9-9½	10	11
GERMANY	35	36	37	38	39	40	41	42

MEN'S CLOTHING SIZES (*Männergrößen*)

SUITES, COATS (*Anzüge, Mäntel*)

U.S.	34	36	38	40	42	44	46	48
GERMANY	44	46	48	50	52	54	56	58

SLACKS (*Hosen*)

U.S.	30	31	32	33	34	35	36	37	38	39
GERMANY	38	39-40	41	42	43	44-45	46	47	48-49	50

SHIRTS (*Hemden*)

U.S.	14	14½	15	15½	16	16½	17	17½	18
GERMANY	36	37	38	39	40	41	42	43	44

SWEATERS (*Pullover*)

U.S.	XS/36	S/38	M/40	L/42	XL/44
GERMANY	42/2	44/3	46-48/4	50/5	52-54/6

SHOES (*Schuhe*)

U.S.	7	7½	8	8½	9	9½	10	10½	11	11½
GERMANY	39	40	41	42	43	43	44	44	45	46

ANSWERS

PRACTICE 1: 1. Deine Schuhe sind teurer (als meine Schuhe).
2. Du bist später dran (als ich). **3.** Die kurze Krawatte ist schöner
(als die lange Krawatte). **4.** Das lange Kleid gefällt mir besser (als
das kurze Kleid). **5.** Dein Mantel ist wärmer (als mein Mantel).

PRACTICE 2: 1. besser, am besten; **2.** wärmsten; **3.** schöner;
4. teurer, am teuersten; **5.** kürzer, am kürzesten

UNIT 7 ESSENTIALS

Kann ich Ihnen helfen?	*Can I help you?*
Ich möchte . . . anprobieren.	*I'd like to try on . . .*
Kann ich . . . anprobieren?	*Can I try on . . . ?*
. . . steht mir gut.	*. . . look(s) good on me. (lit., . . . suit[s] me well.)*
Kann ich . . . umtauschen?	*Can I exchange . . . ?*
Wo ist die Umkleidekabine?	*Where is the fitting room?*
Wo ist die Schuhabteilung?	*Where is the shoe department?*
Haben Sie . . . auch in einer anderen Größe/Farbe?	*Do you have . . . in a different size/color?*
Ich suche . . .	*I am looking for . . .*
Wo ist die Kasse?	*Where is the cash register?*
Kann ich mit Kreditkarte bezahlen?	*Can I pay with a credit card?*
Was darf's denn sein?	*What can I get you?*
Ich möchte gern . . .	*I'd like . . .*

Geschnitten oder am Stück?	*(Would you like this) sliced or in one piece?*
Am Stück, bitte.	*In one piece, please.*
Darf's sonst noch etwas sein?	*Anything else?*

UNIT 8
Let's eat!

──────────── Lesson 29 (words) ────────────

Eating different foods is one of the most enjoyable pleasures of traveling. Here is the vocabulary you'll need to order to your heart's delight.

WORD LIST 1

das Restaurant	*restaurant*
die Kneipe	*(neighborhood) bar*
der Kellner	*waiter*
die Kellnerin	*waitress*
der Ober	*waiter*
die Bedienung	*waitress*
das Essen	*meal*
das Mittagessen	*lunch*
das Abendessen	*dinner*
die Vorspeise	*appetizer*
die Hauptspeise	*main course*
die Nachspeise	*dessert*
der Nachtisch	*dessert*
das Getränk	*beverage*
die Suppe	*soup*
die Süßspeise	*sweets, dessert*
die Spezialität	*specialty*
die Rechnung	*check*
das Trinkgeld	*tip*
bestellen	*to order*
empfehlen	*to recommend*

NUTS & BOLTS 1

SIMPLE PAST OF SEIN, HABEN, AND WERDEN

Even though the present perfect is the most commonly used past tense, the helping verbs **haben** and **sein** often use the simple past tense to refer to events in the past. Here are the forms.

haben (*to have*)			
ich hatte	*I had*	**wir hatten**	*we had*
du hattest	*you had*	**ihr hattet**	*you had*
Sie hatten	*you had*	**Sie hatten**	*you had*
er/sie/es hatte	*he/she/it had*	**sie hatten**	*they had*

sein (*to be*)			
ich war	*I was*	**wir waren**	*we were*
du warst	*you were*	**ihr wart**	*you were*
Sie waren	*you were*	**Sie waren**	*you were*
er/sie/es war	*he/she/it was*	**sie waren**	*they were*

Ich war gestern schon in diesem Restaurant.
I was already in this restaurant yesterday.

Ich hatte Eis zum Nachtisch.
I had ice cream for dessert.

Werden (*to become*) is another verb commonly used in the simple past. Here are the forms.

werden (*to become*)			
ich wurde	*I became*	**wir wurden**	*we became*
du wurdest	*you became*	**ihr wurdet**	*you became*
Sie wurden	*you became*	**Sie wurden**	*you became*
er/sie/es wurde	*he/she/it became*	**sie wurden**	*they became*

Gestern war mein Geburtstag. Ich wurde vierzig Jahre alt.
Yesterday was my birthday. I turned forty years old.

PRACTICE 1
Please rewrite these sentences in the simple past.

1. Das Essen ist heute aber gut.

2. Wir haben keinen Nachtisch.

3. Unser bester Kellner ist krank.

4. Er wird heute zwanzig Jahre alt.

5. Dieses Restaurant ist das teuerste in der ganzen Stadt.

6. Die Kneipe hat keinen Tisch mehr frei.

WORD LIST 2
die Speisekarte	*menu*
die Weinkarte	*wine list*
der Tisch	*table*
das Glas	*glass*
die Tasse	*cup*
der Teller	*plate, bowl*
der Löffel	*spoon*

das Messer	knife
die Gabel	fork
das Besteck	silverware
die Serviette	napkin
der Geburtstag	birthday
feiern	to celebrate

NUTS & BOLTS 2
TIME EXPRESSIONS FOR THE PAST
There are a few important common time expressions used when talking about past events.

gestern	yesterday
vorgestern	the day before yesterday
letzt-	last
vorletzt-	the . . . before last
letzte Woche	last week
vorletzte Woche	the week before last
letzten Monat	last month
vorletzten Monat	the month before last
letztes Jahr	last year
vorletztes Jahr	the year before last
früher	earlier
vor einer Stunde	an hour ago
vor vielen Jahren	many years ago

Note that **letzt-** works like an adjective and adjusts in number, gender, and case to the noun it describes.

Ich war letzte Woche in Tübingen.
I was in Tübingen last week.

In den letzten Tagen war ich oft im Restaurant essen.
In the last few days, I went out to dinner a lot.

Vor vielen Jahren war hier eine Kneipe.
Many years ago, there was a (neighborhood) bar here.

PRACTICE 2
Rephrase the sentence in the simple past using the time expressions in parentheses.

1. Ich bin in Dresden. *(yesterday)*

2. Haben Sie heute Geburtstag? *(last week)*

3. Wo bist du? *(the day before yesterday)*

4. Er wird morgen fünfzig Jahre alt. *(last year)*

5. Hat dein Vater in einer Stunde Zeit? *(an hour ago)*

Tip!
Ask **Wo ist die Toilette?** if you have to use the bathroom. **Das Badezimmer** is where you take your bath or a shower and brush your teeth. Public restrooms are referred to as **Toiletten** or **W.C.** Look for **Herren** for the men's restrooms, and **Damen** for the women's restrooms.

ANSWERS
PRACTICE 1: 1. Das Essen war heute aber gut. **2.** Wir hatten keinen Nachtisch. **3.** Unser bester Kellner war krank. **4.** Er wurde heute zwanzig Jahre alt. **5.** Dieses Restaurant war das teuerste in der ganzen Stadt. **6.** Die Kneipe hatte keinen Tisch mehr frei.

PRACTICE 2: 1. Ich war gestern in Dresden. **2.** Hatten Sie letzte Woche Geburtstag? **3.** Wo warst du vorgestern? **4.** Er wurde letztes Jahr fünfzig Jahre alt. **5.** Hatte dein Vater vor einer Stunde Zeit?

———————— Lesson 3O (phrases) ————————

Here are some phrases you'll often hear and use in a restaurant.

PHRASE LIST 1

einen Tisch bestellen	*to reserve a table, to make reservations*
einen Tisch reservieren	*to reserve a table, to make reservations*
Auf welchen Namen?	*Under which name?*
ein Tisch für vier	*a table for four*
ein Tisch für 20 (zwanzig) Uhr	*a table for 8 P.M.*
ein Tisch am Fenster	*a table at the window*
ein Tisch im Nebenzimmer	*a table in a separate room*
ein Tisch auf der Terrasse	*a table on the terrace*
Wie wär's mit . . . ?	*How about . . . ?*
Darf ich . . . empfehlen?	*May I recommend . . . ?*
Ich empfehle . . .	*I recommend . . .*
als Vorspeise	*as an appetizer*
als Hauptspeise	*as a main course*
als Nachspeise	*for dessert*
Was darf's sein?	*What can I get you?*
Noch etwas?	*Anything else?*

NUTS & BOLTS 1

THE SIMPLE PAST OF REGULAR (WEAK) VERBS

The simple past is mostly used in writing, in speeches that refer to the past, in stories or fairy tales, and, as discussed above, with the auxiliary verbs **haben, sein,** and **werden.**

Weak verbs form their past tense by adding the past tense marker, **-t-,** and the personal endings, **-e, -est, -e, -en, -et,** and **-en,** to the stem of the verb.

ich	*stem* + t + e
du	*stem* + t + est
Sie	*stem* + t + en
er/sie/es	*stem* + t + e
wir	*stem* + t + en
ihr	*stem* + t + et
Sie	*stem* + t + en
sie	*stem* + t + en

If the verb stem ends in **-d** or **-t,** insert **-e-** between the stem and the past tense ending–for example, **antworten → er antwortete.**

Er bestellte den Schweinebraten.
He ordered the pork roast.

Ich hörte viel Gutes über dieses Restaurant.
I heard many good things about this restaurant.

Der Koch öffnete ein neues Restaurant.
The cook opened a new restaurant.

PRACTICE 1
Please rewrite the sentences in the simple past.

1. Wer bestellt die Käsespätzle?

2. Ich arbeite in einer Kneipe.

3. Wir suchen lange nach dem Restaurant.

4. Der Kellner redet zu viel.

5. Der Nachtisch schmeckt mir gut.

PHRASE LIST 2

Eine Speisekarte, bitte.	*A menu, please.*
Ich nehme . . .	*I'll have . . .*
Ich möchte gern . . .	*I'd like . . .*
ein Teller Suppe	*a bowl of soup*
ein Glas Wein	*a glass of wine*
eine Flasche Wein	*a bottle of wine*
eine Tasse Kaffee	*a cup of coffee*
ein Kännchen Kaffee	*a small pot of coffee*
mit Zucker	*with sugar*
ohne Zucker	*without sugar*
mit Milch	*with milk*
ohne Milch	*without milk*
Die Rechnung, bitte.	*The check, please.*
Alles zusammen?	*One check? (lit., All together?)*
ein Trinkgeld geben	*to leave a tip, to tip*
aufrunden	*to round up (the amount)*
Stimmt so.	*Keep the change. (lit., This is correct.)*

NUTS & BOLTS 2

THE SIMPLE PAST OF IRREGULAR (STRONG) VERBS

All strong verbs show a stem-vowel change in the past tense—for example, **bitten** → **ich bat**. In addition, strong verbs add the following endings.

ich	*stem-vowel change* + -
du	*stem-vowel change* + **st**
Sie	*stem-vowel change* + **en**
er/sie/es	*stem-vowel change* + -
wir	*stem-vowel change* + **en**
ihr	*stem-vowel change* + **t**
Sie	*stem-vowel change* + **en**
sie	*stem-vowel change* + **en**

Please note that the first person singular and third person singular do not have an ending.

If the verb stem ends in **-d** or **-t,** insert **-e-** between the stem with stem-vowel change and the ending in the second person singular and plural—for example: **finden → du fand̲e̲st.**

As it is hard to know which verbs are strong verbs, it is best to simply memorize the past tense forms along with the infinitives. Please refer to the appendix for a list of common strong verbs.

Let's look at a few common verbs with stem-vowel changes.

lesen	*to read*	**las**	*read*
finden	*to find*	**fand**	*found*
sprechen	*to speak*	**sprach**	*spoke*
rufen	*to call (to yell)*	**rief**	*called*
trinken	*to drink*	**trank**	*drank*

essen	to eat	aß	ate
nehmen	to take	nahm	took
empfehlen	to recommend	empfahl	recommended
gefallen	to like (lit., to be to one's liking)	gefiel	liked
gehen	to go	ging	went
kommen	to come	kam	came
sitzen	to sit	saß	sat

Nach langem Suchen fanden wir endlich das Restaurant.

After searching for a long time, we finally found the restaurant.

Der Kellner empfahl den Rinderbraten.

The waiter recommended the beef roast.

Dieses Restaurant gefiel mir schon immer.

I always liked this restaurant. (lit., This restaurant always was to my liking.)

PRACTICE 2

Please rewrite the sentences in the simple past.

1. Der Koch empfiehlt den Sauerbraten.

2. Wir finden das Restaurant nicht.

3. Lesen Sie die Speisekarte?

4. Ich sitze am Fenster.

5. Der Kellner gefällt mir.

ANSWERS

PRACTICE 1: 1. Wer bestellte die Käsespätzle? **2.** Ich arbeitete in einer Kneipe. **3.** Wir suchten lange nach dem Restaurant. **4.** Der Kellner redete zu viel. **5.** Der Nachtisch schmeckte mir gut.

PRACTICE 2: 1. Der Koch empfahl den Sauerbraten. **2.** Wir fanden das Restaurant nicht. **3.** Lasen Sie die Speisekarte? **4.** Ich saß am Fenster. **5.** Der Kellner gefiel mir.

―――――――― Lesson 31 (sentences) ――――――――

Here are the sentences you'll need to order the most scrumptious meals on your travels through German-speaking countries.

SENTENCE LIST 1

Ich möchte einen Tisch für zwei Personen reservieren (bestellen).	*I'd like to reserve a table for two people.*
Um welche Uhrzeit?	*For what time?*
Um 19 Uhr.	*For 7 P.M.*
Auf welchen Namen, bitte?	*What's the name?*
(Auf) Schneider.	*(In the name of) Schneider.*
Können wir einen Tisch im Garten haben?	*Could we have a table in the garden?*
Im Garten ist leider nichts mehr frei.	*Unfortunately, there is no more room in the garden.*

| Ich habe eine Reservierung für Schneider. | *I have a reservation for Schneider.* |

NUTS & BOLTS 1
THE SIMPLE PAST OF MODAL VERBS

Modal verbs form the past tense by adding the past tense marker. -t-. and a personal ending, **-e, -est, -e, -en, -et,** or **-en.**

dürfen *(to be allowed to)*			
ich	durfte	wir	durften
du	durftest	ihr	durftet
Sie	durften	Sie	durften
er/sie/es	durfte	sie	durften

können *(to be able to)*			
ich	konnte	wir	konnten
du	konntest	ihr	konntet
Sie	konnten	Sie	konnten
er/sie/es	konnte	sie	konnten

möchten *(to like to)*			
ich	mochte	wir	mochten
du	mochtest	ihr	mochtet
Sie	mochten	Sie	mochten
er/sie/es	mochte	sie	mochten

müssen *(to have to)*			
ich	musste	wir	mussten
du	musstest	ihr	musstet
Sie	mussten	Sie	mussten
er/sie/es	musste	sie	mussten

wollen *(to want to)*			
ich	wollte	wir	wollten
du	wolltest	ihr	wolltet
Sie	wollten	Sie	wollten
er/sie/es	wollte	sie	wollten

The simple past is commonly used with modal verbs.

Ich wollte heute im Restaurant essen.
I wanted to eat in the restaurant today.

Meine Mutter konnte leider nicht mitkommen.
Unfortunately, my mother couldn't come along.

Wir mussten zu Hause bleiben.
We had to stay home.

PRACTICE 1
Please rephrase the sentences in the simple past.

1. Willst du heute im Restaurant essen?
2. Möchten Sie ein Glas Wein trinken?

3. Sie kann nicht mitkommen.

4. Warum müssen wir schon gehen?

5. Der Kellner kann nichts empfehlen.

SENTENCE LIST 2

Können wir bitte eine Speisekarte haben?	*Could we have a menu, please?*
Was darf's denn sein?	*What can I get you?*
Was empfehlen Sie?	*What do you recommend?*
Das klingt aber gut.	*That sounds good.*
Ich nehme den Rostbraten.	*I'll have the roast.*
Wir brauchen noch ein Messer.	*We need a knife.*
An unserem Tisch fehlt eine Gabel.	*We are missing a fork at our table.*
Guten Appetit!	*Enjoy your meal! (Bon Appetit!)*
Bitte bringen Sie mir noch ein Glas Rotwein.	*Please bring me another glass of red wine.*
Die Rechnung, bitte.	*The check, please.*
Ist das Trinkgeld inklusive?	*Is the tip included?*
Stimmt so.	*That's correct.*
Vielen Dank.	*Thank you.*

NUTS & BOLTS 2

THE SIMPLE PAST OF MIXED VERBS

Mixed verbs in the simple past add the past tense marker, **-t-**, and the past tense endings (**-e, -est, -e, -en, -et, -en**) of the weak verbs, and undergo a stem-vowel change like strong verbs.

ich	*stem-vowel change* + **t** + **e**
du	*stem-vowel change* + **t** + **est**
Sie	*stem-vowel change* + **t** + **en**
er/sie/es	*stem-vowel change* + **t** + **e**
wir	*stem-vowel change* + **t** + **en**
ihr	*stem-vowel change* + **t** + **et**
Sie	*stem-vowel change* + **t** + **en**
sie	*stem-vowel change* + **t** + **en**

The simple past is commonly used with mixed verbs.

bringen (*to bring*)			
ich	brachte	wir	brachten
du	brachtest	ihr	brachtet
Sie	brachten	Sie	brachten
er/sie/es	brachte	sie	brachten

denken (*to think*)			
ich	dachte	wir	dachten
du	dachtest	ihr	dachtet
Sie	dachten	Sie	dachten
er/sie/es	dachte	sie	dachten

kennen (*to know*)			
ich	kannte	wir	kannten
du	kanntest	ihr	kanntet
Sie	kannten	Sie	kannten
er/sie/es	kannte	sie	kannten

rennen (*to run*)			
ich	rannte	wir	rannten
du	ranntest	ihr	ranntet
Sie	rannten	Sie	rannten
er/sie/es	rannte	sie	rannten

wissen (*to know*)			
ich	wusste	wir	wussten
du	wusstest	ihr	wusstet
Sie	wussten	Sie	wussten
er/sie/es	wusste	sie	wussten

PRACTICE 2
Please rewrite the sentences in the simple past.

1. Kennen Sie das Restaurant schon?
2. Ich denke an den Salat als Vorspeise.

3. Der Kellner bringt die Rechnung.

4. Die Kinder rennen zwischen den Tischen.

5. Ihr wisst, welches Restaurant ich meine.

Culture note

Das Mittagessen *(lunch)* is the main meal of the day for most people in Germany, Austria, and Switzerland. That's when people eat their **Käsespätzle** or their **Schnitzel**. Many companies offer employees a hot midday meal at the company's cafeteria, and companies without a cafeteria offer meal tickets for local restaurants. School-age children who cannot go home for lunch eat a hot meal in the school cafeteria, which is usually staffed by volunteering parents. **Das Abendessen** *(dinner)* is usually just a light meal consisting of **belegte Brote** *(open-faced sandwiches)* sampling the wide variety of **Wurst** *(cold cuts)* and **Käse** *(cheese)* to be found particularly in the south of Germany and Switzerland. **Das Frühstück** *(breakfast)* consists of **Brötchen** *(fresh baked breakfast rolls)* with **Marmelade** *(marmalade)*, **Gelee** *(jelly)*, or **Wurst** *(cold cuts)* and **Käse** *(cheese)*, or the famous **Müesli** *(granola and dried fruit mixed with either milk or yogurt)*, which originated in Switzerland. Between lunch and dinner, people enjoy **Kaffee und Kuchen** *(coffee and cake)*, particularly on the weekends.

ANSWERS

PRACTICE 1: 1. Wolltest du heute im Restaurant essen?
2. Mochten Sie ein Glas Wein trinken? **3.** Sie konnte nicht mitkommen. **4.** Warum mussten wir schon gehen? **5.** Der Kellner konnte nichts empfehlen.

PRACTICE 2: 1. Kannten Sie das Restaurant schon? **2.** Ich dachte an den Salat als Vorspeise. **3.** Der Kellner brachte die Rechnung. **4.** Die Kinder rannten zwischen den Tischen. **5.** Ihr wusstet, welches Restaurant ich meinte.

Hungry? Let's go out to dinner.

CONVERSATION 1
Rainer wants to take his girlfriend out to dinner for her birthday.

> **Rainer:** *(on the phone)* Ich möchte für heute Abend um 20 Uhr einen Tisch für zwei Personen reservieren. Auf Schäfer.

At the restaurant

> **Rainer:** Zur Feier des Tages trinken wir eine Flasche Champagner. Du hast schließlich nicht jeden Tag Geburtstag.

The waiter returns with the champagne.

> **Rainer:** Auf dein Wohl, Caroline.
>
> **Caroline:** Zum Wohl!
>
> **Rainer:** *(handing her a present)* Alles Gute zum Geburtstag!
>
> **Caroline:** Oh. Warst du schon einmal in diesem Restaurant?
>
> **Rainer:** Nein, aber ich wollte schon immer mal hier essen. Es gehört dem Bruder eines Kollegen.
>
> **Caroline:** Was empfiehlst du?
>
> **Rainer:** Die Spezialität des Hauses sind die Rindsrouladen.
>
> **Caroline:** *(to the waiter)* Ich nehme die Rindsrouladen.
>
> **Rainer:** Für mich bitte das Wiener Schnitzel mit Kartoffelsalat. *(to Caroline)* Wolltest du das Geschenk nicht öffnen?
>
> **Caroline:** Doch, natürlich. *(She opens the present.)* Rainer! Diese Ohrringe wollte ich schon so lange.
>
> **Rainer:** Das wußte ich, mein Schatz.
>
> **Caroline:** Woher wußtest du das?
>
> **Rainer:** Na, wir waren schon oft genug zusammen

bummeln. Und jedes Mal hast du diese
Ohrringe bewundert.

Caroline: Das ist das beste Geschenk meines Lebens.
Das war nicht nötig.

Rainer: Doch. Du bist die Frau meiner Träume.

Rainer: (on the phone) *I'd like to make reservations for
tonight at 8 P.M. for two people. In the name "Schäfer."*

At the restaurant

Rainer: *To honor the day, we'll have a bottle of champagne.
After all, it's not your birthday every day.*

The waiter returns with a bottle of champagne.

Rainer: *To your health, Caroline.*

Caroline: *Cheers!*

Rainer: (handing her a present) *Happy birthday!*

Caroline: *Have you been to this restaurant before?*

Rainer: *No, but I've always wanted to eat here. It belongs to the
brother of a colleague.*

Caroline: *What do you recommend?*

Rainer: *The specialty of the house is the Rindsrouladen.*

Caroline: (to the waiter) *I'll have the Rindsrouladen.*

Rainer: *The Wiener Schnitzel with potato salad for me.* (to
Caroline) *Didn't you want to open your present?*

Caroline: *Yes, of course.* (She opens the present.) *Rainer! I've
wanted these earrings for so long.*

Rainer: *I knew that, my darling.*

Caroline: *How did you know?*

Rainer: *Well, we've been window-shopping often enough. And
every time, you have admired those earrings.*

Caroline: *This is the best present of my life. That wasn't necessary.*

Rainer: *Yes, it was. You are the woman of my dreams.*

NOTES

There is good reason why the German cuisine is considered meat-
and-potatoes fare. There are many excellent meat dishes. **Rindsrouladen,** for example, are a German specialty. They are made
with thinly sliced beef, rolled up with onions, green peppers, and

mustard. They are usually served with mashed potatoes and a green salad or a vegetable medley. And the famous **Wiener Schnitzel** is a breaded veal cutlet, often served with nothing but **Kartoffelsalat** *(potato salad).*

NUTS & BOLTS 1
EXPRESSING POSSESSION: THE GENITIVE

German uses the possessive or the genitive case to show possession or close relationship.

Das ist der Bruder eines Kollegen.

That is a colleague's brother. (lit., That is the brother of a colleague.)

Eines Kollegen is in the genitive case and translates as *a colleague's* or *of a colleague.*

Here are all the forms of nouns in the genitive case.

m.	f.	n.	pl.
des Vaters	der Mutter	des Kindes	der Väter, der Mütter, der Kinder
eines Vaters	einer Mutter	eines Kindes	-
meines Vaters	meiner Mutter	meines Kindes	meiner Väter, meiner Mütter, meiner Kinder
keines Vaters	keiner Mutter	keines Kindes	keiner Väter, keiner Mütter, keiner Kinder

m.	f.	n.	pl.
des netten Vaters	der netten Mutter	des netten Kindes	der netten Väter, der netten Mütter, der netten Kinder

Note that most masculine and neuter nouns simply add an **-s** ending in the genitive, whereas most feminine nouns do not add an ending at all—for example, **der Vater** → **des Vaters,** but **die Frau** → **der Frau.** Masculine and neuter nouns ending in **-t, -d, -s, -f,** and **-g** add an **-e-** before the **-s** to facilitate pronunciation—for example: **der Tag** → **des Tages.**

Zur Feier des Tages trinken wir Champagner.
As a celebration of the day, we'll have champagne.

The n-nouns, such as **der Herr** *(man, mister, sir)* and **der Patient** *(patient),* add an **-n** ending in all cases, including the genitive. For example: **der Kollege** → **des Kollegen.**

Das ist der Bruder eines Kollegen.
That is the brother of a colleague.

The genitive answers the question **Wessen?** *(Whose?)*

Wessen Bruder gehört das Restaurant?
Whose brother does the restaurant belong to?

Es gehört dem Bruder einer Kollegin.
It belongs to the brother of a colleague.

Das ist das beste Geschenk meines Lebens.
This is the best present of my life.

Du bist die Frau meiner Träume.

You are the woman of my dreams.

German, like English, can also express possession by adding an **s** to a noun. In German, however, the **s** is only added to proper names and is not preceded by an apostrophe.

Das ist Rainers Freundin.

This is Rainer's girlfriend.

Das sind Carolines Ohrringe.

These are Caroline's earrings.

PRACTICE 1
Please complete the sentences.

1. Das ist die Freundin _____. *(of a colleague)*

2. Wo ist _____ Restaurant? *(Mr. Schneider's)*

3. Du bist der Mann _____. *(of my dreams)*

4. Zur Feier _____ gehen wir essen. (dein Geburtstag)

5. Das ist der Kellner _____. *(of the year)*

CONVERSATION 2
Rainer and Caroline have finished their dinner.

Rainer: Hat's geschmeckt?

Caroline: Oh ja. Es war ausgezeichnet. Wie wär's mit einem Nachtisch oder einer Tasse Kaffee?

Rainer: *(to the waiter)* Ich nehme eine Tasse Kaffee. Schwarz bitte.

Caroline: Ich auch. Aber mit Milch und Zucker. *(to Rainer)* Du warst so still während des Essens. Ist alles in Ordnung?

Rainer: Ja, natürlich. Es ist nur . . .

Caroline: Was ist denn?

Rainer:	Wie ich vorhin schon sagte, du bist die Frau meiner Träume.
Caroline:	Ja?
Rainer:	Und ich wollte einen perfekten Abend ...
Caroline:	Ja?
Rainer:	Aber leider habe ich ...
Caroline:	Was wolltest du denn sagen?
Rainer:	Leider habe ich meinen Geldbeutel zu Hause vergessen. Kannst du die Rechnung bezahlen?
Caroline:	Aber selbstverständlich, Rainer. Und der Abend war trotz des vergessenen Geldbeutels perfekt.

Rainer:	*Did you enjoy it?*
Caroline:	*Oh, yes, it was excellent. How about some dessert or a cup of coffee?*
Rainer:	*(to the waiter) I'll have a cup of coffee. Black, please.*
Caroline:	*Me, too. But with milk and sugar. (to Rainer) You were so quiet during dinner. Is everything okay?*
Rainer:	*Yes, of course. It's just ...*
Caroline:	*What's up?*
Rainer:	*As I said earlier, you are the woman of my dreams.*
Caroline:	*Yes?*
Rainer:	*And I wanted a perfect evening ...*
Caroline:	*Yes?*
Rainer:	*But unfortunately, I ...*
Caroline:	*What did you want to say?*
Rainer:	*Unfortunately, I forgot my wallet at home. Could you take care of the check?*
Caroline:	*But of course, Rainer. And the evening was perfect despite the forgotten wallet.*

NOTES

Rainer's embarrassment is endearingly old-fashioned. In Europe it is much more common for a man and a woman to share the check, even on a date, or for a woman to treat her man.

NUTS & BOLTS 2
PREPOSITIONS WITH THE GENITIVE
There are four prepositions that are followed by the genitive case in the German language.

wegen	**Wir sind wegen der Spezialitäten in diesem Restaurant.**
because	*We are in this restaurant for (lit., because of) its specialties.*
während	**Wir haben während des Essens telefoniert.**
during	*We made calls during dinner.*
(an)statt	**Sie hat das Wiener Schnitzel statt der Rindsrouladen gegessen.**
instead of	*She ate the Wiener Schnitzel instead of the Rindsrouladen.*
trotz	**Er hat die Ohrringe trotz des Preises gekauft.**
despite	*He bought the earrings despite their price.*

You will notice that, in spoken German, these prepositions are often followed by the dative case. So you may also hear **Wir haben während <u>dem</u> Essen telefoniert.**

PRACTICE 2
Please fill in the blanks.

1. Während _____ rief meine Mutter an. (das Essen)

2. Ich hatte trotz _____ zu viel Arbeit. (deine Hilfe)

3. Der Kellner brachte einen Rotwein statt _____. (ein Weißwein)

4. Trotz _____ war das Restaurant leer. (das gute Essen)

5. Ich konnte wegen _____ nicht pünktlich kommen. (der Verkehr)

Culture note

Even though Germans are known as a time-conscious people, when it comes to eating out, Germans like to take their time. In most restaurants in Germany, Austria, and Switzerland, it is customary to seat yourself, and, once you are seated, it may take the **Kellner** *(waiter)* or **Kellnerin** *(waitress)* several minutes to greet you and bring the menu. The idea is to allow the guests to settle in and chat for a few minutes before ordering. Once you have ordered, the food is usually served as it is ready rather than to all parties at the same time. After the main course, people tend to stay and chat, sometimes over dessert or coffee. It is not at all unusual to spend well over an hour for lunch. A **Kellner** or **Kellnerin** will not expect a large tip, as gratuity is automatically included in the price of the meal. While additional tipping is customary, you usually just add a Euro or two, rounding up to the next five- or ten-Euro amount. **Guten Appetit!** *(Enjoy your meal!)*

ANSWERS

PRACTICE 1: 1. eines Kollegen; **2.** Herrn Schneiders; **3.** meiner Träume; **4.** deines Geburtstages; **5.** des Jahres

PRACTICE 2: 1. des Essens/dem Essen; **2.** deiner Hilfe; **3.** eines Weißweins; **4.** des guten Essens; **5.** des Verkehrs

UNIT 8 ESSENTIALS

Ich möchte einen Tisch für zwei Personen reservieren.	*I'd like to reserve a table for two people.*
Ich möchte einen Tisch für zwei Personen bestellen.	*I'd like to reserve a table for two people.*
Um welche Uhrzeit?	*For what time?*

Um 19 (neunzehn) Uhr.	*For 7 P.M.*
Auf welchen Namen, bitte?	*What's the name?*
(Auf) Schneider.	*(In the name of) Schneider.*
Können wir einen Tisch im Garten haben?	*Could we have a table in the garden?*
Im Garten ist leider nichts mehr frei.	*Unfortunately, there is no more room in the garden.*
Können wir bitte eine Speisekarte haben?	*Could we have a menu, please?*
Was darf's denn sein?	*What can I get you?*
Was empfehlen Sie?	*What do you recommend?*
Ich nehme . . .	*I'll have . . .*
An unserem Tisch fehlt . . .	*We are missing . . . at our table.*
Guten Appetit!	*Enjoy your meal! (Bon Appetit!)*
Bitte bringen Sie mir noch ein Glas Rotwein.	*Please bring me another glass of red wine.*
Die Rechnung, bitte.	*The check, please.*
Alles zusammen?	*One check? (lit., All together?)*
Ist das Trinkgeld inklusive?	*Is the tip included?*
Stimmt so.	*Keep the change. (lit., That's correct.)*

UNIT 9
School and work

---------- Lesson 33 (words) ----------

If you are on a business trip, words and expressions about work and the workplace are very important. Or, you may be studying at a German school and want to know more vocabulary to talk about your academic subjects. We'll learn all about work and school in this lesson. Additionally, you'll learn the passive voice, the imperative, and compound nouns to help you discuss these topics.

WORD LIST 1

der Beruf	*profession, job*
beruflich	*professionally*
der Angestellte	*employee*
der Arbeiter	*worker*
der Vorgesetzte	*superior*
die Beförderung	*promotion*
die Arbeitsstelle	*workplace, job*
die Stellenanzeige	*job announcement, help-wanted ad*
die Berufschancen	*professional outlook (chances)*
die Berufserfahrung	*professional experience*
die Karriere	*career*
die Arbeitszeit	*work hours, working hours*
die Überstunden	*overtime*
die Teilzeitbeschäftigung	*part-time employment*
die Vollzeitbeschäftigung	*full-time employment*
die Arbeitslosenrate	*unemployment rate*
das Gehalt	*salary*
die Gehaltserhöhung	*raise*
die Rente	*retirement*

einstellen	*to hire*
befördern	*to promote*
entlassen	*to let go, to fire*
arbeitslos	*unemployed*

NUTS & BOLTS 1
THE PASSIVE VOICE 1

All of the German sentences you have heard or read so far were in the active voice. This means that the subject of the sentence performs the action specified by the verb.

Der Chef befördert den Angestellten.
The boss promotes the employee.

In the passive voice, the subject does not perform the action; instead, it is the person or object acted on. It is *passive*. Accordingly, the verb comes in a special form called the *passive voice*.

Der Angestellte wird befördert.
The employee is being promoted.

The German passive is formed with the verb **werden** *(to become)* and the past participle of the main verb. Here are the present tense forms of **werden**.

werden *(to become)*			
ich	werde	wir	werden
du	wirst	ihr	werdet
Sie	werden	Sie	werden
er/sie/es	wird	sie	werden

In the passive voice, the person or thing performing the action (the agent) may or may not be mentioned.

Der Angestellte wird befördert. *(no agent)*
The employee is being promoted.

Der Angestellte wird vom Chef befördert. *(agent = der Chef)*
The employee is being promoted by the boss.

The passive voice is more common in the German language than it is in English.

Werden Sie befördert?
Will you be promoted?

Ich werde entlassen.
I will be let go.

Viele Arbeiter werden von InterCorp neu eingestellt.
Many workers are being newly employed by InterCorp.

The passive voice is often used with modal verbs. In this case, the modal verb forms the tense and takes the position of the conjugated verb, and the passive consists of the past participle of the verb plus **werden** in the infinitive at the very end of the sentence.

Kann er entlassen werden?
Can he be fired?

Ich will besser bezahlt werden.
I want to be paid better.

PRACTICE 1
Please rewrite the sentences below in the passive voice.

1. Die Firma stellt neue Arbeiter ein.

2. Die andere Firma entlässt viele Angestellte.

3. Ich will meinen neuen Assistenten besser bezahlen.

4. Wir reservieren einen Tisch für Sie.

5. Mein Mann bestellt den Wein.

WORD LIST 2

die Schule	*school*
die Universität	*university*
die Ausbildung	*professional training, apprenticeship*
das Praktikum	*internship*
das Volontariat	*internship (newspaper)*
der Schüler	*pupil*
der Mitschüler	*classmate*
der Kommilitone	*fellow university student (male)*
die Komilitonin	*fellow university student (female)*
der Auszubildende	*apprentice*
der Azubi	*apprentice*
das Fach	*subject*
das Lieblingsfach	*favorite subject*
das Zeugnis	*report card*
die Beurteilung	*evaluation*
der Hauptschulabschluß	*school-leaving exam (lower level)*
die Realschulprüfung	*middle school exam*
das Abitur	*high school exam*
studieren	*to study (at a university)*

NUTS & BOLTS 2
THE PASSIVE VOICE 2

The passive voice can be formed in all tenses. The verb **werden** changes to express different tenses, whereas the past participle of the main verb remains the same.

Present tense

Ich werde befördert.
I am being promoted.

Die Angestellten werden entlassen.
The employees are being let go.

Future tense

Even though it is possible to form the future tense in the passive voice, the present tense is much more common.

Ich werde befördert (werden).
I will be promoted.

Die Angestellten werden entlassen (werden).
The employees will be let go.

Past tense

Ich wurde befördert.
I was promoted.

Die Angestellten wurden entlassen.
The employees were let go.

Present perfect

Werden forms the present perfect with the conjugated form of **sein** plus the past participle **worden**. Note that in the present perfect, the conjugated form of **sein** takes the second position in the sentence, whereas the past participle of the main verb and the past participle of **werden**–**worden**–follow at the very end of the sentence.

Ich bin befördert worden.
I have been promoted.

Die Angestellten sind entlassen worden.
The employees have been let go.

PRACTICE 2

Please rewrite each sentence below in the passive voice, retaining the tense of the active sentence.

1. Die Firma hat neue Arbeiter eingestellt.

2. Die andere Firma hat viele Angestellte entlassen.

3. Ich wollte meinen neuen Assistenten besser bezahlen.

4. Wir werden einen Tisch für Sie reservieren.

5. Mein Mann hat den Wein bestellt.

ANSWERS

PRACTICE 1: 1. Neue Arbeiter werden (von der Firma) eingestellt. **2.** Viele Angestellte werden (von der anderen Firma) entlassen. **3.** Mein neuer Assistant will (von mir) besser bezahlt werden. **4.** Ein Tisch wird (von uns) für Sie reserviert. **5.** Der Wein wird (von meinem Mann) bestellt.

PRACTICE 2: 1. Neue Arbeiter sind (von der Firma) eingestellt worden. **2.** Viele Angestellte sind (von der anderen Firma) entlassen worden. **3.** Mein neuer Assistant wollte (von mir) besser bezahlt werden. **4.** Ein Tisch wird (von uns) für Sie reserviert (werden). **5.** Der Wein ist (von meinem Mann) bestellt worden.

——————— Lesson 34 (phrases) ———————

PHRASE LIST 1

die gleitende Arbeitszeit	*flexible working hours*
von . . . bis arbeiten	*to work from . . . to*
laut Statistik	*based on statistics*
Überstunden machen	*to work overtime*
Karriere machen	*to advance (lit., to make a career)*
sich Urlaub nehmen	*to take a vacation/time off*
die (Berufs)Erfahrung sammeln	*to collect (professional) experience*
freiberuflich arbeiten	*to freelance*
freiberuflich tätig sein	*to freelance*
selbstständig sein	*to be self-employed*
arbeitslos sein	*to be unemployed*
in Rente gehen	*to retire*
in Pension gehen	*to retire*

NUTS & BOLTS 1
ALTERNATIVES TO THE PASSIVE VOICE

We just learned how to make passive sentences, such as *He has been fired*. Whereas in the active voice, the subject of the sentence performs the action that the verb describes, the subject in the passive voice is the person or object acted on. It is passive. The passive voice, which is rather common in the German language, can be replaced by other constructions.

Man + active verb

The construction using **man** is the most common way to express the passive, particularly if the agent has not been named in the passive sentence.

Der Arbeiter wurde entlassen.	Man hat den Arbeiter entlassen.
The worker was let go.	*One/They let the worker go.*
Die Schüler wurden gelobt.	**Man hat die Schüler gelobt.**
The students were praised.	*One/They praised the students.*

Sein + zu + infinitive

Passive constructions with **können** and **müssen** can be replaced with **sein + zu + infinitive**. You will come across both versions in many newspaper articles.

Das kann so nicht gesagt werden.	Das ist so nicht zu sagen.
That cannot be said like that.	*That cannot be said like that.*

So viele Entlassungen können nicht aufrecht erhalten werden.	So viele Entlassungen sind nicht aufrecht zu erhalten.
This many firings cannot continue. (lit., So many firings cannot be kept up.)	*This many firings are not to continue. (lit., So many firings are not to be kept up.)*

Sich lassen + infinitive

This can replace **können** and a passive infinitive. You will hear this often if the speaker does not want to name a specific agent.

Das kann besser gemacht werden.	Das lässt sich besser machen.
That can be done better.	*That can be done better.*
Diese Meinung kann nicht bewiesen werden.	Diese Meinung lässt sich nicht beweisen.
This opinion cannot be backed up.	*This opinion cannot be backed up.*

PRACTICE 1

Please transform the following story using the alternatives to the passive guided by the clues in parentheses. Watch your tenses.

Gestern haben Schneiders angerufen. Herr Schneider ist befördert worden (man). Das muss gross gefeiert werden (sein + zu + *infinitive*). Es wurde mir gesagt, dass ich Wein mitbringen soll (man). Ich habe eine Flasche Weißwein mitgebracht. Das Essen wurde um 20 Uhr serviert (man). Es schmeckte hervorragend.

PHRASE LIST 2

ein guter Schüler sein	*to be a good (school) student*
ein guter Student sein	*to be a good (college) student*
ein schlechter Schüler sein	*to be a bad (school) student*
ein schlechter Student sein	*to be a bad (college) student*
die Hausaufgaben machen	*to do homework*
eine Pause machen	*to take a break*
eine Ausbildung machen	*to apprentice*
ein Volontariat machen	*to intern at a newspaper*
die Realschulprüfung machen	*to take the middle school exam*
das Abitur machen	*to take the high school exam*
einen Magister machen	*to study for a master's degree*
einen Magister haben	*to have a master's degree*
einen Doktor machen	*to study for a Ph.D.*
einen Doktor haben	*to have a Ph.D.*
viel zu tun haben	*to have a lot to do*
viel zu lernen haben	*to have a lot to learn*
eine Stelle suchen	*to look for a job*
eine Ausbildungsstelle suchen	*to look for an apprenticeship*
sich auf eine Stelle bewerben	*to apply for a job, to apply for a position*
den Lebenslauf schreiben	*to prepare one's résumé*
eine Familie gründen	*to start a family*

NUTS & BOLTS 2
Compound nouns

The German language likes putting long nouns together to make an even longer one. If a new noun is made of one or more nouns, it is called a compound noun—for example,

die Realschule with **die Prüfung** makes **die Realschulprüfung** (*middle school exam*, from *middle school + exam*).

Please note that the second noun dictates the gender of the compound noun.

das Leben + der Lauf = der Lebenslauf *(résumé, curriculum vitae)*

das Haus + die Aufgabe = die Hausaufgabe *(homework)*

die Arbeitslosen + die Rate = die Arbeitslosenrate *(unemployment rate)*

Many compound nouns have a possessive connection, which could be expressed by using the genitive case: **die Erhöhung des Gehalts** *(the raise of the payment)*. The possessive connection is often still noticeable in a compound noun by the possessive **-s-** (or in case of **n**-nouns, by the possessive **-n-**) that attaches to the first word in the compound.

das Gehalt + die Erhöhung = die Gehaltserhöhung *(raise)*

die Arbeit + die Stelle = die Arbeitsstelle *(workplace)*

die Arbeitslosen + die Rate = die Arbeitslosenrate *(unemployment rate)*

German also creates compounds from a noun and an adjective or from two adjectives. If a noun is combined with an adjective, the second word in the compound dictates whether the new word is a noun or an adjective.

der Zucker + süß = zuckersüß *(sugary sweet)*

süß + sauer = süßsauer *(sweet-and-sour)*

One of the most curious German spelling rules requires that a compound word retains all individual letters, even if they are identical, in order to keep the old word stem intact.

das Schiff + die Fahrt = die Schifffahrt *(cruise)*

Note that it is okay in this situation to have three identical consonants in a row.

schnell + lebig = schnelllebig *(fast-paced)*

der Schluss + der Satz = der Schlusssatz *(final sentence)*

To avoid this, you can use a hyphen: **der Schluss-Satz.** If the compound consists of two nouns, capitalize both.

PRACTICE 2
Create the compound.

1. die Arbeit + der Kollege =

2. die Pause + das Brot =

3. die Zeitung + der Artikel =

Find the individual parts.

4. die Teilzeitbeschäftigung =

5. die Rentenfrage =

6. der Lebenslauf =

Discovery activity

Go to the website of one of the newspapers listed earlier. Read any article you find interesting. Go through the article and find five compound nouns. Write them down. Did you understand what the article is about? Rewrite it in your own words. And, as a bonus activity, how many passive constructions did you find in the article?

If you don't have access to a computer, see if your local library has any German newspapers that you might be able to browse for articles.

ANSWERS

PRACTICE 1: Gestern haben Schneiders angerufen. Man hat Herrn Schneider befördert. Das ist gross zu feiern. Man hat mir gesagt, dass ich Wein mitbringen soll. Ich habe eine Flasche Weißwein mitgebracht. Man hat das Essen um 20 Uhr serviert. Es schmeckte hervorragend.

PRACTICE 2: 1. der Arbeitskollege; **2.** das Pausenbrot; **3.** der Zeitungsartikel; **4.** die Teilzeit + die Beschäftigung; **5.** die Rente + die Frage; **6.** das Leben + der Lauf

---

Lesson 35 (sentences)

SENTENCE LIST 1

Ich suche eine neue Stelle.	*I am looking for a new job. (lit., I am looking for a new position.)*
Ich möchte mich beruflich verbessern.	*I want to get ahead in my profession. (lit., I want to better myself professionally.)*
Wollen Sie Karriere machen oder eine Familie gründen?	*Do you want to have a career or start a family?*
Kann man denn nicht beides machen?	*Can't one/you do both?*
Heutzutage muss man viele Überstunden machen.	*These days, you have to work overtime a lot.*
Wo haben Sie Ihre Berufserfahrung gesammelt?	*Where have you gained your professional experience?*
Ich war freiberuflich tätig.	*I freelanced.*
Bitte bringen Sie Ihren Lebenslauf mit.	*Please bring your résumé along.*
Man kann im Alter von siebenundsechzig in Rente gehen.	*One/You can retire at the age of sixty-seven.*

NUTS & BOLTS 1
THE IMPERATIVE 1

The imperative forms are used to give commands, instructions, suggestions, and requests. English has only one imperative, because there is only one word for *you*. But German has three words for *you*–**Sie, du,** and **ihr**–and therefore needs three imperative forms.

du-*form:*	**Unterbrich mich nicht, Martin!**
	Don't interrupt me, Martin!
Sie-*form:*	**Unterbrechen Sie mich nicht, mein Herr!**
	Don't interrupt me, sir!
ihr-*form:*	**Unterbrecht mich nicht, Kinder!**
	Don't interrupt me, children!

If you want to soften the request, add **bitte.**

Bitte unterbrechen Sie mich nicht, mein Herr!
Please don't interrupt me, sir!

Let's first look at the informal and formal singular imperative.

Du-form

If you are giving commands to just one person–a friend no less–use the **du**-form. The **du**-form is basically the stem of the verb, which you get by taking off the infinitive ending **-en: sagen** minus **-en** becomes **sag.** Do not use the pronoun **du.**

Schreib deinen Lebenslauf.
Write your résumé.

Irregular (strong) verbs, such as **unterbrechen** *(to interrupt)* and **bewerben** *(to apply),* which take vowel changes in the second and third person singular in the present tense, take the same vowel change in the imperative.

Du unterbrichst mich.
You are interrupting me.

Unterbrich mich nicht, Martin!
Don't interrupt me, Martin!

Du bewirbst dich auf diese Stelle.
You are applying for this job.

Bewirb dich auf diese Stelle!
Apply for this job!

However, verbs with vowel changes from **a** to **ä** in the second and third person singular present, such as **laufen** *(to run)* and **fahren** *(to drive),* do not add the umlaut in the imperative.

Du fährst schnell.
You are driving fast.

Fahr nicht so schnell!
Don't drive so fast!

Verbs with a stem ending in **-t, -d,** or **-g,** such as **wart(en)** or **antwort(en),** always add an **-e** in the imperative.

Warte auf mich!
Wait for me!

Antworte mir!
Answer me!

Sie-form

The **Sie**-form is used to command or make suggestions to those you would generally refer to with the polite **Sie**. The imperative form is identical to the **Sie**-form of the present tense. You have to use the personal pronoun **Sie,** but note that subject **(Sie)** and verb (e.g., **unterbrechen**) trade places.

Unterbrechen Sie mich nicht, mein Herr!
Don't interrupt me, sir!

Bewerben Sie sich doch!
Apply! (Why don't you apply?)

Note that the verb **sein** *(to be)* is the only irregular imperative form.

Bitte seien Sie pünktlich, Herr Müller.
Please be punctual, Mr. Müller.

Bitte sei leise, Klaus!
Please be quiet, Klaus!

PRACTICE 1
Rewrite the sentences in the imperative.

1. Du gehst jetzt in die Schule.

2. Sie bringen den Lebenslauf mit.

3. Sie kommen pünktlich.

4. Du machst Überstunden.

5. Du suchst eine Stelle.

SENTENCE LIST 2

Meine Tochter geht auf das Gymnasium.	*My daughter goes to high school.*

Ohne Abitur findet man keine Stelle.	*Without the high school exit exam, one/you won't find a job.*
Wo sind Sie zur Schule gegangen?	*Where did you go to school?*
Eine gute Ausbildung ist wichtig.	*A good education is important.*
Nach dem Abitur mache ich erst mal Pause.	*After my high school exit exam, I'll first take a break.*
Ich möchte einen Doktor in Psychologie machen.	*I want to get a Ph.D. in psychology.*
Ich muss meinen Lebenslauf schreiben.	*I have to prepare my résumé.*
Ich möchte mich als Auszubildender bei Ihrer Firma bewerben.	*I want to apply for an apprenticeship (lit., as an apprentice) with your company.*

NUTS & BOLTS 2
THE IMPERATIVE 2
Let's take a look at the plural command forms.

Ihr-form

When you are issuing commands or asking suggestions to a group of people **(ihr),** simply use the regular present tense form for the second person plural. Do not use the pronoun.

Unterbrecht mich nicht, Kinder!
Don't interrupt me, children!

Macht die Hausaufgaben!
Do your homework!

If you want to make suggestions and include yourself, use the German verb **lassen** *(to let)* similarly to the way you would use the English verb *let's* in comparable sentences.

Lass uns eine neue Stelle suchen.
Let's look for a new job.

You can also simply use the **wir**-form of the verb and switch subject and verb.

Suchen wir eine neue Stelle.
Let's look for a new job.

The verb **sein** *(to be)* is irregular in the plural imperative as well.

Seid nicht so laut, Kinder!
Don't be so loud, children!

PRACTICE 2
Rewrite these imperatives in the plural.

1. Schreib deinen Lebenslauf!

2. Sei nicht böse!

3. Laß uns Biologie studieren!

4. Sammel erst mal Berufserfahrung!

5. Unterbrich mich nicht!

Culture note

Education in Germany, Austria, and Switzerland is free from **Kindergarten** *(kindergarten)* all the way to high school. Once a student reaches **Universität** *(university)*, he or she is required to pay a low fee, which is but a fraction of the tuition in the United States. A typical school career starts with **die Grundschule** *(elementary school, first grade through fourth grade)* and goes to either **die Hauptschule** *(junior high school, fifth grade through ninth grade)*, **die Realschule** *(middle school, fifth grade through tenth grade)*, or the **Gymnasium** *(high school, fifth grade through twelfth grade)*.

Students graduating from the **Hauptschule** usually go on to **die Berufsschule** *(vocational school)* to learn a trade, those graduating from the **Realschule** often choose administrative careers, and only those graduating with the **Abitur** from the **Gymnasium** can go on to the **Universität.** This threefold school system has been criticized for locking children into a certain career based on their academic performance at too early an age—in grade school. Therefore, **Gesamtschulen** *(comprehensive schools),* which keep all students together until the tenth grade and thus eliminate the **Hauptschule** altogether, have become more and more popular. These days, job opportunities for students without the **Abitur** are becoming rather scarce.

ANSWERS
PRACTICE 1: 1. Geh jetzt in die Schule! **2.** Bringen Sie den Lebenslauf mit! **3.** Kommen Sie pünktlich! **4.** Mach Überstunden! **5.** Such eine Stelle!

PRACTICE 2: 1. Schreibt euren Lebenslauf! **2.** Seid nicht böse! **3.** Laßt uns Biologie studieren! **4.** Sammelt erst mal Berufserfahrung! **5.** Unterbrecht mich nicht!

—————— Lesson 36 (conversations) ——————

Let's listen to a couple at the breakfast table.

CONVERSATION 1
Martin and Maria Huber are sitting at the breakfast table, reading the newspaper.

Maria: Hör mal zu: "Schon wieder sind Hunderte von Arbeitnehmern entlassen worden. Die Arbeitslosenrate ist auf fast zehn Prozent gestiegen."

Martin: Ja, heutzutage sind die Berufsaussichten

schlecht. Man kann nicht mehr so einfach
Karriere machen. Wenn man kein Abitur hat,
bekommt man keine Ausbildungsstelle. Ohne
gute Ausbildung wird man nicht eingestellt.
Und wenn man nicht ständig Überstunden
macht, wird man nicht befördert. Heute heißt
es entweder Familie gründen oder Karriere
machen.

Maria: Na, ich weiß nicht. War das nicht schon immer
so?

Martin: Aber nein. Ich habe eine Familie und eine
erfolgreiche Karriere.

Maria: Ja, das stimmt. Aber sag mal ganz ehrlich, hast
du nicht mehr Zeit im Büro als mit deiner
Familie verbracht?

Martin: Äh . . .

Maria: Man muss einen Partner haben, wenn man
Karriere erfolgreich mit einem Familienleben
vereinbaren will.

Martin: Aber du hast doch auch eine Karriere.

Maria: Ja, aber um die Kinder muss ich mich
kümmern.

Marin: Aber Maria, das lässt sich so nicht sagen.

Maria: Ach nein? Wann hast du dir das letzte Mal
Urlaub genommen wenn die Kinder krank
waren?

Martin: Ich . . . ah . . . hmmm . . .

Maria: Na bitte.

Maria: *Listen to this: "Once again, hundreds of employees have
been laid off. The unemployment rate has risen to
almost ten percent."*

Martin: *Yes, these days, job opportunities are scarce. It is not
that easy to have a career. If you don't have the high
school exam, you won't get an apprenticeship. Without
a good education, you won't be employed. And if you*

don't work overtime constantly, you will not get
promoted. Today it is either family or career.

Maria: Well, I don't know. Hasn't it always been like that?

Martin: Well, no. I have a family and a successful career.

Maria: Yes, that's true. But be honest, didn't you spend more
time in the office than with your family?

Martin: Uh . . .

Maria: One has to have a partner to combine a career with
family life successfully.

Martin: But you have a career, too.

Maria: Yes, but I am the one who takes care of the children.

Marin: But Maria, you can't say that (lit., this can't be said
like that)!

Maria: Oh no? When was the last time you took time off when
the kids were sick?

Martin: I . . . uh . . . hmmm . . .

Maria: See!

NOTES

Ach is a versatile interjection, similar to the English *oh*. The English *well* can be translated into the German **na. Na also!** is
equivalent to the English *See!* or *There you have it!*

NUTS & BOLTS 1

WENN-SENTENCES

In German, **wenn**-sentences introduce a condition on which the
main clause depends. In English, these sentences can be expressed with either *if-* or *when*-clauses.

Wenn die Kinder krank sind, muss ich Urlaub nehmen.

When/If the kids are sick, I have to take time off.

If the **wenn**-sentence is mentioned first, subject and verb change
places in the main clause. Compare the following sentences.

Man muss einen Partner haben, wenn man erfolgreich sein will.
You have to have a partner when/if you want to be successful.

Wenn man erfolgreich sein will, **muss man** einen Partner haben.
If/When you want to be successful, you have to have a partner.

PRACTICE 1
Please connect the following sentences with **wenn**.

1. Die Kinder sind krank. Ich muss Urlaub nehmen.

2. Man braucht eine gute Ausbildung. Man will eine gute Stelle.

3. Du musst lernen. Du willst ein gutes Zeugnis.

4. Sie wollen befördert werden. Sie müssen Überstunden machen.

5. Du brauchst meine Hilfe. Du willst erfolgreich sein.

CONVERSATION 2
Susi is applying for a job as an editor with a newspaper. She has an interview with Lars Hochut.

Lars Hochut: Ihr Lebenslauf ist sehr beeindruckend.
Susi: Danke.
Lars Hochut: Warum wollen Sie denn bei uns arbeiten?
Susi: Ich glaube, dass meine Ausbildung mich gut auf diese Stelle vorbereitet hat.
Lars Hochut: Wo haben Sie denn Ihre Berufserfahrung gesammelt?
Susi: Nach meinem Studium habe ich bei der Hohenloher Tageszeitung ein Volontariat gemacht. Und dann bin ich zur Assistentin des Herausgebers befördert worden.
Lars Hochut: Die Stelle einer Redakteurin ist viel Arbeit. Sie wissen, dass Sie manchmal Überstunden machen müssen.
Susi: Ja.

Lars Hochut:	Aber wir haben gleitende Arbeitszeit. Wenn Sie abends spät arbeiten, können Sie am nächsten Tag später ins Büro kommen.
Susi:	Die Stelle interessiert mich sehr. Ich möchte mich beruflich verbessern.
Lars Hochut:	Gut. Wir melden uns.

Lars Hochut:	*Your résumé is very impressive.*
Susi:	*Thank you.*
Lars Hochut:	*Why do you want to work for us?*
Susi:	*I think my education has prepared me well for this position.*
Lars Hochut:	*Where did you gain your job experience?*
Susi:	*After my studies I did an internship with the Hohenloher newspaper. And then I was promoted to the assistant of the publisher.*
Lars Hochut:	*The position of editor is a lot of work. You know that you have to work overtime sometimes.*
Susi:	*Yes.*
Lars Hochut:	*But we have flexible working hours. If you work late at night, you can come in later the next day.*
Susi:	*I am very interested in this position. I want to get ahead in my profession.*
Lars Hochut:	*Good. We will contact you.*

NOTES

Almost every larger company in Germany offers **gleitende Arbeitszeit**. This means that as long as the employees are at their workplace during the so-called **Kernzeit** *(core/base hours)*, usually between 9:00 A.M. and 2:00 P.M., they can choose whether they'd like to work early or late in the day.

NUTS & BOLTS 2
DASS-SENTENCES AND OB-SENTENCES

Dass introduces a clause that is dependent on a main clause and cannot stand alone. It is equivalent to the English *that*.

Ich weiss, dass ich viel arbeiten muss.
I know (that) I have to work a lot.

Unlike in English, it is not possible to drop **dass**.

Ich glaube, dass ich die richtige Ausbildung habe.
I believe (that) I have the right education.

Ob-sentences also introduce a dependent clause; **ob** is equivalent to the English *if* or *whether*.

Ich weiß nicht, ob ich die richtige Ausbildung habe.
I don't know whether I have the right education.

Ich bin nicht sicher, ob ich Karriere machen oder eine Familie gründen will.
I'm not sure whether I want a career or to start a family.

Please note that the verb in the **dass**-clauses and **ob**-clauses always takes the final position in the sentence.

PRACTICE 2
Please put the two sentences together with **dass** or **ob**.

1. Ich habe eine gute Ausbildung. Ich hoffe, _____.

2. Die Stelle ist frei. Ich weiß nicht, _____.

3. Ich bewerbe mich. Du weißt, _____.

4. Ich bin befördert worden. Haben Sie gehört, _____?

5. Er arbeitet hier. Ich bin nicht sicher, _____.

Language link

If you ever decide to enter the German job market, you'll need to adapt your application to the customs and standards of the country. *Focus*, a popular German magazine, offers a few excellent tips on the dos and don'ts of German job applications. They discuss how to put your résumé together, how to interview successfully, and how to follow up. Go to **www.focus.de/jobs/bewerbung**.

ANSWERS

PRACTICE 1: 1. Wenn die Kinder krank sind, muss ich Urlaub nehmen. **2.** Man braucht eine gute Ausbildung, wenn man eine gute Stelle will. **3.** Du musst lernen, wenn du ein gutes Zeugnis willst. **4.** Wenn Sie befördert werden wollen, müssen Sie Überstunden machen. **5.** Du brauchst meine Hilfe, wenn du erfolgreich sein willst.

PRACTICE 2: 1. Ich hoffe, dass ich eine gute Ausbildung habe. **2.** Ich weiß nicht, ob die Stelle frei ist. **3.** Du weißt, dass ich mich bewerbe. **4.** Haben Sie gehört, dass ich befördert worden bin? **5.** Ich bin nicht sicher, ob er hier arbeitet.

UNIT 9 ESSENTIALS

Ich suche eine neue Stelle.	*I am looking for a new job. (lit., I am looking for a new position.)*
Ich möchte mich beruflich verbessern.	*I want to get ahead in my profession. (lit., I want to better myself professionally.)*
Ich möchte mich bei Ihrer Firma bewerben.	*I want to apply with your company.*
Haben Sie Ihren Lebenslauf mitgebracht?	*Did you bring your résumé?*
Eine gute Ausbildung ist wichtig.	*A good education is important.*
Ich habe einen Doktor.	*I have a Ph.D.*

Wo sind Sie zur Schule gegangen?	*Where did you go to school?*
Wo haben Sie Ihre Berufserfahrung gesammelt?	*Where have you gotten your professional experience?*
Ich war freiberuflich tätig.	*I freelanced.*
Ich habe lange bei Bosch gearbeitet.	*I have been employed at Bosch for a long time.*
Ich bin befördert worden.	*I was promoted.*
Ich bin entlassen worden.	*I was let go.*

UNIT 10
Sports and hobbies

―――――――――― Lesson 37 (words) ――――――――――

Now that you know how to get a job and a promotion using your German, it's time for some relaxation.

WORD LIST 1

der Sport	*sports*
Sportler	*athlete*
Freizeitsportler	*hobby athlete*
das Sportstudio	*sports center*
der Fitnessclub	*fitness club*
das Schwimmbad	*(public) pool*
das Skigebiet	*ski resort*
der Verein	*club*
das Mitglied	*member*
Rad fahren	*to bicycle*
Motorrad fahren	*to ride a motorcycle*
Ski fahren	*to ski*
snowboarden	*to snowboard*
schwimmen	*to swim*
tauchen	*to (scuba) dive*
Karate	*karate*
Yoga	*yoga*
joggen	*to jog*
wandern	*to hike*
Berg steigen	*to go mountain climbing*

NUTS & BOLTS 1
RELATIVE CLAUSES 1

Relative clauses give additional information about a noun.

Der Mann, der joggt, ist sehr sportlich.

The man who is jogging is very athletic.

The pronoun *who* is used to refer back to the noun **der Mann** *(the man)*, which the relative clause describes further: **der joggt** *(who is jogging)*. In other words, *who* is the relative pronoun *relating* back to the noun mentioned in the main clause: **Der Mann ist sehr sportlich.** *(The man is very athletic.)*

Die Frau, die eine rote Mütze trägt, fährt Ski.

The woman who is wearing a red cap is skiing.

In English, the relative pronoun can be omitted. In German, it cannot be omitted.

Das Snowboard, das du benutzt, gehört mir.

The snowboard (that) you are using is mine.

In German, the relative pronoun agrees in gender and number with the noun it refers to. The relative pronoun is usually identical to the definite article.

Der Fitnessclub, der *(m. sg.)* neu aufgemacht hat, ist prima.

The fitness club, which recently opened, is great.

Die Tasse, die *(f. sg.)* auf dem Tisch steht, habe ich getöpfert.

The cup that is standing on the table was made by me.

Note that the verb stands in the last position in a relative clause.

Das Motorrad, das *(n.sg.)* in der Garage steht, war sehr teuer.

The motorbike that is standing in the garage was very expensive.

Make sure not to mix up **dass** and **das**. Even though they are pronounced the same, they are spelled differently and have very different meanings. **Das** is the definite article for singular neuter nouns and also a relative pronoun.

Das Motorrad, das in der Garage steht, war sehr teuer.
The motorbike that is standing in the garage was very expensive.

Dass, on the other hand, does not refer to a noun but to the information conveyed by the entire sentence.

Bist du sicher, dass das Motorrad noch in der Garage steht?
Are you sure (that) the motorbike is still in the garage?

PRACTICE 1
Please complete the sentences with the appropriate relative pronoun.

1. Das Motorrad, _____ ich fahre, ist weiß.

2. Der Fitnessclub, _____ neu aufgemacht hat, ist immer voll.

3. Das Schwimmbad, _____ in der Innenstadt liegt, ist immer kalt.

4. Ich kann in Schuhen, _____ neu sind, nicht joggen.

5. Der Mann, _____ Karate unterrichtet, ist sehr sportlich.

WORD LIST 2

die Freizeitbeschäftigung	*leisure time activity*
das Hobby	*hobby*
fotografieren	*to photograph*
malen	*to paint*
zeichnen	*to draw*
töpfern	*to make pottery*
stricken	*to knit*
häkeln	*to crochet*

kochen	to cook
backen	to bake
die Musik	music
die Gitarre	guitar
das Klavier	piano

NUTS & BOLTS 2
RELATIVE CLAUSES 2

A relative pronoun can be the subject or the object of the relative clause. Above we only dealt with relative pronouns in the subject case (nominative). If the relative pronoun refers to an object in the relative clause, it has to change accordingly. Let's compare the following two sentences.

Der Mann, der Karate unterrichtet, ruft dich.
The man who is teaching karate is calling you.

Der Mann, den du rufst, unterrichtet Karate.
The man whom you are calling is teaching karate.

Just as the English relative pronoun changes from *who* to *whom* in the second sentence to signify the change from subject to object in the relative clause, the German relative pronoun changes from **der** to **den.** Let's look at another example.

Der Fußball, den du hältst, gehört mir.
The soccer ball (that) you are holding is mine.

In the relative clause, the subject is **du,** and **der Fußball,** represented by the relative pronoun **den,** is the direct object: **Du hältst den Fußball.** *(You are holding the soccer ball.)* → **Der Fußball, den du hältst . . .** *(The soccer ball that you are holding . . .)* Hence, the relative pronoun needs to be in the masculine singular accusative form: **den.**

A relative clause can begin with a preposition followed by a relative pronoun. The case of the relative pronoun is dictated by the preposition.

Das ist der Fitnessclub, bei dem ich Mitglied bin. (bei *takes dative*)
This is the fitness club where I am a member.

PRACTICE 2
Please insert the appropriate relative pronoun.

1. Der Fußball, mit _____ ich am liebsten spiele, ist schwarz.

2. Das Bild, _____ ich male, wird verkauft.

3. Der Pullover, _____ ich stricke, ist bald fertig.

4. Das Fahrrad, mit _____ ich fahre, gehört meiner Freundin.

5. Die Kekse, _____ du gegessen hast, habe ich gebacken.

Culture note

They say Germans work hard—and play hard. As a result of strong unions in virtually all professions, along with the trend towards part-time and freelance employment, employees in Germany have more leisure time than do employees in most other industrialized countries. While in Great Britain, people work an average of 43.6 hours a week, and in Spain, Portugal, Austria, and Sweden, about 41 hours, Germans only work an average of 39 hours per week, leaving ample time to get involved in sports or take up a hobby—on average, around six hours a day. Note that men seem to have about 30 minutes more leisure time a day than women.

ANSWERS
PRACTICE 1: 1. das; **2.** der; **3.** das; **4.** die; **5.** der

PRACTICE 2: 1. dem; **2.** das; **3.** den; **4.** dem; **5.** die

A few phrases will make it easier for you to discuss leisure activities with your newfound friends and colleagues in Germany.

PHRASE LIST 1

Sport treiben	*to do sports*
einem Verein beitreten	*to join a club*
Fußball spielen	*to play soccer*
Handball spielen	*to play handball*
Basketball spielen	*to play basketball*
Volleyball spielen	*to play volleyball*
Tennis spielen	*to play tennis*
Squash spielen	*to play squash*
Golf spielen	*to play golf*
einen Marathon laufen	*to run a marathon*
(keine) Lust haben	*(not) to feel like*
fit bleiben	*to stay in shape*
das Wetter	*weather*
bei gutem Wetter	*in good weather*
bei schlechtem Wetter	*in bad weather*
bei Regenwetter	*in rainy weather*
bei Schneewetter	*in snowy weather*
Es regnet.	*It is raining.*
Es schneit.	*It is snowing.*
Die Sonne scheint.	*The sun is shining.*

NUTS & BOLTS 1

INFINITIVES WITH ZU

Infinitive constructions with **zu** are subordinate clauses that never have their own subject. Instead, they relate to the subject and action of the introductory main clause.

Hast du Lust, mit mir joggen zu gehen?
Do you feel like going for a jog with me?

Glaubst du, schnell genug zu laufen?
Do you believe you run fast enough?

Note that separable verbs place the **zu** between the separable prefix and the stem.

Hast du Lust mit<u>zu</u>spielen.
Do you want to play along?

Bei Regenwetter habe ich keine Lust hinaus<u>zu</u>gehen.
In rainy weather I don't feel like going out.

Constructions with **um** followed by **zu** and the infinitive are comparable to the English *in order to*.

Ich muss nicht schnell laufen, um mit dir zu joggen.
I don't have to run fast in order to jog with you.

Just like any infinitive with **zu, um . . . zu** demands that the main clause and the subordinate clause share the same subject.

Ohne . . . zu and **anstatt . . . zu** are other infinitive constructions.

Er spielt im Verein Tennis, ohne bei<u>zu</u>treten.
He plays tennis at the club without joining.

Die Kinder spielen Fußball, anstatt Hausaufgaben zu machen.
The kids are playing soccer instead of doing their homework.

PRACTICE 1
Answer the questions in German with an infinitive construction.

1. *Do you feel like playing tennis? (no)*

2. *Do you believe you play the piano well? (yes)*

3. *Do you feel like dancing? (yes)*

4. *Do you prefer to play golf instead of working? (yes)*

5. *Do you run fast enough to run with me? (yes)*

PHRASE LIST 2

einem Hobby nachgehen	*to have a hobby*
Gitarre spielen	*to play the guitar*
Klavier spielen	*to play the piano*
Briefmarken sammeln	*to collect stamps*
im Garten arbeiten	*to work in the garden*
Blumen pflanzen	*to plant flowers*
einen Kuchen backen	*to bake a cake*
dick machen	*to be fattening*
Tango tanzen	*to dance the tango*
Ballettunterricht nehmen	*to take ballet classes*
stricken lernen	*to learn (how) to knit*
Leute kennenlernen	*to meet people*
Es macht Spaß.	*It is fun.*

NUTS & BOLTS 2
WEIL-SENTENCES

Weil-sentences introduce the reason for a particular action in the main clause with **weil** *(because)*. In other words, **weil** answers the question **warum?** *(why?)*.

Warum sollte ich Sport treiben?
Why should I play sports?

Du solltest Sport treiben, weil es gesund ist.
You should play sports because it's healthy.

Ich will nicht Tennis spielen, weil ich müde bin.
I don't want to play tennis, because I am tired.

Remember that in the subordinate clause, the verb is moved to the end. And finally, as you may have noticed, all subordinate clauses in German have to be separated from the main clause by a comma.

PRACTICE 2
Connect the sentences using **weil**.

1. Ich lerne stricken. Es macht Spaß.

2. Ich gehe gern tanzen. Ich lerne Leute kennen.

3. Wir essen nie Kuchen. Es macht dick.

4. Er sammelt Briefmarken. Er hat viel Zeit.

5. Sie sind müde. Sie arbeiten zu viel.

Discovery activity

Let's walk down memory lane. Which sports did you play when you were younger? Were you on a high school or college team? Which sports are you still playing? Did you participate in other leisure activities when you were growing up? Any favorites? Make a list! **Auf Deutsch, natürlich!** Then, interview your family members and friends about their favorite sports and leisure activities. Who knows; perhaps you'll end up going back to that long-forgotten hobby.

ANSWERS
PRACTICE 1: 1. Nein, ich habe keine Lust, Tennis zu spielen. **2.** Ja, ich glaube, gut Klavier zu spielen. **3.** Ja, ich habe Lust zu tanzen. **4.** Ja, ich spiele lieber Golf, anstatt zu arbeiten. **5.** Ja, ich laufe schnell genug, um mit dir/Ihnen zu laufen.

PRACTICE 2: 1. Ich lerne stricken, weil es Spaß macht. **2.** Ich gehe gern tanzen, weil ich Leute kennenlerne. **3.** Wir essen nie Kuchen, weil es dick macht. **4.** Er sammelt Briefmarken, weil er viel Zeit hat. **5.** Sie sind müde, weil Sie zu viel arbeiten.

Let's put together the phrases and vocabulary you have learned to create sentences that will get you off the couch and into the gym.

SENTENCE LIST 1

Treiben Sie Sport?	*Do you play sports?*
Ich spiele Tennis.	*I play tennis.*
Meine Kinder möchten gern Fußball spielen.	*My children would like to play soccer.*
Ich habe früher Golf gespielt.	*I used to play golf.*
Wenn Sie Golf spielen wollen, müssen Sie dem Verein beitreten.	*If you want to play golf, you have to join the club.*
Gibt es hier einen Fitnessclub in der Nähe?	*Is there a fitness club nearby?*
Wo kann ich hier in der Nähe joggen gehen?	*Where can I go for a jog around here?*
Gibt es hier ein Schwimmbad?	*Is there a pool around here?*
Haben Sie Lust, Squash zu spielen?	*Do you feel like playing squash?*
Leider habe ich keine Zeit, um heute wandern zu gehen.	*Unfortunately, I don't have time to go hiking today.*

NUTS & BOLTS 1
Subordinate clauses with question pronouns
It is also possible to form subordinate clauses with question words such as **warum** *(why)*, **wer** *(who)*, **wann** *(when)*, **wie** *(how)*, and **wo** *(where)*.

Ich weiß nicht, wo man hier Squash spielen kann.

I don't know where you can play squash around here.

Wissen Sie, wann das Schwimmbad aufmacht?

Do you know when the pool opens?

Können Sie mir zeigen, wie man strickt?

Can you show me how to knit?

Es ist mir egal, warum man Sport treiben soll.

I don't care why you are supposed to play sports.

As with all of the subordinate clauses you've learned so far (**wenn-, dass-,** and **ob-**sentences and relative clauses), the verb moves to the final position in subordinate clauses with question words, as well.

Wer <u>will</u> Fußball spielen?

Who wants to play soccer?

Ich weiß nicht, wer Fußball spielen <u>will</u>.

I don't know who wants to play soccer.

PRACTICE 1
Please form a subordinate clause.

1. Wo kann man hier joggen? Wissen Sie, _____?

2. Wann wollen Sie Golf spielen? Es ist mir egal, _____.

3. Warum brauche ich einen neuen Tennisschläger? Ich weiß nicht, _____.

4. Wie komme ich am besten zum Schwimmbad? Können Sie mir sagen, _____?

5. Wer hat Zeit, Fußball zu spielen? Ich weiß nicht, _____.

SENTENCE LIST 2

Haben Sie ein Hobby?	*Do you have a hobby?*
Ich arbeite gern in meinem Garten.	*I enjoy working in my garden.*
Meine Mutter töpfert.	*My mother does pottery.*
Sie macht Vasen aus Ton.	*She makes vases from clay.*
Können Sie stricken?	*Do you know how to knit?*
Nein, aber ich häkle gern.	*No, but I enjoy crocheting.*
Ich bin Hobbyfotograf.	*I am an amateur photographer.*
Ich wäre gern Amateur-Filmemacher.	*I'd like to be an amateur filmmaker.*
Das ist aber ein teures Hobby.	*That's an expensive hobby.*

NUTS & BOLTS 2

POLITE SPEECH: THE WÜRDE-FORM AND THE SUBJUNCTIVE OF HABEN AND SEIN

The subjunctive, the form expressing hypothetical conditions, is not very common in everyday German speech, except in polite requests. All you need to know are **hätte, wäre,** and **würde,** which are the subjunctive II forms of **haben, sein,** and **werden,** respectively. They are used very much like the English *would.* Let's take a look.

Würde + infinitive

In polite speech, most verbs take the subjunctive of **werden** and the infinitive of the main verb. This is similar to the English *would.* A request like **Hilf mir bitte!** *(Help me!)* becomes more polite by saying, **Würdest du mir bitte helfen?** *(Would you help me, please?)*

Würden Sie mir sagen, wie ich zum Golfplatz komme?
Would you please tell me how to get to the golf course?

Würdest du mir zeigen, wie man strickt?
Would you show me how to knit?

Here are the subjunctive forms of **werden.**

ich	würde	wir	würden
du	würdest	ihr	würdet
Sie	würden	Sie	würden
er/sie/es	würde	sie	würden

The subjunctive II of **haben** and **sein**

Haben and *sein* do not need to use the **würde**-form. Their subjunctive II forms, **hätte** and **wäre,** are rather common.

Hätten Sie Zeit, mit mir Tennis zu spielen?
Would you have time to play tennis with me?

Wie wäre es, wenn wir heute joggen gehen?
How about going jogging today? (lit., How about it if we go jogging today?)

Here are the subjunctive forms of **haben** and **sein.**

ich	hätte	wir	hätten
du	hättest	ihr	hättet
Sie	hätten	Sie	hätten
er/sie/es	hätte	sie	hätten

ich	wäre	wir	wären
du	wärst	ihr	wärt
Sie	wären	Sie	wären
er/sie/es	wäre	sie	wären

PRACTICE 2

Please make these requests more polite.

1. Zeigen Sie mir bitte, wie ich zum Schwimmbad komme.

2. Haben Sie Lust, mit mir Golf zu spielen?

3. Sind Sie bitte so freundlich!

4. Beeilen Sie sich bitte!

5. Hilf mir bitte!

Culture note

Getting involved in sports is a great icebreaker in a foreign country, and it keeps you fit! There are many opportunities to get involved in Germany. German leisure activities and sports are more organized than they are in the English-speaking world. Most sports are organized in a **Verein** or **Club,** whether you are talking about team sports, like soccer and German **Handball,** or more individual sports, such as gymnastics or tennis. To become a member of a **Verein,** you pay an annual fee and often a one-time initiation fee. Some clubs require that you be recommended by a member in good standing, but usually, this is but a formality. Many clubs and associations have frequent social gatherings, regular meetings, and club events, which may demand active participation. The exceptions to this rule are the fitness studios and sports clubs that offer instruction in karate, yoga, and many other more individual sports. All it takes is signing up for a class, and you can participate as your own schedule permits.

ANSWERS

PRACTICE 1: 1. Wissen Sie, wo man hier joggen kann? **2.** Es ist mir egal, wann Sie Golf spielen wollen. **3.** Ich weiß nicht, warum ich einen neuen Tennisschläger brauche. **4.** Können Sie mir sagen, wie ich am besten zum Schwimmbad komme? **5.** Ich weiß nicht, wer Zeit hat, Fußball zu spielen.

PRACTICE 2: 1. Würden Sie mir bitte zeigen, wie ich zum Schwimmbad komme? **2.** Hätten Sie Lust, mit mir Golf zu spielen? **3.** Wären Sie bitte so freundlich! **4.** Würden Sie sich bitte beeilen? **5.** Würdest du mir bitte helfen?

———————— Lesson 40 (conversations) ————————

Ready for a jog? Or a cooking class? Let's make plans for your leisure time in Germany.

CONVERSATION 1

Dan Andrews has just moved to Germany. He is chatting with a neighbor.

> **Dan:** Ich kenne mich hier noch nicht so gut aus. Was kann man denn hier in der Freizeit machen?
>
> **Roswitha:** Das kommt darauf an, was Sie gerne machen. Treiben Sie Sport?
>
> **Dan:** Ja, ich spiele Golf.
>
> **Roswitha:** Wenn Sie Golf spielen wollen, müssen Sie einem Club beitreten.
>
> **Dan:** Wissen Sie, ob es hier in der Nähe einen Golfclub gibt?
>
> **Roswitha:** Es gibt einen Golfclub in Büttchen. Büttchen ist das Dorf, das beim Flughafen liegt. Sie könnten mit meinem Mann Golf spielen. Er ist Mitglied.

Dan: Spielen Sie auch Golf?

Roswitha: Nein, ich spiele nicht Golf, weil ich nicht genug Zeit habe. Ich jogge lieber. Das hält mich fit.

Dan: So ein Zufall, ich laufe auch gern. Hätten Sie Lust, mit mir joggen zu gehen?

Roswitha: Ich weiß nicht . . .

Dan: Sie könnten mir zeigen, wo man hier am besten joggen gehen kann.

Roswitha: Ja, das stimmt.

Dan: Wie wär's mit Samstag?

Roswitha: Das wäre gut. Am Samstag könnte sich mein Mann um die Kinder kümmern.

Dan: Gut.

Roswitha: Wenn es regnet, verschieben wir unseren Lauf.

Dan: *I don't know my way around here yet. What can you do here in your leisure time?*

Roswitha: *That depends on what you enjoy doing. Do you play sports?*

Dan: *Yes, I play golf.*

Roswitha: *If you want to play golf, you need to join a club.*

Dan: *Do you know if there's a golf club near here?*

Roswitha: *There is a golf club in Büttchen. Büttchen is the village that is near the airport. You could play golf with my husband. He is a member.*

Dan: *Do you play golf, too?*

Roswitha: *No, I don't play golf, because I don't have enough time. I'd rather jog. That keeps me in shape.*

Dan: *What a coincidence—I enjoy running too. Would you feel like going jogging with me?*

Roswitha: *I don't know . . .*

Dan: *You could show me where you can go jogging around here.*

Roswitha:	Yes, that's true.
Dan:	How about Saturday?
Roswitha:	That would be good. On Saturday my husband could take care of the kids.
Dan:	Good.
Roswitha:	If it's raining, we'll postpone our run.

NOTES

Golf is not at all as common in Germany as it is in the U.S. Usually, you have to be a member in good standing of a golf club to get some tee-time. Membership fees can be rather high. It is not unusual for a golf club to ask for membership fees of thousands of dollars per year.

NUTS & BOLTS 1

THE SUBJUNCTIVE OF MODAL VERBS

As you already know, modal verbs are used frequently in polite requests. To make these requests extra polite, use their subjunctive form. Compare the two following sentences.

Darf ich Sie etwas fragen?

Can I ask you something?

Dürfte ich Sie etwas fragen?

May I ask you something?

Kann ich Sie fotografieren?

Can I photograph you?

Könnte ich Sie fotografieren?

Could I photograph you?

Even though **wollen** has its own subjunctive form, which can be used in polite speech, **möchten** often takes its place.

Wollen Sie heute noch Tennis spielen?

Do you want to play tennis today?

Wollten Sie heute noch Tennis spielen?

Would you want to play tennis today?

Möchten Sie heute noch Tennis spielen?

Would you like to play tennis today?

The second sentence in the pairs above all use the subjunctive of the modal verb. Here are the subjunctive forms of the modal verbs.

	können *(to be able to)*	**müssen** *(to have to)*	**dürfen** *(to be allowed to)*
ich	könnte	müsste	dürfte
du	könntest	müsstest	dürftest
Sie	könnten	müssten	dürften
er/sie/es	könnte	müsste	dürfte
wir	könnten	müssten	dürften
ihr	könntet	müsstet	dürftet
Sie	könnten	müssten	dürften
sie	könnten	müssten	dürften

	wollen (to want to)	mögen (to like to)	sollen (to be supposed to)
ich	wollte	möchte	sollte
du	wolltest	möchtest	solltest
Sie	wollten	möchten	sollten
er/sie/es	wollte	möchte	sollte
wir	wollten	möchten	sollten
ihr	wolltet	möchtet	solltet
Sie	wollten	möchten	sollten
sie	wollten	möchten	sollten

PRACTICE 1
Please make these requests more polite.

1. Können Sie mir helfen?

2. Darf ich Sie etwas fragen?

3. Müssen wir nicht einen Schläger mitbringen?

4. Wir sollen langsamer laufen.

5. Können Sie mir zeigen, wie man strickt?

CONVERSATION 2
Roswitha and Dan never went jogging that Saturday. Let's find out what happened.

> **Dan:** Wo waren Sie denn gestern? Ich habe bei Ihnen geklingelt.

Roswitha: Das ist mir aber peinlich. Leider ist etwas dazwischen gekommen. Ich musste meinen Sohn zum Arzt bringen, weil er krank war. Tut mir leid.

Dan: Macht nichts. Darf ich fragen, wie es ihm jetzt geht?

Roswitha: Ach, viel besser. Es ist erstaunlich, wie schnell Kinder gesund werden. Er ist schon wieder im Garten und geht seinem Hobby nach.

Dan: Was macht er denn gern?

Roswitha: Gartenarbeit. Er pflanzt gerade Blumen.

Dan: Haben Sie auch ein Hobby?

Roswitha: Ja, ich backe gern. Deshalb muss ich ja joggen. *(They both laugh.)* Mmmh . . . Sie sollten meinen Marmorkuchen probieren. Wie wär's mit einer Tasse Kaffee und einem Stück Kuchen, der gar nicht dick macht?

Dan: Nicht's wäre mir lieber. Aber leider muss ich ins Büro.

Roswitha: An einem Sonntag?

Dan: Leider ja. Tut mir leid.

Roswitha: Kein Problem. Hätten Sie heute Nachmittag Zeit?

Dan: Ja, gern.

Roswitha: Prima, dann lernen Sie auch meinen Mann kennen. Er freut sich schon, mit Ihnen Golf zu spielen.

Dan: *Where were you yesterday? I rang your doorbell.*

Roswitha: *That's embarrassing. Unfortunately, something came up. I had to take my son to the doctor, because he was sick. I'm sorry.*

Dan: *No harm done. May I ask how he is doing now?*

Roswitha: *Oh, much better. It is amazing how quickly children recuperate. He is in the backyard already, pursuing his hobby.*

Dan: *What does he like to do?*

Roswitha:	Garden work. He is planting flowers just now.
Dan:	Do you have a hobby, too?
Roswitha:	Yes, I enjoy baking. That's why I have to go jogging. Mmmh . . . you should try my marble cake. How about a cup of coffee and a piece of cake, which is not fattening?
Dan:	There's nothing I'd rather do. But unfortunately, I have to go to the office.
Roswitha:	On a Sunday?
Dan:	Unfortunately, yes. I'm sorry.
Roswitha:	No problem. Would you have time this afternoon?
Dan:	Yes, I'd like that.
Roswitha:	Great, then you'll meet my husband. He is looking forward to a round of golf with you.

NOTES

Germans don't *ring a doorbell;* they just *ring.*

Ich habe bei Ihnen geklingelt.

I rang your doorbell.

You could also use **läuten.**

Ich habe zweimal geläutet.

I rang your doorbell twice.

NUTS & BOLTS 2

APOLOGIES

You are bound to find yourself in a situation where an apology will save the day. Here are the essentials of apologizing.

(Es) tut mir leid.

I'm sorry.

Entschuldigung.

Sorry./Forgive me.

Verzeihung.
Forgive me.

Leider kann ich heute nicht.
Unfortunately, I can't make it today.

Leider ist etwas dazwischen gekommen.
Unfortunately, something came up.

Das wollte ich nicht.
I didn't mean for that to happen.

Das war nicht meine Absicht.
This was not my intention.

Das ist mir aber peinlich.
That is embarrassing.

Wie kann ich das wieder gut machen?
How can I make this up to you?

Reacting graciously if somebody else apologizes will help you make friends.

(Das) macht nichts.
It doesn't matter.

Kein Problem.
No problem.

Schon gut.
It's okay.

Nichts passiert.
No harm done.

PRACTICE 2

Please translate the following sentences into German.

1. *I am sorry.*
2. *It's okay.*
3. *Unfortunately, something came up.*
4. *How can I make this up to you?*
5. *No harm done.*

Language link

If you are planning to go to Germany with your kids and want to make sure ahead of time that they can participate in the sports and hobbies they enjoy at home, visit the joint website of the **Auswärtige Amt** *(the German foreign relations office)* and the German embassy in Washington, D.C. Visit **www.germany.info/relaunch/culture/life/life.html** to read more about life in Germany, what sports your kids can expect to enjoy, or even what you can expect yourself.

ANSWERS

PRACTICE 1: 1. Könnten Sie mir helfen? **2.** Dürfte ich Sie etwas fragen? **3.** Müssten wir nicht einen Schläger mitbringen? **4.** Wir sollten langsamer laufen. **5.** Könnten Sie mir zeigen, wie man strickt?

PRACTICE 2: 1. (Es) tut mir leid./Entschuldigung. **2.** Schon gut. **3.** Leider ist etwas dazwischen gekommen. **4.** Wie kann ich das wieder gut machen? **5.** Nichts passiert.

Treiben Sie Sport?	*Do you play sports?*
Ich spiele Tennis.	*I play tennis.*
Ich habe früher Golf gespielt.	*I used to play golf.*
Gibt es hier einen Fitnessclub in der Nähe?	*Is there a fitness club nearby?*
Wo kann man hier in der Nähe joggen gehen?	*Where can you go for a jog around here?*
Gibt es hier ein Schwimmbad?	*Is there a pool around here?*
Hätten Sie Lust, Squash zu spielen?	*Do you feel like playing squash?*
Haben Sie ein Hobby?	*Do you have a hobby?*
Ich arbeite gern in meinem Garten.	*I enjoy working in my garden.*
Würden Sie mir helfen?	*Would you help me?*
Ich bin Hobbyfotograf.	*I am an amateur photographer.*
Das ist aber ein teures Hobby.	*That's an expensive hobby.*
Hätten Sie Lust auf eine Tasse Kaffee?	*Would you feel like a cup of coffee?*
Leider ist etwas dazwischen gekommen.	*Unfortunately, something came up.*
(Es) tut mir leid.	*I'm sorry.*

Entschuldigung.	Sorry./Forgive me.
Verzeihung.	Forgive me.
Leider kann ich heute nicht.	Unfortunately, I can't make it today.
Das war nicht meine Absicht.	This was not my intention.
Wie kann ich das wieder gut machen?	How can I make this up to you?
Das macht nichts.	It doesn't matter.
Kein Problem.	No problem.

Grafenau-Döffingen   €498 000,00
Gepfl. EFH m. ELW naturnaher Aussichtslage am Waldfried-
hof, Grdst. ca. 1 100 m², Bj. 1973, ges. Wohnfläche ca. 204 m²,
ELW ca. 53 m², Doppelgarage, momentan vermietet, frei ab
Sommer.

Grafenau-Döffingen   €498,000.-
Well-maintained single-family house in the country with separate studio,
beautiful views, lot about 11,840 square feet, house built in 1973, living
quarters about 2,195 square feet, studio about 570 square feet, two-car
garage, tenant-occupied until summer.

ABBREVIATIONS AND VOCABULARY

gepfl.	gepflegt	*well-maintained*
EFH	das Einfamilienhaus	*single-family house*
Grdst.	das Grundstück	*lot*
ca.	circa	*about*
Bj.	das Baujahr	*year built*
Ges.	gesamt	*complete, total*
ELW	die Einliegerwohnung	*separate studio*

Please answer the following questions.

1. What is this?

2. Does the ad speak of a house, an apartment, or an office building?

3. Is it for rent or for sale?

4. How much is it?

5. When was it built?

6. How large is the living space?

7. How many cars does the garage hold?

8. When can you move in?

ANSWERS

1. A real estate ad

2. A house

3. For sale

4. €498.000,-

5. In 1973

6. 204 m²

7. Two

8. In the summer

―――――――― GERMAN IN ACTION 2 ――――――――

Marmorkuchen
Zutaten

- **300 g Butter**
- **300 g Zucker**
- **8 Eier**
- **500 g Mehl**
- **1 Päckchen Backpulver**
- **5 Eßlöffel Kakaopulver**

Zubereitung

- **Backofen auf 180 Grad vorheizen**
- **Butter, Eier, Zucker schaumig rühren**
- **Mehl mit Backpulver vermischen und langsam unterrühren**

- 1/3 des Teiges in eine andere Schüssel geben, und den Kakao unterrühren
- Teig in Form füllen: erst den Boden mit hellem Teig bedecken, dann den dunklen Teig auflegen, und wieder mit hellem Teig abdecken. Eine Gabel nehmen und ein Muster machen
- Ab in den vorgeheizten Ofen

<u>Backzeit</u>

- 1 Stunde bei 180 Grad

<u>Vor dem Servieren</u>

- Wenn der Kuchen abgekühlt ist, mit Puderzucker besträuen

Marble cake
<u>*Ingredients*</u>

- *10 ounces butter*
- *10 ounces sugar*
- *8 eggs*
- *1 lb. flour*
- *1 small package of baking powder*
- *5 tablespoons of cocoa*

<u>*Preparation*</u>

- *preheat oven to 360 degrees Fahrenheit*
- *mix butter, eggs, and sugar until foamy*
- *mix flour with baking powder and slowly add to butter-egg-sugar mixture*

- *in a separate bowl, mix a third of the dough with the cocoa*
- *add the dough to the baking form in layers, mixing light and dark dough. Use a fork to create a pattern*
- *place in preheated oven*

Baking time

- *bake for 1 hour at 360 degrees Fahrenheit*

Before you serve

- *once the cake has cooled down, sprinkle with powdered sugar*

VOCABULARY

die Zutaten	*ingredients*
das Backpulver	*baking powder*
vorheizen	*to preheat*
schaumig	*foamy*
rühren	*to stir*
unterrühren	*mix, stir under*
der Teig	*dough*
der Puderzucker	*powdered sugar*

Please answer the following questions.

1. How many eggs do you need?
2. How much milk do you need?
3. Do you put the whole dough into the form all at once?

4. How long does it take for the cake to bake?

5. What do you need to do before you serve the cake?

ANSWERS

1. 8

2. none

3. no

4. 1 hour

5. sprinkle powdered sugar on it

———— GERMAN IN ACTION 3 ————

LEBENSLAUF
PERSÖNLICHE DATEN
Claudia Schimmel
11.11.1960 in Sandhausen/Thüringen geboren
verheiratet, zwei erwachsene Kinder
stellv. Leiterin einer Kindertagesstätte
ausgebildete Krankenschwester

BERUFSTÄTIGKEIT
seit 1.1.1994 Pädagogische Mitarbeiterin im Kindergarten
Köln-Mitte
seit 1.1.1998 in der Funktion einer stellv. Leiterin
1990–1994 Familienphase
Geburt und Erziehung der Kinder

Berufliche/außerberufliche Weiterbildung
1990 Fortbildungsseminare im Haus des Erziehers
1984–1989 Studium der Sozialpädagogik/Univ. Köln
1979–1983 Geriatrielehrgänge im Kölner Uniklinikum

Ausbildungsweg und Schule
1979–1984 Besuch der Abendschule Heinrich Heine
Abschluss Abitur (Durchschnittsnote 2,0)
1979–1983 Ausbildung zur Krankenschwester im Diakonissen-
krankenhaus Köln-Nord
1966–1979 Volks-, Mittelschule, Gymnasium

KENNTNISSE/FÄHIGKEITEN/INTERESSEN

Computerkenntnisse: Word Office, Internet
Fremdsprachen: Gute Englisch- und Französisch-Kenntnisse
Ehrenamt: Mitarbeit bei der Telefonseelsorge
Interessen: Klassische Musik, Klavier
Sonstiges: Führerschein Klasse 3
Mannheim, 12.1.2008

CURRICULUM VITAE
PERSONAL DATA
Claudia Schimmel
DOB: 11/11/60
POB: Sandhausen/Thüringen
Marital status: married, two adult children
Deputy director of a day care center
trained nurse

WORK EXPERIENCE

since 1/1/94 Kindergarten teacher in Köln
since 1/1/98 Deputy director
1990–1994 Leave of Absence to raise own children

PROFESSIONAL TRAINING

1990 Professional training at the House of Education
1984–1989 Graduate studies in social studies at the University of Cologne
1979–1983 Courses in Geriatrics at the University Hospital in Cologne

EDUCATION

1979–1984 Attended evening classes at the Heinrich Heine Evening School
High School Exam (Average grade 2)
1979–1983 Nursing School at the Deaconesses Hospital in Cologne-North
1966–1979 Attended elementary school through high school

ADDITIONAL ABILITIES AND INTERESTS

Computer: Word Office, Internet
Languages: English and French
Volunteer activities: Local Samaritans hotline service
Interests: Classical music, piano
Miscellaneous: Driver's license
Mannheim, 1/12/08

VOCABULARY

der Mitarbeiter/die Mitarbeiterin	*coworker*
stellv. Leiterin (stellvertretende Leiterin)	*deputy director*
Geriatrie	*geriatrics*
der Lehrgang	*course*
die Weiterbildung	*further education*
das Ehrenamt	*volunteer position*
der Führerschein	*driver's license*
die Telefonseelsorge	*Samaritans*

Please answer the questions below.

1. Where does Frau Schimmel live?

2. Does Frau Schimmel have children?

3. Does she work now?

4. Does she volunteer?

5. Which foreign languages does she speak?

ANSWERS

1. In Köln

2. Yes, she has two.

3. Yes, at a Kindergarten

4. Yes, she works for the Samaritans.

5. English and French

———— GERMAN IN ACTION 4 ————

This just in . . .

Nächtlicher Einkauf ist wenig gefragt
Esslingen (adi)—Nach dem Fall des Ladenschlussgesetzes nutzen in Esslingen bislang nur wenige die neue Einkaufsfreiheit, die nun möglich wäre. In den einzelnen Geschäften wird noch höchst unterschiedlich Feierabend gemacht, und diejenigen, die auch am späten Samstagabend noch geöffnet haben, können zu nächtlicher Stunde bislang noch keinen allzu großen Andrang der Kundschaft vermelden.

Frühwarnsystem für junge Familien
Kreis Esslingen (rok)—Ein soziales Frühwarnsystem soll im Kreis Esslingen dafür sorgen, dass kleine Kinder nicht mehr misshandelt und missbraucht werden. ProjuFa heißt das Projekt, das ein Netzwerk knüpft von der Entbindungsklinik über die Hebammen bis zur Kindertagesstätte und den Beratungsstellen. Außerdem sollen ehrenamtliche Paten besonders gefährdete Familien unterstützen.

Shopping at Night Not Popular
Esslingen (adi)—Now that the mandatory closing hours are no longer in effect, only few shoppers use the now possible flexible store-opening hours in Esslingen. The individual stores close at very different times, and those who are still open late on Saturday evenings do not report a rush of customers at such late hours.

Early Warning System for Young Families
Esslingen County (rok)–A social early warning system in Esslingen is meant to help prevent child abuse. ProjuFa is the name of the project, which creates a network from the maternity ward to midwives, to day care centers, to parent education centers. In addition, volunteer mentors are helping to support at-risk families.

VOCABULARY

nächtlich	*nightly, at night*
das Ladenschlussgesetz	*store-closing laws*
der Feierabend	*end of work, closing time*
der Andrang	*rush*
die Kundschaft	*customers*
das Frühwarnsystem	*early warning system*
misshandeln	*to abuse*
missbrauchen	*to abuse sexually*
das Netzwerk	*network*
die Entbindungsklinik	*maternity ward*
die Hebamme	*midwife*
ehrenamtlich	*volunteer*
der Pate	*mentor*
gefährdet	*endangered, at risk*

Please answer these questions.

1. What changed with regards to store closing hours?
2. Do all stores now close at the same time?
3. Do many customers shop late?
4. Who is ProjuFa supposed to protect?
5. Who is included in the network to portect small children?

ANSWERS

1. Stores can now stay open late.
2. No, the **Ladenschlussgesetze** are no longer in effect.
3. No
4. Small children
5. The maternity ward, midwives, day care centers, and social services, including volunteer mentors

Supplemental Vocabulary

1. WEATHER

das Wetter	*weather*
Es regnet.	*It's raining.*
Es schneit.	*It's snowing.*
Es hagelt.	*It's hailing.*
Es ist windig.	*It's windy.*
Es ist heiß.	*It's hot.*
Es ist kalt.	*It's cold.*
Es ist sonnig.	*It's sunny.*
Es ist bewölkt.	*It's cloudy.*
Das Wetter ist schön.	*It's/The weather is beautiful.*
der Sturm (die Stürme)	*storm*
der Wind (die Winde)	*wind*
die Sonne (die Sonnen)	*sun*
der Donner (die Donner)	*thunder*
der Blitz (die Blitze)	*lightning*
der Sturm (die Stürme)	*storm*
die Temperatur (die Temperaturen)	*temperature*
das Grad (die Grade)	*degree*
der Regen	*rain*
der Schnee	*snow*
die Wolke (die Wolken)	*cloud*
der Nebel (die Nebel)	*fog*
der Smog	*smog*
der Schirm (die Schirme)	*umbrella*

2. FOOD

das Essen (die Essen), die Speise (die Speisen)	*food*
das Abendessen (die Abendessen)	*dinner*
das Mittagessen (die Mittagessen)	*lunch*
das Frühstück (die Frühstücke)	*breakfast*
das Fleisch	*meat*
das Hühnchen (die Hühnchen)	*chicken*
das Rindfleisch	*beef*
das Schweinefleisch	*pork*
der Fisch (die Fische)	*fish*
die Garnele (die Garnelen)	*shrimp*
der Hummer (die Hummer)	*lobster*
das Brot (die Brote)	*bread*
das Ei (die Eier)	*egg*
der Käse (die Käse)	*cheese*
der Reis	*rice*
das Gemüse (die Gemüse)	*vegetable*
der grüne Salat (die grünen Salate)	*lettuce*
die Tomate (die Tomaten)	*tomato*
die Karotte (die Karotten), die Möhre (die Möhren)	*carrot*
die Salatgurke (die Salatgurken)	*cucumber*
die Paprikaschote (die Paprikaschoten)	*green pepper, red pepper*
die Frucht (die Früchte, das Obst)	*fruit*

der Apfel (die Äpfel)	*apple*
die Orange (die Orangen), die Apfelsine (die Apfelsinen)	*orange*
die Banane (die Bananen)	*banana*
die Birne (die Birnen)	*pear*
die Weintraube (die Weintrauben)	*grape*
der Drink (die Drinks)	*drink (alcoholic)*
das Wasser	*water*
die Milch	*milk*
der Saft (die Säfte)	*juice*
der Kaffee	*coffee*
der Tee	*tea*
der Wein (die Weine)	*wine*
das Bier (die Biere)	*beer*
das Getränk (die Getränke)	*soft drink*
der Sprudel (die Sprudel)	*soda water*
das Mineralwasser (die Mineralwasser)	*mineral water*
das Salz (die Salze)	*salt*
der Pfeffer (die Pfeffer)	*pepper*
der Zucker	*sugar*
der Honig	*honey*
heiß/kalt	*hot/cold*
süß/sauer	*sweet/sour*

3. PEOPLE

Leute	*people*
die Person (die Personen)	*person*
der Mann (die Männer)	*man*
die Frau (die Frauen)	*woman*
der/die Erwachsene (die Erwachsenen)	*adult*

das Kind (die Kinder)	*child*
der Junge (die Jungen)	*boy*
das Mädchen (die Mädchen)	*girl*
der Teenager (die Teenager), der/die Jugendliche (die Jugendlichen)	*teenager*
groß/klein	*tall/short*
alt/jung	*old/young*
dick/dünn	*fat/thin*
freundlich/unfreundlich	*friendly/unfriendly*
glücklich/traurig	*happy/sad*
schön/hässlich	*beautiful/ugly*
krank/gesund	*sick/healthy*
stark/schwach	*strong/weak*
berühmt	*famous*
intelligent	*intelligent*
talentiert	*talented*

4. AT HOME

zu Hause	*at home*
das Haus (die Häuser)	*house*
die Wohnung (die Wohnungen)	*apartment*
das Zimmer (die Zimmer)	*room*
das Wohnzimmer (die Wohnzimmer)	*living room*
das Esszimmer (die Esszimmer)	*dining room*
die Küche (die Küchen)	*kitchen*
das Schlafzimmer (die Schlafzimmer)	*bedroom*
das Badezimmer (die Badezimmer)	*bathroom*

die Diele (die Dielen), die Eingangshalle (die Eingangshallen)	*hall*
der Schrank (die Schränke)	*closet*
das Fenster (die Fenster)	*window*
die Tür (die Türen)	*door*
der Tisch (die Tische)	*table*
der Stuhl (die Stühle)	*chair*
das Sofa (die Sofas)	*sofa, couch*
der Vorhang (die Vorhänge)	*curtain*
der Teppich (die Teppiche)	*carpet*
der Fernseher (die Fernseher)	*television*
der CD-Spieler (die CD-Spieler)	*CD player*
die Lampe (die Lampen)	*lamp*
der DVD-Spieler (die DVD-Spieler)	*DVD player*
die Lautsprecheranlage (die Lautsprecheranlagen)	*sound system*
das Gemälde (die Gemälde)	*painting*
das Bild (die Bilder)	*picture*
das Regal (die Regale)	*shelf*
die Treppe (die Treppen)	*staircase*
die Stufe (die Stufen)	*stair, step*
die Decke (die Decken)	*ceiling*
die Wand (die Wände)	*wall*
der Boden (die Böden)	*floor*
groß/klein	*big/small*
neu/alt	*new/old*
das Holz	*wood*
hölzern	*wooden*
das Plastik	*plastic*
aus Plastik	*made from plastic*

5. THE HUMAN BODY

der menschliche Körper	*the human body*
der Kopf (die Köpfe)	*head*
das Gesicht (die Gesichter)	*face*
die Stirn (die Stirnen)	*forehead*
das Auge (die Augen)	*eye*
die Augenbraue (die Augenbrauen)	*eyebrow*
die Wimper (die Wimpern)	*eyelash*
das Ohr (die Ohren)	*ear*
die Nase (die Nasen)	*nose*
der Mund (die Münder, die Munde)	*mouth*
der Zahn (die Zähne)	*tooth*
die Zunge (die Zungen)	*tongue*
die Wange (die Wangen)	*cheek*
das Kinn (die Kinne)	*chin*
das Haar (die Haare)	*hair*
der Nacken (die Nacken)	*nape of the neck*
der Hals (die Hälse)	*throat, neck*
der Brustkorb (die Brustkörbe)	*chest*
die Brust (die Brüste)	*breast*
die Schulter (die Schultern)	*shoulders*
der Arm (die Arme)	*arm*
der Ellbogen (die Ellbogen)	*elbow*
das Handgelenk (die Handgelenke)	*wrist*
die Hand (die Hände)	*hand*
der Magen (die Mägen)	*stomach, abdomen*
der Penis (die Penisse)	*penis*
die Vagina (die Vaginas)	*vagina*

der Hintern (die Hintern)	*buttocks*
das Bein (die Beine)	*leg*
das Knie (die Knie)	*knee*
der Knöchel (die Knöchel)	*ankle*
der Fuß (die Füße)	*foot*
der Finger (die Finger)	*finger*
die Zehe (die Zehen)	*toe*
die Haut (die Häute)	*skin*
das Blut	*blood*
das Gehirn (die Gehirne)	*brain*
das Herz (die Herzen)	*heart*
die Lunge (die Lungen)	*lungs*
der Knochen (die Knochen)	*bone*
der Muskel (die Muskeln)	*muscle*
die Sehne (die Sehnen)	*tendon*

6. TRAVEL AND TOURISM

Reise und Tourismus	*travel and tourism*
der Tourist (die Touristen)	*tourist*
das Hotel (die Hotels)	*hotel*
die Jugendherberge (die Jugendherbergen)	*youth hostel*
die Hotelrezeption (die Hotelrezeptionen)	*reception desk*
sich anmelden	*to check in*
sich abmelden	*to check out*
die Reservierung (die Reservierungen)	*reservation*
der Pass (die Pässe)	*passport*
der Reisebus (die Reisebusse)	*tour bus*
die Führung (die Führungen)	*guided tour*

der Fotoapparat (die Fotoapparate), die Kamera (die Kameras)	*camera*
die Touristeninformation	*information center*
der Stadtplan (die Stadtpläne)	*map*
die Broschüre (die Broschüren)	*brochure*
das Monument (die Monumente)	*monument*
Sehenswürdigkeiten besichtigen	*to go sightseeing*
ein Foto machen	*to take a picture*
Könnten Sie ein Foto von uns machen?	*Can you take our picture?*

7. IN THE OFFICE

im Büro	*in the office*
das Büro (die Büros)	*office*
der Schreibtisch (die Schreibtische)	*desk*
der Computer (die Computer)	*computer*
das Telefon (die Telefone)	*telephone*
die Faxmaschine (die Faxmaschinen)	*fax machine*
das Fax	*fax*
das Bücherregal (die Bücherregale)	*book shelf*
der Aktenschrank (die Aktenschränke)	*file cabinet*
die Akte (die Akten)	*file*
der Chef (die Chefs)	*boss*
der Kollege (die Kollegen)	*colleague*

der/die Angestellte (die Angestellten)	employee
die Belegschaft	staff
die Firma (die Firmen)	company
das Geschäft (die Geschäfte)	business
die Fabrik (die Fabriken), das Werk (die Werke)	factory
das Konferenzzimmer (die Konferenzzimmer)	meeting room, conference room
das Meeting (die Meetings), die Sitzung (die Sitzungen)	meeting
der Termin (die Termine)	appointment
das Gehalt (die Gehälter)	salary
der Arbeitsplatz (die Arbeitsplätze)	job
beschäftigt	busy
arbeiten	to work
verdienen	to earn

8. AT SCHOOL

in der Schule	at school
die Schule (die Schulen)	school
die Universität (die Universitäten)	university
das Klassenzimmer (die Klassenzimmer)	classroom
der Kurs (die Kurse)	course
der Lehrer (die Lehrer)	teacher (male)
die Lehrerin (die Lehrerinnen)	teacher (female)
der Professor (die Professoren)	professor (male)
die Professorin (die Professorinnen)	professor (female)

der Schüler (die Schüler)	*(school) student (male)*
die Schülerin (die Schülerinnen)	*(school) student (female)*
der Student (die Studenten)	*(college) student (male)*
die Studentin (die Studentinnen)	*(college) student (female)*
das Fach (die Fächer)	*subject*
das Notizbuch (die Notizbücher)	*notebook*
das Fachbuch (die Fachbücher)	*textbook*
die Mathematik	*math*
die Geschichte	*history*
die Chemie	*chemistry*
die Biologie	*biology*
die Literatur	*literature*
die Sprache (die Sprachen), die Sprachwissenschaft (-en)	*language* *linguistics*
die Kunst	*art*
die Musik	*music*
der Sport	*gym*
die Ferien	*break, recess (from school)*
die Semesterferien	*break, recess (from college)*
die Klassenarbeit (die Klassenarbeiten)	*test*
die Klausur (die Klausuren)	*test, exam (in college)*
die Zensur (die Zensuren)	*grade*
das Zeugnis (die Zeugnisse)	*report card*
das Diplom (die Diplome)	*diploma*
der Abschluss (die Abschlüsse)	*degree*
schwierig/leicht	*difficult/easy*
studieren	*to study*

lernen	*to learn*
bestehen	*to pass*
nicht bestehen	*to fail*

9. SPORTS AND RECREATION

Sport und Erholung	*sports and recreation*
(der) Fußball	*soccer*
(der) Basketball	*basketball*
(der) Baseball	*baseball*
(der) Football	*American football*
(das) Hockey	*hockey*
(das) Tennis	*tennis*
(das) Skifahren, das Skilaufen	*skiing*
(das) Landlaufen	*cross-country skiing*
(das) Bergsteigen	*mountain climbing*
das Spiel (die Spiele)	*game*
die Mannschaft (die Mannschaften)	*team*
das Stadion (die Stadien)	*stadium*
der Trainer (die Trainer)	*coach*
der Spieler (die Spieler)	*player*
der Champion (die Champions)	*champion*
der Ball (die Bälle)	*ball*
Wandern	*(to go) hiking*
Zelten (gehen)	*(to go) camping*
Sport treiben	*to play (a sport)*
ein Spiel austragen	*to play (a game)*
gewinnen	*to win*
verlieren	*to lose*
unentschieden spielen	*to draw, to tie*
die Karten	*cards*
(das) Billiard	*pool, billiards*

10. NATURE

die Natur	*nature*
der Baum (die Bäume)	*tree*
die Blume (die Blumen)	*flower*
der Wald (die Wälder)	*forest*
der Berg (die Berge)	*mountain*
das Feld (die Felder)	*field*
der Fluss (die Flüsse)	*river*
der See (die Seen)	*lake*
der Ozean (die Ozeane)	*ocean*
das Meer (die Meere)	*sea*
der Strand (die Strände)	*beach*
die Wüste (die Wüsten)	*desert*
der Fels(en) (die Felsen)	*rock*
der Sand	*sand*
der Himmel	*sky*
die Sonne (die Sonnen)	*sun*
der Mond (die Monde)	*moon*
der Stern (die Sterne)	*star*
das Wasser	*water*
das Land (die Länder)	*land*
die Pflanze (die Pflanzen)	*plant*
der Hügel (die Hügel)	*hill*
der Teich (die Teiche)	*pond*

11. COMPUTERS AND THE INTERNET

Computer und Internet	*computer and internet*
der Computer (die Computer)	*computer*
die Tastatur (die Tastaturen)	*keyboard*
der Monitor (die Monitore)	*monitor*
der Bildschirm (die Bildschirme)	*screen*

der Drucker (die Drucker)	*printer*
die Maus (die Mäuse)	*mouse*
das Modem (die Modems)	*modem*
der Speicher (die Speicher)	*memory*
die CD-ROM (die CD-ROMs)	*CD-ROM*
das CD-ROM Laufwerk (die CD-ROM Laufwerke)	*CD-ROM drive*
die Datei (die Dateien)	*file*
das Dokument (die Dokumente)	*document*
das Internet	*internet*
die Website (die Websites)	*website*
die Webseite (die Webseiten)	*webpage*
die E-Mail (die E-Mails)	*e-mail*
der Chatroom (die Chatrooms)	*chatroom*
das Einloggen	*log-in*
einloggen	*to log in*
sich abmelden	*to log off*
die Sofortnachricht (die Sofortnachrichten)	*instant message*
die angehängte Datei (die angehängten Dateien), die Anlage (die Anlagen)	*attachment*
eine Mail schicken	*to send an e-mail*
eine Datei schicken (beifügen)	*to send a file*
weiterleiten	*to forward*
antworten	*to reply*
löschen	*to delete*
ein Dokument abspeichern	*to save a document*
eine Datei öffnen	*to open a file*

eine Datei schließen	*to close a file*
eine Datei anhängen	*to attach a file*

12. FAMILY AND RELATIONSHIPS

Familie und Beziehungen	*family and relationships*
die Mutter (die Mütter)	*mother*
der Vater (die Väter)	*father*
der Sohn (die Söhne)	*son*
die Tochter (die Töchter)	*daughter*
die Schwester (die Schwestern)	*sister*
das Baby (die Babys)	*baby*
der Bruder (die Brüder)	*brother*
der Ehemann (die Ehemänner)	*husband*
die Ehefrau (die Ehefrauen)	*wife*
die Tante (die Tanten)	*aunt*
der Onkel (die Onkel)	*uncle*
die Großmutter (die Großmütter), die Oma (die Omas)	*grandmother*
der Großvater (die Großväter), der Opa (die Opas)	*grandfather*
der Vetter (die Vettern)	*cousin (male)*
die Kusine (die Kusinen)	*cousin (female)*
die Schwiegermutter (die Schwiegermütter)	*mother-in-law*
der Schwiegervater (die Schwiegerväter)	*father-in-law*
die Stiefmutter (die Stiefmütter)	*stepmother*
der Stiefvater (die Stiefväter)	*stepfather*

der Stiefsohn (die Stiefsöhne)	*stepson*
die Stieftochter (die Stieftöchter)	*stepdaughter*
der Freund (die Freunde)	*boyfriend*
die Freundin (die Freundinnen)	*girlfriend*
der/die Verlobte (die Verlobten)	*fiancé(e)*
der Freund (die Freunde)	*friend*
der/die Verwandte (die Verwandten)	*relative*
lieben	*to love*
kennen	*to know (a person)*
(sich) treffen	*to meet (a person)*
heiraten	*to marry (someone)*
sich scheiden lassen (von)	*to divorce (someone)*
sich scheiden lassen, die Scheidung einreichen	*to get a divorce, to file for divorce*
erben	*to inherit*

13. ON THE JOB

der Beruf (die Berufe)	*job*
der Polizist (die Polizisten)	*policeman*
die Polizistin (die Polizistinnen)	*policewoman*
der Rechtsanwalt (die Rechtsanwälte)	*lawyer (male)*
die Rechtsanwältin (die Rechtsanwältinnen)	*lawyer (female)*
der Arzt (die Ärzte)	*doctor (male)*
die Ärztin (die Ärztinnen)	*doctor (female)*
der Ingenieur (die Ingenieure)	*engineer (male)*

die Ingenieurin (die Ingenieurinnen)	*engineer (female)*
der Geschäftsmann (die Geschäftsmänner)	*businessman*
die Geschäftsfrau (die Geschäftsfrauen)	*businesswoman*
der Verkäufer (die Verkäufer)	*salesman*
die Verkäuferin (die Verkäuferinnen)	*saleswoman*
der Lehrer (die Lehrer)	*teacher (male)*
die Lehrerin (die Lehrerinnen)	*teacher (female)*
der Professor (die Professoren)	*professor (male)*
die Professorin (die Professorinnen)	*professor (female)*
der Bankier (die Bankiers)	*banker*
der Architekt (die Architekten)	*architect (male)*
die Architektin (die Architektinnen)	*architect (female)*
der Tierarzt (die Tierärzte)	*veterinarian (male)*
die Tierärztin (die Tierärztinnen)	*veterinarian (female)*
der Zahnarzt (die Zahnärzte)	*dentist (male)*
die Zahnärztin (die Zahnärztinnen)	*dentist (female)*
der Tischler (die Tischler)	*carpenter*
der Bauarbeiter (die Bauarbeiter)	*construction worker*
der Taxifahrer (die Taxifahrer)	*taxi driver (male)*
die Taxifahrerin (die Taxifahrerinnen)	*taxi driver (female)*
der Künstler (die Künstler)	*artist (male)*

die Künstlerin (die Künstlerinnen)	*artist (female)*
der Schriftsteller (die Schriftsteller)	*writer (male)*
die Schriftstellerin (die Schriftstellerinnen)	*writer (female)*
der Klempner (die Klempner)	*plumber*
der Elektriker (die Elektriker)	*electrician*
der Journalist (die Journalisten)	*journalist (male)*
die Journalistin (die Journalistinnen)	*journalist (female)*
der Schauspieler (die Schauspieler)	*actor*
die Schauspielerin (die Schauspielerinnen)	*actress*
der Musiker (die Musiker)	*musician (male)*
die Musikerin (die Musikerinnen)	*musician (female)*
der Landwirt (die Landwirte), der Bauer (die Bauern)	*farmer (male)*
die Bäuerin (die Bäuerinnen)	*farmer (female)*
der Sekretär (die Sekretäre)	*secretary (male)*
die Sekretärin (die Sekretärinnen)	*secretary (female)*
der Assistent (die Assistenten)	*assistant (male)*
die Assistentin (die Assistentinnen)	*assistant (female)*
arbeitslos	*unemployed*
in Rente, pensioniert	*retired*
Vollzeit-	*full-time*

Teilzeit-	*part-time*
das Angestelltenverhältnis (die Angestelltenverhältnisse)	*steady job*
der Sommerjob (die Sommerjobs)	*summer job*

14. CLOTHING

Kleidung	*clothing*
das Hemd (die Hemden)	*shirt*
die Hose (die Hosen)	*pants*
die Jeans (die Jeans)	*jeans*
das T-Shirt (die T-Shirts)	*T-shirt*
der Schuh (die Schuhe)	*shoe*
die Socke (die Socken)	*sock*
der Gürtel (die Gürtel)	*belt*
der Turnschuh (die Turnschuhe)	*sneaker*
der Tennisschuh (die Tennisschuhe)	*tennis shoe*
das Kleid (die Kleider)	*dress*
der Rock (die Röcke)	*skirt*
die Bluse (die Blusen)	*blouse*
der Anzug (die Anzüge)	*suit*
der Hut (die Hüte)	*hat*
der Handschuh (die Handschuhe)	*glove*
der Schal (die Schals)	*scarf*
die Jacke (die Jacken)	*jacket (casual)*
das Jackett (die Jacketts)	*jacket (formal)*
der Mantel (die Mäntel)	*coat*
der Ohrring (die Ohrringe)	*earring*
das Armband (die Armbänder)	*bracelet*

die Halskette (die Halsketten)	*necklace*
die Brille (die Brillen)	*eyeglasses*
die Sonnenbrille (die Sonnenbrillen)	*sunglasses*
die Armbanduhr (die Armbanduhren)	*wrist watch*
der Ring (die Ringe)	*ring*
die Unterhose (die Unterhosen)	*underpants*
das Unterhemd (die Unterhemden)	*undershirt*
der Unterrock (die Unterröcke)	*slip*
die Badehose (die Badehosen)	*bathing trunks*
der Badeanzug (die Badeanzüge)	*bathing suit*
der Schlafanzug (die Schlafanzüge)	*pyjamas*
die Baumwolle	*cotton*
das Leder	*leather*
die Seide	*silk*
die Größe (die Größen)	*size*
tragen	*to wear*

15. IN THE KITCHEN

in der Küche	*in the kitchen*
der Kühlschrank (die Kühlschränke)	*refrigerator*
die Spüle (die Spülen)	*(kitchen) sink*
die Arbeitsfläche (die Arbeitsflächen)	*counter*

der Herd (die Herde)	*stove*
der Backofen (die Backöfen)	*oven*
der Mikrowellenherd (die Mikrowellenherde)	*microwave*
der Geschirrschrank (die Geschirrschränke)	*cupboard*
die Schublade (die Schubladen)	*drawer*
der Teller (die Teller)	*plate*
die Tasse (die Tassen)	*cup*
die Schüssel (die Schüsseln)	*bowl*
das Glas (die Gläser)	*glass*
der Löffel (die Löffel)	*spoon*
das Messer (die Messer)	*knife*
die Dose (die Dosen)	*can*
die Schachtel (die Schachteln)	*box*
die Flasche (die Flaschen)	*bottle*
der Karton (die Kartons)	*carton*
die Kaffeemaschine (die Kaffeemaschinen)	*coffee maker*
der Teekessel (die Teekessel)	*tea kettle*
der Mixer (die Mixer)	*blender*
das Bügeleisen (die Bügeleisen)	*iron*
das Bügelbrett (die Bügelbretter)	*ironing board*
der Besen (die Besen)	*broom*
die Spülmaschine (die Spülmaschinen)	*dishwasher*
die Waschmaschine (die Waschmaschinen)	*washing machine*
der Trockner (die Trockner)	*dryer*
kochen	*to cook*

abwaschen/spülen	*to do the dishes*
waschen	*to do the laundry*
das Geschirrspülmittel (die Geschirrspülmittel)	*dishwashing detergent*
das Waschpulver (die Waschpulver)	*laundry detergent*
das Bleichmittel (die Bleichmittel)	*bleach*
sauber/schmutzig	*clean/dirty*

16. IN THE BATHROOM

im Badezimmer	*in the bathroom*
die Toilette (die Toiletten)	*toilet*
das Waschbecken (die Waschbecken)	*sink (wash basin)*
die Badewanne (die Badewannen)	*bath tub*
die Dusche (die Duschen)	*shower*
der Spiegel (die Spiegel)	*mirror*
der Badezimmerschrank (die Badezimmerschränke)	*medicine cabinet*
das Handtuch (die Handtücher)	*towel*
das Toilettenpapier	*toilet paper*
das Shampoo	*shampoo*
die Seife (die Seifen)	*soap*
das Bademittel (die Bademittel)	*bath gel*
die Rasiercreme	*shaving cream*
der Rasierapparat (die Rasierapparate)	*razor*
sich waschen	*to wash onself*
duschen/baden	*to take a shower/bath*
sich rasieren	*to shave*

das Parfüm (die Parfüms), das Kölnischwasser (die Kölnischwasser)	*cologne*
das Parfüm (die Parfüms)	*perfume*
das Deodorant (die Deodorants)	*deodorant*
der Verband (die Verbände)	*bandage*
der Puder (die Puder)	*powder*

17. AROUND TOWN

in der Stadt	*around town*
der Ort (die Orte)	*town*
die Stadt (die Städte)	*city*
das Dorf (die Dörfer)	*village*
das Auto (die Autos)	*car*
der Bus (die Busse)	*bus*
der Zug (die Züge)	*train*
das Taxi (die Taxis/Taxen)	*taxi*
die U-Bahn (die U-Bahnen)	*subway, metro*
der Verkehr	*traffic*
das Gebäude (die Gebäude)	*building*
das Wohngebäude (die Wohngebäude)	*apartment building*
die Bibliothek (die Bibliotheken)	*library*
das Restaurant (die Restaurants)	*restaurant*
das Geschäft (die Geschäfte)	*store*
der Laden (die Läden)	*shop, small store*
die Straße (die Straßen)	*street*
der Park (die Parks)	*park*
der Bahnhof (die Bahnhöfe)	*train station*
der Flughafen (die Flughäfen)	*airport*

das Flugzeug (die Flugzeuge)	*airplane*
die Kreuzung (die Kreuzungen)	*intersection*
der Laternenpfahl (die Laternenpfähle)	*lamp post*
die Straßenlaterne (die Straßenlaternen)	*street light*
die Bank (die Banken)	*bank*
die Kirche (die Kirchen)	*church*
der Tempel (die Tempel)	*temple*
die Moschee (die Moscheen)	*mosque*
der Gehsteig (die Gehsteige)	*sidewalk*
die Bäckerei (die Bäckereien)	*bakery*
der Metzgerladen (die Metzgerläden)	*butcher shop*
das Café (die Cafés)	*café, coffee shop*
die Apotheke (die Apotheken)	*drugstore, pharmacy*
der Supermarkt (die Supermärkte)	*supermarket*
der Markt (die Märkte)	*market*
das Schuhgeschäft (die Schuhgeschäfte)	*shoe store*
das Bekleidungsgeschäft (die Bekleidungsgeschäfte)	*clothing store*
das Elektrogeschäft (die Elektrogeschäfte)	*electronics store*
die Buchhandlung (die Buchhandlungen)	*bookstore*
das Kaufhaus (die Kaufhäuser)	*department store*
der Bürgermeister (die Bürgermeister)	*mayor*

das Rathaus (die Rathäuser)	*city hall, municipal building*
kaufen	*to buy*
Einkaufen gehen	*to go shopping*
nah/weit	*near/far*
städtisch, urban	*urban*
vorstädtisch	*suburban*
ländlich	*rural*

18. ENTERTAINMENT

Unterhaltung	*entertainment*
der Film (die Filme)	*movie, film*
ins Kino gehen	*to go to the movies*
einen Film sehen	*to see a movie*
das Theater (die Theater)	*theater*
ein Theaterstück sehen	*to see a play*
die Oper (die Opern)	*opera*
das Konzert (die Konzerte)	*concert*
der Club (die Clubs), der Klub (die Klubs)	*club*
der Zirkus (die Zirkusse)	*circus*
die Eintrittskarte (die Eintrittskarten)	*ticket (for an event)*
das Museum (die Museen)	*museum*
die Galerie (die Galerien)	*gallery*
das Gemälde (die Gemälde)	*painting*
die Skulptur (die Skulpturen)	*sculpture*
das Fernsehprogramm (die Fernsehprogramme)	*television program*
fernsehen	*to watch television*
die Kommödie (die Kommödien)	*comedy*

die Dokumentation (die Dokumentationen)	*documentary*
das Drama (die Dramen)	*drama*
das Buch (die Bücher)	*book*
die Zeitschrift (die Zeitschriften)	*magazine*
ein Buch lesen	*to read a book*
eine Zeitschrift lesen	*to read a magazine*
Musik hören	*to listen to music*
der Song (die Songs), das Lied (die Lieder)	*song*
die Band (die Bands), die Musikgruppe (die Musikgruppen)	*band*
die Nachrichten	*the news*
die Talk-Show (die Talk-Shows)	*talk show*
die Sender wechseln	*to flip channels*
Vergnügen haben, Spaß haben	*to have fun*
gelangweilt sein	*to be bored*
lustig, witzig	*funny*
interessant	*interesting*
aufregend, spannend, fesselnd	*exciting*
gruselig, schaurig	*scary*
die Party (die Partys)	*party*
das Restaurant (die Restaurants)	*restaurant*
auf eine Party gehen	*to go to a party*
eine Party haben	*to have a party*
tanzen	*to dance*

Summary of
German Grammar

1. THE ALPHABET

LETTER	NAME	LETTER	NAME	LETTER	NAME
a	*ah*	j	*yot*	s	*ess*
b	*beh*	k	*kah*	t	*teh*
c	*tseh*	l	*ell*	u	*oo*
d	*deh*	m	*em*	v	*fauh*
e	*eh*	n	*en*	w	*veh*
f	*eff*	o	*oh*	x	*iks*
g	*geh*	p	*peh*	y	*üpsilon*
h	*hah*	q	*ku*	z	*tsett*
i	*ee*	r	*err*		

2. THE GERMAN DECLENSION
2.1. NOMINATIVE (SUBJECT, NOUN)
Das Buch ist hier.

The book is here.

2.2. GENITIVE (POSSESSIVE CASE)
der Name des Lehrers

The name of the teacher

2.3. DATIVE (INDIRECT OBJECT)
Er gibt dem Kind einen Apfel.

He gives an apple to the child.

2.4. ACCUSATIVE (DIRECT OBJECT)
Sie hält den Stift.

She is holding the pen.

3. PLURALS OF NOUNS

3.1. MASCULINE

a. nominative plus -e

der Abend	die Abende
der Freund	die Freunde

b. nominative plus -er

der Geist	die Geister
der Leib	die Leiber

c. nominative plus -e and ¨ (umlaut) on the last vowel

der Hut	die Hüte
der Fall	die Fälle

d. nominative plus -er and ¨ (umlaut) on the last vowel

der Mann	die Männer
der Rand	die Ränder

e. no change (masculine nouns ending in el, en, er)

der Schlüssel	die Schlüssel
der Kuchen	die Kuchen
der Maler	die Maler

3.2. FEMININE

a. nominative plus -n or -en

die Tür	die Türen
die Frage	die Fragen

b. nominative plus -e; nominative plus -e and umlaut on the last vowel

die Kenntnis	die Kenntnisse
die Frucht	die Früchte

(Note: An -s ending will double in the plural.)

c. in becomes innen

die Schülerin	die Schülerinnen
die Freundin	die Freundinnen

3.3. Neuter
Most neuter nouns form their plural like the masculine, the majority of them in **e** or **er.**

das Heft	die Hefte
das Licht	die Lichter

4. GENDER
German nouns can be masculine, feminine, or neuter. There is no rule to determine the gender of a specific noun; however, here are a few hints.

4.1. Masculine
a. designations of trade or profession: **der Maler, der Arzt, der Künstler**

b. titles of nobility: **der Fürst, der Graf, der König**

c. nouns ending in **ling: der Sperling, der Jüngling**

d. days of the week and months: **der Montag, der April**

4.2. Feminine
a. feminine designations of trade: **die Malerin, die Ärztin**

b. feminine titles of nobility: **die Königin, die Fürstin**

c. names of numbers: **die Drei, die Null**

d. many names of trees: **die Tanne, die Eiche**

e. nouns ending in **ei, heit, keit, schaft, sucht,** or **ung: die Freiheit, die Gesellschaft, die Ahnung**

4.3. Neuter
a. diminutives ending in **chen** or **lein: das Mädchen, das Büchlein**

b. many nouns ending in **tum: das Altertum**

c. most names of metals: **das Gold, das Eisen**

d. most cities: **das schöne Berlin**

e. most countries: **das schöne Amerika**

f. colors: **das Rot**

g. most collective nouns beginning with **ge: das Gebirge** *(mountains)*

4.4. STRESS

German words generally have one strongly accented syllable or even two if the word is very long.

a. Short words: The stress is generally on the first syllable.

<u>Va</u>ter   **<u>Mu</u>tter**   **<u>Bru</u>der**

b. Long words: The stress is generally on the root of the word.

Emp<u>feh</u>lung   **Ge<u>bir</u>ge**   **Ge<u>bäu</u>de**

c. Separable prefixes are always stress.

<u>ab</u>machen   **<u>zu</u>geben**   **<u>mit</u>gehen**

d. Inseparable prefixes **(be, emp, ent, er, ge, ver, zer)** are never accented. The stress always falls on the following syllable.

er<u>hal</u>ten   **ver<u>ges</u>sen**   **zer<u>bre</u>chen**

5. THE DEFINITE ARTICLE

5.1. IN FRONT OF A FIRST NAME *(informal)*
Der Hans und die Margarete

Hans and Margaret

5.2. IN FRONT OF A TITLE
Ist der Herr Doktor da?

Is the (Mr.) doctor at home/in?

Nein, aber die Frau Doktor ist zu Hause.

No, but the (Ms.) doctor is at home.

5.3. DECLENSION OF DEFINITE ARTICLES

	Nom.	Gen.	Dat.	Acc.
m.	der	des	dem	den
f.	die	der	der	die
n.	das	des	dem	das
pl.	die	der	den	die

6. THE INDEFINITE ARTICLE

	Nom.	Gen.	Dat.	Acc.
m.	ein	eines	einem	einen
f.	eine	einer	einer	eine
n.	ein	eines	einem	ein

Notice that in a negation, **ein** becomes **kein**.

Er war kein Arzt, sondern ein Zahnarzt.
He was not a physician but a dentist.

	Nom.	Gen.	Dat.	Acc.
m.	kein	keines	keinem	keinen
f.	keine	keiner	keiner	keine
n.	kein	keines	keinem	kein
pl.	keine	keiner	keinen	keine

7. ADJECTIVES

Adjectives are declined in three ways: strong declension, weak declension, and mixed declension.

7.1. WITHOUT ARTICLE OR PRONOUN (STRONG DECLENSION)

	Nom.	Gen.	Dat.	Acc.
m.	roter Wein	roten Weines	rotem Wein	roten Wein
f.	rote Tinte	roter Tinte	roter Tinte	rote Tinte
n.	rotes Licht	roten Lichtes	rotem Licht	rotes Licht
pl.	rote Weine	roter Weine	roten Weinen	rote Weine

7.2. WITH THE DEFINITE ARTICLE (WEAK DECLENSION)

	Nom.	Gen.	Dat.	Acc.
m.	der rote Wein	des roten Weines	dem roten Wein	den roten Wein
f.	die rote Tinte	der roten Tinte	der roten Tinte	die rote Tinte
n.	das rote Licht	des roten Lichtes	dem roten Licht	das rote Licht
pl.	die roten Weine	der roten Weine	den roten Weinen	die roten Weine

7.3. WITH THE INDEFINITE ARTICLE, POSSESSIVE ADJECTIVE, OR *KEIN* WORDS (MIXED DECLENSION)

	Nom.	Gen.	Dat.	Acc.
m.	ein rot<u>er</u> Wein	eines roten Weines	einem roten Wein	einen roten Wein
f.	seine rot<u>e</u> Tinte	seiner roten Tinte	seiner roten Tinte	seine rot<u>e</u> Tinte
n.	kein rot<u>es</u> Licht	keines roten Lichtes	keinem roten Licht	kein rot<u>es</u> Licht
pl.	meine roten Weine	meiner roten Weine	meinen roten Wein<u>en</u>	meine roten Weine

8. COMPARATIVE AND SUPERLATIVE

8.1. The comparative and the superlative are formed as in English by adding **-er** to the adjective for the comparative and **-st** (or **-est**) for the superlative.

Some short adjectives also take an umlaut on their vowels.

schlecht, schlechter, schlechtest

bad, worse, worst

alt, älter, ältest

old, older, oldest

8.2. There are a few adjectives that have irregular comparatives. The following chart lists the most common ones.

POSITIVE	COMPARATIVE	SUPERLATIVE
gut	besser	der (die, das) beste, am besten
groß	größer	der (die, das) größte, am größten

POSITIVE	COMPARATIVE	SUPERLATIVE
hoch	höher	der (die, das) höchste, am höchsten
nahe	näher	der (die, das) nächste, am nächsten
viel	mehr	der (die, das) meiste, am meisten
gern	lieber	der (die, das) liebste, am liebsten

9. THE PARTITIVE

9.1. The partitive is generally not translated.

Geben Sie mir Brot!

Give me some bread.

Geben Sie mir ein Glas Wein.

Give me a glass of wine.

9.2. Etwas can also be used to mean a part of something.

Ich gebe ihm etwas zu trinken.

I am giving him something to drink.

Ich gebe ihm etwas davon.

I give him some of it.

9.3. The negative **kein** is declined like the indefinite article.

Ich habe ein Messer, aber keine Gabel.

I have a knife but no fork.

10. POSSESSIVE ADJECTIVES

10.1. Possessive adjectives agree in gender and number with the thing possessed.

M./N. Sg. Nom.	F. Sg. Nom.	Pl. Nom.	
mein	meine	meine	*my*
dein	deine	deine	*your (infml.)*
sein	seine	seine	*his, its*
ihr	ihre	ihre	*her*
unser	unsere	unsere	*our*
euer	eure	eure	*your (infml. pl.)*
Ihr	Ihre	Ihre	*your (fml.)*
ihr	ihre	ihre	*their*

mein Hund
my dog

meine Tante
my aunt

ihr Vater
her father

seine Mutter
his mother

Ihr Buch
your (fml.) book

ihre Bleistife
their pencils

10.2. Notice that these adjectives agree in gender not only with the possessor but also with the noun they modify. **Sein** and **seine** may mean *his* or *its*.

Hans spricht mit seiner Mutter.

Hans is talking to his mother.

Das Bier hat seinen Geschmack verloren.

The beer has lost its taste.

Sie liest ihren Roman.

She is reading her (their) novel.

11. POSSESSIVE PRONOUNS

M. Nom.	F. Nom.	N. Nom.	
meiner	meine	meines	*mine*
deiner	deine	deines	*yours (infml.)*
seiner	seine	seines	*his*
ihrer	ihre	ihres	*hers*
unser	unsere	unseres	*ours*
euer	eure	eures	*yours (infml.)*
Ihrer	Ihre	Ihres	*yours (fml.)*
ihrer	ihre	ihres	*theirs*

Ist das mein Hut?—Ja, das ist Ihrer. (deiner)

Is that my hat?—Yes, that is yours.

Ist das deine Krawatte?—Ja, das ist meine.

Is that your tie?—Yes, that is mine.

Ist das sein Buch?—Nein, das ist meins. (Note: The **e** of the neuter **es** can be dropped.)

Is that his book?—No, that is mine.

Ist das ihr Schirm?—Nein, das ist seiner.

Is that her umbrella?—No, that is his.

12. DEMONSTRATIVE ADJECTIVES

	Nom.	Gen.	Dat.	Acc.
m.	dieser	dieses	diesem	diesen
f.	diese	dieser	dieser	diese
n.	dieses	dieses	diesem	dieses
pl.	diese	dieser	diesen	diese

Dieses Haus ist schön.

This (that) house is beautiful.

Er sieht diesen Mann.

He sees this man.

Das Haus ist hässlich.

That house is ugly.

Er gibt dieser Frau ein Geschenk.

He gives this woman a present.

13. DEMONSTRATIVE PRONOUNS

Although these forms exist in German, they are not commonly used.

	Nom.	Gen.	Dat.	Acc.
m.	derjenige	desjenigen	demjenigen	denjenigen
f.	diejenige	derjenigen	derjenigen	diejenige
n.	dasjenige	desjenigen	demjenigen	dasjenige
pl.	diejenigen	derjenigen	denjenigen	diejenigen

Mein Buch ist blau. Dasjenige meiner Schwester ist grün.
My book is blue. The one of my sister (My sister's) is green.

14. RELATIVE PRONOUNS

The relative pronoun is like the demonstrative pronoun, but its declension varies in the genitive singular of all genders, and in the genitive and dative plural.

	Nom. *(who)*	Gen. *(whose)*	Dat. *(to whom)*	Acc. *(whom)*
m.	der	dessen	dem	den
f.	die	deren	der	die
n.	das	dessen	dem	das
pl.	die	deren	denen	die

Der Junge, dessen Vater ich kenne, heißt Richard.
The boy whose father I know is named Richard.

Die Frau, deren Tochter die Universität besucht, arbeitet in einen Kaufhaus.
The woman whose daughter attends the university works in a department store.

Welcher can also be used and is declined in the same way as the article **der**.

Der Freund, welcher morgen kommt, heißt Max.
The friend who is coming tomorrow is named Max.

14.1. These pronouns must agree in gender and number with the noun they refer to.

Das Mädchen, das auf der Straße spielt . . .
The little girl who is playing on the street . . .

14.2. A comma should always be used before relative pronouns.

14.3. The verb is always placed at the end of the clause that a relative pronoun introduces.

14.4. Relative pronouns can never be omitted as in English.

Das Buch, das ich lese . . .
The book (that) I am reading . . .

15. PERSONAL PRONOUNS
15.1. SINGULAR

Nom.	Gen.	Dat.	Acc.
ich	meiner	mir	mich
du	deiner	dir	dich
er	seiner	ihm	ihm
sie	ihrer	ihr	sie
es	seines	ihm	es
Sie	Ihrer	Ihr	Sie

Nom.	Gen.	Dat.	Acc.
wir	unserer	uns	uns
ihr	eurer	euch	euch
sie	ihrer	ihnen	sie
Sie	Ihrer	Ihnen	Sie

Wir geben ihr Blumen.
We are giving her flowers.

Du sprichst mit ihm.
You are speaking with him.

Wir sprechen von Ihnen.
We're talking about you (fml.).

Diese Geschenke sind für dich.
These presents are for you.

16. INDEFINITE PRONOUNS

man	*one*
jeder(man)	*everybody, everyone*
jemand	*somebody, someone*
niemand	*nobody*
etwas	*something, some*

Jemand steht vor der Tür.
Someone is standing in front of (before) the door.

Es muss etwas geschehen.
Something has to be done.

Man spricht hier nur Deutsch.
One speaks only German here.

17. POSITION OF PRONOUNS

17.1. In a German sentence, the subject pronoun usually comes first, and the indirect object generally precedes the direct object.

Subj.	Verb	Indir. Obj.	Dir. Obj.
Er	**gibt**	**dem Bruder**	**einen Roman.**
He	*gives*	*the brother*	*a novel.*

Sie schenkt der Mutter eine Ledertasche.

She gives her mother a leather handbag.

Dem Bruder and **der Mutter** are the indirect objects. If we substituted indirect object pronouns for each indirect object, the sentences would read as follows:

Er gibt <u>ihm</u> einen Roman.

He gives <u>him</u> a novel.
(He gives a novel to <u>him</u>.)

Er schenkt <u>ihr</u> eine Ledertasche.

He gives <u>her</u> a leather handbag.
(He gives a leather handbag to <u>her</u>.)

17.2. If we substituted a direct object pronoun for each direct object, the two sentences would read as follows:

Er gibt <u>ihn</u> dem Bruder.

He gives it to the brother.

Er schenkt <u>sie</u> der Mutter.

He gives it to (his) mother.

17.3. If we substitute pronouns for both objects in each sentence, we get:

Er gibt ihn ihm.

He gives it to him.

Er schenkt sie ihr.
He gives it to her.

18. THE NEGATIVE

A sentence is made negative by using the word **nicht,** generally following the verb. Words may come between the verb and **nicht.**

Ich weiß.
I know.

Ich weiß nicht.
I do not know.

Ich weiß es nicht.
I don't know it.

The negative of **ein** is **kein.**

19. ADVERBS

19.1. ADJECTIVES AS ADVERBS

Almost all adjectives can be used as adverbs.

19.2. REGULAR COMPARITIVES AND SUPERLATIVES

The comparative of adverbs is formed the same way as the adjectives.

Their superlative is preceded by **am** instead of the article, and has the ending **en.**

Fritz ist ein guter Tänzer.
Fritz is a good dancer.

Fritz tanzt gut.
Fritz dances well.

Karl ist ein besserer Tänzer als Fritz.
Karl is a better dancer than Fritz./Karl dances better than Fritz.

Fred Astaire ist der beste Tänzer.
Fred Astaire is the best dancer.

Fred Astaire tanzt am besten.
Fred Astaire dances the best.

19.3. COMMON ADVERBS WITH IRREGULAR COMPARATIVES AND SUPERLATIVES

viel	**mehr**	**am meisten**
much	*more*	*most*
gern	**lieber**	**am liebsten**
gladly	*preferably*	*most preferably*
bald	**eher**	**am ehesten**
soon	*sooner*	*soonest*

19.4. ADVERBS OF PLACE

hier	*here*
dort	*there*
fort	*away*
links	*on the left*
rechts	*on the right*
vorne	*in front of*
nirgends	*nowhere*
irgendwo	*somewhere*
weg	*aside, away*
hinten	*behind, in the back*
unten	*down(stairs)*
drinnen	*inside*
draußen	*outside*
überall	*everywhere*
nirgendwo, nirgends	*nowhere*
weit	*far*

nahe	near
dort oben	up there
dort drüben	over there

19.5. ADVERBS OF TIME

heute	today
bald	soon
ab und zu	now and then
gerade	just
morgen	tomorrow
gestern	yesterday
vorgestern	the day before yesterday
übermorgen	the day after tomorrow
jetzt	now
dann	then
vorher	before
damals	once, at that time
einmal, ehemals	once, formerly
früh	early
spät	late
oft	often
niemals, nie	never
immer, je, jemals	always, ever
lang, lange	long, for a long time
sofort	at once, right away
manchmal	sometimes
noch	still, yet
nicht mehr	no longer, no more
nachher	afterwards

19.6. ADVERBS OF MANNER

deshalb	*therefore*
fast	*almost*
genau	*exactly*
sehr	*very*
sogar	*even*
überhaupt	*at all*
sowieso	*anyway*
gut	*well*
schlecht	*ill, badly*
so, somit	*thus, so*
ähnlich	*similarly*
andererseits	*on the other hand*
zusammen	*together*
viel	*much*
besonders	*above all, especially*
absichtlich	*on purpose, purposely*
ausdrücklich	*expressly*
gewöhnlich	*usually*

19.7. ADVERBS OF QUANTITY OR DEGREE

viel	*much, many*
genug	*enough*
auf einmal	*all of a sudden*
kaum	*not much, hardly*
wenig	*little*
mehr	*more*
nicht mehr	*no more*
weniger	*less*
noch mehr	*more, even more*
zu viel	*too much, too many*
so viel	*so much, so many*

19.8. PARTICLES AND INTENSIFIERS

allerdings	*certainly*
also	*so, well*
doch	*yes, indeed*
eben	*exactly, just*
ja	*certainly, to be sure*
mal	*just, simply*
nämlich	*namely*
nur	*only*
schon	*already, I/we suppose*
wohl	*probably*
zwar	*to be sure*

20. PREPOSITIONS

20.1. PREPOSITIONS WITH THE GENITIVE

während	*during*
wegen	*because of*
statt, anstatt	*instead of*
trotz	*in spite of*

20.2. PREPOSITIONS WITH THE ACCUSATIVE

durch	*through, by*
für	*for*
gegen	*against, toward*
ohne	*without*
um	*round, about, at (time)*

20.3. PREPOSITIONS WITH THE DATIVE

aus	*from, out of*
bei	*at, by, near, with*
außer	*besides, except*
mit	*with*
nach	*after, to (a place)*

seit	*since*
von	*of, from, by*
zu	*to, at*

20.4. Prepositions with the dative or accusative

an	*at, to*
auf	*on, upon, in*
hinter	*behind*
in	*in, into, at*
neben	*beside, near*
über	*over, across*
unter	*under, among*
vor	*before, ago*
zwischen	*between*

21. CONTRACTIONS

am	an dem
ans	an das
im	in dem
ins	in das
beim	bei dem
vom	von dem
zum	zu dem
zur	zu der
ins	in das
fürs	für das
aufs	auf das

23. PREFIXES

Many German verbs have certain prefixes. These often correspond to English prefixed verbs (*overcome*, *remake*) or phrasal verbs (*come out, do over, go in*). They are divided into three groups.

23.1. INSEPARABLE PREFIXES

Inseparable prefixes remain attached to the verb and are never stressed (just like the English verbs *overthrow, understand*, etc.). The past participles of these verbs do not take the prefix **ge**. These prefixes are **be, emp, ent, er, ge, miss, ver, zer, hinter,** and **wider**.

empfehlen	*to recommend*
gefallen	*to like*
verstehen	*to understand*

23.2. SEPARABLE PREFIXES

Separable prefixes are linked to the verb in the compound tenses; in the other tenses, they are separated and generally placed at the end of the sentence. Their past participles place the **ge** between the prefix and the verb form—for example, **mitgegangen**. They are always stressed. The most common such prefixes are **ab, an, auf, aus, bei, ein, fort, mit, nach, vor, weg, zu, frei, los, wahr,** and **statt**. There are also compound separable prefixes added to verbs, such as **hinaus, herauf, hinein, herein, zurück,** and **zusammen**.

mitkommen	*to come along*
weggehen	*to go away*
zuschliessen	*to lock up*

Her indicates a movement toward the person who is speaking.

Kommen Sie herunter!
Come down!

Hin indicates a movement away from the person speaking.

Geh hinaus!
Go out!

The separable prefix is so important in the sentence that the verb is sometimes omitted in short statements.

Herein!
(Come) in!

23.3. SEPARABLE AND INSEPARABLE PREFIXES
Some prefixes are sometimes separable and sometimes inseparable, depending on the meaning of the verb. These prefixes are **wieder, voll, durch, um, unter,** and **über.**

Der Schüler wiederholt seine Lektion.
The student repeats his lesson.

Holen Sie das wieder!
Take it back!

Die Polizei hat das ganze Hause durchsucht.
The police searched whole house.

24. THE TENSES OF THE INDICATIVE
24.1. SIMPLE TENSES
a. The present tense expresses an uncompleted action in the present. It has several English translations.

ich spreche
I speak, I am speaking, I do speak

ich esse
I eat, I am eating, I do eat

Remember that regular verbs are conjugated with a set of endings, and irregular verbs take the same endings but also have a vowel change.

b. The simple past (narrative past) is mostly used in writing. It sometimes indicates an action that was happening when something else happened. The weak verbs add the following endings to their stems: **-te, -test, -te, -tet,** and **-ten.**

The strong verbs usually change their stem vowels. The first and third person singular have no ending. The others take the same endings as in the present.

Er schlief, als Hans eintrat.
He was sleeping when Hans entered.

Er sprach oft davon.
He often spoke about that.

Es war dunkel, als er ausging.
It was night (dark) when he went out.

24.2. COMPOUND TENSES
a. The future tense is formed by using the auxiliary **werden** plus the infinitive of the verb. It indicates a future action.

Er wird morgen ankommen.
He'll arrive tomorrow.

Ich werde ihm morgen schreiben.
I'll write him (to him) tomorrow.

b. The conversational past tense (also known as the present perfect) is formed by adding the past participle to the present indicative of **haben** or, in some cases, **sein.** It is usually used in spoken German to indicate a past action.

Er hat mir nichts gesagt.
He didn't tell me anything.

Ich habe meine Arbeit beendet.
I finished my work./I have finished my work.

Haben Sie ihn gesehen?
Have you seen him?/Did you see him?

Sie sind angekommen.
They arrived.

c. The pluperfect tense is formed by adding the past participle to the imperfect of **haben** or, in some cases, **sein.**

Er hatte es getan.
He had done it.

Als ich zurückkam, war er schon fort gewesen.
When I came back, he had already left.

d. The future perfect tense is formed by adding the past participle to the future of **haben** or, in some cases, **sein.**

Er wird bald seine Arbeit beendet haben.
He will soon have finished his work.

In zwei Wochen wird er schon in Spanien gewesen sein.
In two weeks he will already have been in Spain.

Sometimes it indicates probability.

Er wird es ihm zweifellos gesagt haben.
No doubt he will have told him.

Er wird krank gewesen sein.
He probably was sick.

Ich werde mich geirrt haben.
I must have been mistaken.

24.3. *HABEN* **AND** *SEIN* **IN THE COMPOUND PAST TENSES**
a. Most compound past tenses are made up of **haben** and the past participle. Some verbs use **sein** instead—namely, intransitive

verbs of motion and verbs that express a state of being or a change of state.

Er hat gesprochen.
He has spoken.

Sie haben gegessen.
You have eaten.

Ich habe ein Geschenk erhalten.
I received a present.

Er hat zuviel getrunken.
He drank too much.

b. The most common intransitive verbs conjugated with the verb **sein** are **gehen, ankommen, absteigen, eintreten, einsteigen, sterben, abreisen, bleiben, kommen, fallen, zurückkommen, laufen,** and **geboren.**

Ich bin gekommen.
I have come.

Er ist angekommen.
He has come (arrived).

Wir sind abgereist.
We have left.

Sie ist geboren.
She was born.

Er ist durch ganz Europa gefahren.
He traveled through Europe.

The verb **fahren** can also be used as a transitive verb, requiring a direct object. In that case, it is conjugated with **haben.**

Er hat den Mercedes nach Hamburg gefahren.
He drove the Mercedes to Hamburg.

In the above sentence, **Mercedes** is the direct object of the verb **fahren**.

25. THE PAST PARTICIPLE

The first syllable of the past participle of both weak and strong verbs is usually **ge** when the verbs have no prefix whatsoever. If they do have a separable prefix, then the syllable **ge** stands between the prefix and the past participle. If the verbs have an inseparable prefix, the past participle has no additional **ge**. Most verbs that end in **-ieren** have no **ge** in the past participle.

	INFINITIVE	PAST PARTICIPLE
strong verb without a prefix	**ziehen** *(to pull)*	**gezogen**
strong with a separable prefix	**vorziehen** *(to prefer)*	**vorgezogen**
weak without a prefix	**warten** *(to wait)*	**gewartet**
weak with a separable prefix	**abwarten** *(to wait and see)*	**abgewartet**
strong with an inseparable prefix	**verlieren** *(to lose)*	**verloren**
weak with an inseparable prefix	**entdecken** *(to discover)*	**entdeckt**
ieren-verb	**studieren** *(to study)*	**studiert**

In the weak verbs, the past participle ends in **-t** or **-et**.

arbeiten	**gearbeitet**
lernen	**gelernt**

In the strong verbs, the past participle ends in **en,** but the vowel of the infinitive stem generally changes. Therefore, when you study the verbs, do not forget to memorize the past participle as well as the other tenses. See the table of irregular verbs.

26. USE OF THE AUXILIARIES HABEN AND SEIN

Notice that most verbs form the perfect, pluperfect, and future perfect with the auxiliary **haben.**

Ich habe gesehen.
I have seen.

Du hast gesehen.
You have seen.

Ich habe mich gewaschen.
I have washed myself.

However, quite a few verbs, chiefly intransitive, form these tenses with the auxiliary **sein:**

a. The verbs **sein, werden,** and **bleiben.**

b. Verbs indicating a change of place (chiefly, verbs of motion, such as **gehen, kommen, eilen, fallen, fließen, laufen, reisen, rollen, steigen, sinken, aufstehen, fliegen, begegnen,** etc.).

c. Verbs indicating a change in the condition of a thing or a person, such as **aufwachen, einschlafen, wachsen, aufbleiben, verblühen, vergehen, verschwinden, sterben, erhalten, platzen,** and **erkranken.**

27. THE SUBJUNCTIVE

27.1. Present of **haben** *(to have)*, **sein** *(to be)*, and **werden** *(to become)*.

HABEN	SEIN	WERDEN
ich habe (hätte)	ich sei	ich werde (würde)
du habest	due seiest	du werdest
er, sie, es habe	er, sie, es sei	er, sie, es werde
wir haben (hätten)	wir seien	wir werden (würden)
ihr habet	ihr seiet	ihr werdet
Sie, sie haben (hätten)	Sie, sie seien	Sie, sie werden (würden)

The endings of both weak and strong verbs are **e, est, e, en, et,** and **en.** The strong verbs keep the stem vowel in each person.

27.2. When the present subjunctive verb forms are identical to the indicative, the imperfect subjunctive verb forms can be used: **Er sagte, dass ich ihn nicht begrüsst hätte** (instead of **begrüsst habe**).

IMPERFECT SUBJUNCTIVE		
ich hätte	ich wäre	ich würde
du hättest	du wärest	du würdest
er, sie, es hätte	er, sie, es wäre	er, sie, es würde
wir hätten	wir wären	wir würden
ihr hättet	ihr wäret	ihr würdet
Sie, sie hätten	Sie, sie wären	Sie, sie würden

Notice that the imperfect tense of the weak verbs is identical in both the indicative and subjunctive. When this occurs, the structure **würde** and a main verb are used. The substitution is therefore with the present conditional tense.

INDIRECT DISCOURSE
Er sagte, dass er es nicht lernen würde.
He said that he would not learn it.

UNREAL CONDITIONS
Wenn er mit mir ins Kino ginge, dann würde ich mich freuen.
If he went with me to the movies, I'd be happy.

Strong verbs have the same endings as the present subjunctive, but take the umlaut if their stem vowel is **a, e,** or **u.**

ich tat	**ich täte**
I did	*that I did*

27.3. The past tenses: The past, pluperfect, and the future are formed with the past participle of the indicative of the verb plus the auxiliaries **haben, sein,** and **werden** in their respective subjunctive forms.

27.4 The subjunctive is used to express doubt, wish, eventuality, or unreality.

27.5. The subjunctive is used in indirect discourse.

27.6. The subjunctive is used after certain conjunctions and expressions.

als ob	*as if*
es sei denn, dass	*unless*

Er glaubte, dass er käme.
He believed that he was coming.

Wir helfen ihm, damit er gesund werde.

We help him, so that he may be healthy again.

27.7. A contrary-to-fact condition in reference to the present or a future time is usually introduced by the conjunction wenn (if) and the imperfect subjunctive followed by the result clause in the present conditional.

Wenn er morgen käme, dann würde ich mit ihm in die Stadt fahren.

If he came tomorrow, I would go to the city with him.

The *if*-clause **(wenn-clause)** has transposed word order (verb in last position), and the main clause has inverted word order (subject after the verb) whenever it stands after the subordinate clause. The above sentence may also be expressed as follows:

a. **Ich würde mit ihm in die Stadt fahren, wenn er morgen käme.**

b. **Ich führe mit ihm in die Stadt, wenn er käme.**

c. **Ich würde mit ihm in die Stadt fahren, wenn er kommen würde.**

The construction in sentence *c* is used less frequently because it employs one conditional verb form in each clause.

27.8. The subjunctive is used to express a wish.
Mögen Sie glücklich sein!

May you be happy!

Wärest du doch hier!

Wish you were here!

27.9. Unreal conditions in reference to past time are formed by the past perfect subjunctive in the **wenn**-clause, followed by the conditional perfect. In modern German, the conditional perfect is usually replaced by the pluperfect subjunctive. Note that the **helping** verb may be a form of **haben** or **sein**.

Wenn ich Zeit gehabt hätte, wäre ich mit dir zum Strand gekommen.
If I had had the time, I would have come to the beach with you.

Wenn ich die Bahn genommen hätte, (dann) hätte ich ihn rechtzeitig getroffen.
If I had taken the train, (then) I would have met him on time.

28. THE CONDITIONAL

The conditional is most often formed with the auxiliary **werden** in its imperfect subjunctive form.

ich würde	wir würden
du würdest	ihr würdet
er, sie, es würde	sie (Sie) würden

It is generally used in connection with the conjunction **wenn** instead of the subjunctive to express a condition.

Wenn wir Geld hätten, würden wir eine lange Reise machen.
If we had any money, we would go on a long trip.

The past conditional is formed like the future perfect, but using **würde** instead of **werde**.

29. THE PASSIVE VOICE

The passive voice is formed with the past participle of the verb and the auxiliary **werden** used in the present and in the past.

Die Erde wird von der Sonne beleuchtet.
The earth is lit by the sun.

By is translated by the German **von** (plus dative).

Amerika wurde von Kolumbus entdeckt.

America was discovered by Columbus.

In the past tense (perfect tense), the participle of the auxiliary **werden, geworden** drops the prefix **ge-** and becomes simply **worden.**

Das Buch ist von ihm geschrieben worden.

The book has been written by him.

Er war von ihr gesehen worden.

He had been seen by her.

30. THE IMPERATIVE

The imperative of verbs is formed from the present indicative tense.

30.1. SECOND PERSON SINGULAR

Drop the ending **-n** from the infinitive. However, strong verbs that change the vowel **e** to **i** or **ie** in the present indicative form their imperative by dropping the **-st** from this tense.

Lerne! (du lernst)

Learn!

Nimm! (du nimmst)

Take!

30.2. FIRST PERSON PLURAL

Invert the infinitive form with the personal pronoun.

Singen wir! (wir singen)

We sing!

30.3. SECOND PERSON PLURAL

Simply insert the second person plural of the present indicative tense and omit the pronoun.

Gebt! (ihr gebt)
Give!

30.4. POLITE SECOND PERSON

Same as the first person plural.

Nehmen Sie! Geben Sie!
Take! Give!

30.5. To express the imperative, the verb **lassen** can also be used; it corresponds to the English *let*.

Lassen Sie das sein!
Let it be!

30.6. IMPERATIVE OF sein AND haben

sein	to be
sei! *(infml.)*	be!
seid! *(infml. pl.)*	be!
seien wir!	let us be!
seien Sie! *(fml.)*	be!

haben	to have
habe! *(infml.)*	have!
habt! *(infml. pl.)*	have!
haben wir!	let us have!
haben Sie! *(fml.)*	have!

31. THE INFINITIVE

The infinitive is usually preceded by **zu** when used in connection with another verb; however, **zu** is in most instances omitted when the infinitive is used in connection with the following verbs: **werden, können, dürfen, wollen, mögen, müssen, sollen, lassen, machen, hören, sehen, heißen, helfen, lehren,** and **lernen.**

Er bittet ihn, den Brief zu schreiben.

He asks him to write the letter.

Ich werde ihr schreiben.

I shall write to her (future).

Ich helfe ihm den Wagen waschen.

I'm helping him wash the car.

Er lehrt uns schwimmen.

He teaches us to swim.

The infinitive is also used after certain prepositions in connection with **zu.**

um . . . zu *(in order to)*
ohne . . . zu *(without)*
anstatt . . . zu *(instead of)*

The **zu** can be used alone.

Wir gehen zur Schule, um zu lernen.

We go to school to learn.

Ich kann nicht essen, ohne etwas zu trinken.

I cannot eat without drinking something.

Er faulenzt, anstatt uns zu helfen.

He is lazy instead of helping us.

Words with a separable prefix have the **zu** between the prefix and the infinitive.

Er bittet ihn, die Tür aufzumachen. (aufmachen)

He asks him to open the door.

32. COMPLEMENTS OF VERBS

32.1. VERBS FOLLOWED BY A PREPOSITION

Their complement should be put in the case required by the preposition—for example, **bedecken mit,** *to cover with* (always dative).

Der Tisch ist mit Staub bedeckt.
The table is covered with dust.

32.2. Verbs followed by an object without a preposition

The genitive, accusative, or dative is used, depending on the verb.

Er ist des Mordes beschuldigt. (genitive)
He is accused of murder.

Sie glauben mir nicht. (dative)
You don't believe me.

Wir lieben ihn. (accusative)
We love him.

33. CHANGES IN THE NORMAL SEQUENCE OF WORDS WITHIN A SENTENCE

33.1. By transposition

Transposition means placing the verb at the end of the sentence. In a subordinate clause—that is, a clause beginning with a relative pronoun or a subordinating conjunction—the verb is always placed at the end of the clause.

Die Sprache, die wir lernen, ist Deutsch.
The language that we are learning is German.

Ich kann nicht sehen, weil es dunkel ist.
I cannot see because it is dark.

Ich glaube, dass das Essen in diesem Restaurant gut ist.
I believe that the food in this restaurant is good.

Notice also that a comma is always used before the relative pronoun or conjunction. If the verb is in a compound tense, the **auxiliary** is placed at the end of the sentence.

Ich glaube nicht, dass es morgen regnen wird.
I do not believe that it will rain tomorrow.

In the case of an indirect question or subordinate clause introduced by an interrogative word—such as the pronouns **wer, was,** or **welcher,** the adverbs **wo, wann,** etc., or the conjunction **ob**—the verb is also placed at the end of the sentence.

Wir wissen nicht, ob er morgen kommt.

We don't know whether he is coming tomorrow.

Können Sie mir sagen, wie weit es von hier bis zum Bahnhof ist?

Can you tell me how far it is from here to the train station?

33.2. BY INVERSION

Inversion means placing the verb before the subject. The inversion is necessary in the following instances.

a. Usually, when a question is asked:
(affirmative)

Er schreibt den Brief.

He writes the letter.

(interrogative)

Schreibt er den Brief?

Does he write the letter?

b. In the main clause of any sentence, when it is preceded by a subordinate clause:

Wenn wir die Augen schließen, können wir nicht sehen.

If we close our eyes, we cannot see.

c. Whenever the main clause opens with a word other than the subject:

Morgen werden die Kinder ins Kino gehen.

Tomorrow the children will go to the movies.

Here we have inversion because the sentence does not start with its subject, **die Kinder,** but with an adverb: **morgen.**

Die Kinder werden morgen ins Kino gehen.
The children will go to the movies tomorrow.

The above does not take any inversion because the sentence is started by its subject, **die Kinder.**

34. INDIRECT DISCOURSE

34.1. When you want to tell a story or make an indirect quotation in German, you use indirect discourse.

DIRECT DISCOURSE
Hans sagt: "Ich gehe zum Bahnhof."
Hans says, "I am going to the station."

INDIRECT DISCOURSE
Hans sagt, dass er zum Bahnhof gehe.
Hans says that he is going to the station.

IMPERFECT
Hans sagte, dass er zum Bahnhof ginge.
Hans said that he was going to the station.

34.2. The subjunctive should be used (even though you can use the indicative, as many Germans do).

34.3. The conjunction **dass** *(that)* can be used or omitted.
If it is used, the verb should be placed at the end of the sentence, as in the regular case of transposition.

Er sagt, dass er zum Bahnhof gehe.

34.4. If **dass** is omitted, the order of the words remains unchanged.
Hans sagt, er gehe zum Bahnhof.
Hans says he is going to the station.

Hans sagte, er ginge zum Bahnhof.
Hans said he was going to the station.

The tense of the verb in indirect discourse does not affect the tense of the inflected verb form in the indirect statement.

Er berichtet, er nehme (nähme) den Bus. (action in present)

Er berichtet, er habe (hätte) den Bus genommen. (action in past)

Er erzählt uns, er sei (wäre) eine Meile gelaufen. (action in past with an intransitive verb)

Er berichtet, er werde (würde) den Bus nehmen. (action in future)

The subjunctive of indirect discourse is normally used after the following verbs: **behaupten** *(to claim)*, **berichten** *(to report)*, **erklären** *(to explain)*, **glauben** *(to believe)*, **meinen** *(to mean)*, **sagen** *(to say)*, and **schreiben** *(to write)*.

34.5. Notice that in both instances, a comma is used at the beginning of the second clause.

34.6. A certain sequence of tenses is generally observed in expressing conditional sentences.

FOR REAL CONDITIONS

The *if*-clause (**wenn**-clause)	result clause
Present indicative	future or present indicative

FOR UNREAL CONDITIONS IN REFERENCE TO PRESENT OR FUTURE TIME

The *if*-clause (**wenn**-clause)	result clause
Imperfect subjunctive	present conditional or imperfect subjunctive

FOR UNREAL CONDITIONS IN REFERENCE TO PAST TIME

The *if*-clause (**wenn**-clause)	result clause
Pluperfect subjunctive	pluperfect subjunctive or conditional perfect

35. CONSTRUCTION OF THE SENTENCE

35.1. MAIN CLAUSES OR SIMPLE SENTENCES

a. Affirmative sentence

Das Buch ist rot.
The book is red.

b. Interrogative

Ist das Buch rot?
Is the book red?

c. Negative

Das Buch ist nicht rot.
The book is not red.

d. Past tenses

Ich habe ein Gedicht gelernt.
I have learned a poem.

Ich lernte ein Gedicht.
I learned a poem.

Ich hatte ein Gedicht gelernt.
I had learned a poem.

e. Infinitive

Sie brauchen das nicht zu wissen.
You do not need to know that.

35.2. SUBORDINATE CLAUSES
a. Transposition

Ich sehe, dass das Buch rot ist.
I see that the book is red.

Ich kenne den Schüler, der das Gedicht liest.
I know the student who is reading the poem.

b. Inversion

Wenn das Wetter schön ist, gehe ich gern spazieren.
When the weather is fine, I like to take a walk.

The second clause has inverted word order.

c. Indirect discourse

Sie antwortet ihm, dass sie eine Schülerin sei/ist.
Sie antwortet ihm, sie sei/ist eine Schülerin.
She answers (him) that she is a pupil.

36. THE MOST COMMON IRREGULAR VERBS

SEIN *to be*

PRESENT INFINITIVE	PAST INFINITIVE	PRESENT PARTICIPLE	PAST PARTICIPLE
sein	gewesen sein	seiend	gewesen

	PRESENT	CONVERSATIONAL PAST	SIMPLE PAST	PAST PERFECT	FUTURE	PAST FUTURE
ich	bin	bin gewesen	war	war gewesen	werde sein	werde gewesen sein
du	bist	bist gewesen	warst	warst gewesen	wirst sein	wirst gewesen sein
er/sie/es	ist	ist gewesen	war	war gewesen	wird sein	wird gewesen sein
wir	sind	sind gewesen	waren	waren gewesen	werden sein	werden gewesen sein
ihr	seid	seid gewesen	wart	wart gewesen	werdet sein	werdet gewesen sein
sie/Sie	sind	sind gewesen	waren	waren gewesen	werden sein	werden gewesen sein

	PRESENT CONDITIONAL	PERFECT CONDITIONAL	PRESENT SUBJUNCTIVE	PRESENT PERFECT SUBJUNCTIVE	IMPERFECT SUBJUNCTIVE	PAST PERFECT SUBJUNCTIVE
ich	würde sein	würde gewesen sein	sei	sei gewesen	wäre	wäre gewesen
du	würdest sein	würdest gewesen sein	seiest	seiest gewesen	wärest	wärest gewesen
er/sie/es	würde sein	würde gewesen sein	sei	sei gewesen	wäre	wäre gewesen
wir	würden sein	würden gewesen sein	seien	seien gewesen	wären	wären gewesen
ihr	würdet sein	würdet gewesen sein	seiet	seiet gewesen	wäret	wäret gewesen
sie/Sie	würden sein	würden gewesen sein	seien	seien gewesen	wären	wären gewesen

Imperative: sei! seien wir! seid! seien Sie!

HABEN *to have*

PRESENT INFINITIVE	PAST INFINITIVE	PRESENT PARTICIPLE	PAST PARTICIPLE
haben	gehabt haben	habend	gehabt

	PRESENT	CONVERSATIONAL PAST	SIMPLE PAST	PAST PERFECT	FUTURE	FUTURE PERFECT
ich	habe	habe gehabt	hatte	hatte gehabt	werde haben	werde gehabt haben
du	hast	hast gehabt	hattest	hattest gehabt	wirst haben	wirst gehabt haben
er/sie/es	hat	hat gehabt	hatte	hatte gehabt	wird haben	wird gehabt haben
wir	haben	haben gehabt	hatten	hatten gehabt	werden haben	werden gehabt haben
ihr	habt	habt gehabt	hattet	hattet gehabt	werdet haben	werdet gehabt haben
sie/Sie	haben	haben gehabt	hatten	hatten gehabt	werden haben	werden gehabt haben

	PRESENT CONDITIONAL	PERFECT CONDITIONAL	PRESENT SUBJUNCTIVE	PRESENT PERFECT SUBJUNCTIVE*	IMPERFECT SUBJUNCTIVE	PAST PERFECT SUBJUNCTIVE
ich	würde haben	würde gehabt haben	habe	habe (hätte) gehabt	hätte	hätte gehabt
du	würdest haben	würdest gehabt haben	habest	habest gehabt	hättest	hättest gehabt
er/sie/es	würde haben	würde gehabt haben	habe	habe gehabt	hätte	hätte gehabt
wir	würden haben	würden gehabt haben	haben	haben (hätten) gehabt	hätten	hätten gehabt
ihr	würdet haben	würdet gehabt haben	habet	habet gehabt	hättet	hättet gehabt
sie/Sie	würden haben	würden gehabt haben	haben	haben (hätten) gehabt	hätten	hätten gehabt

Imperative: Habe!, Haben wir!, Habt!, Haben Sie!

* When the subjunctive forms are identical to the indicative forms, you have to use an alternate subjunctive form. These alternates are in parentheses.

WERDEN *to become*

PRESENT INFINITIVE	PAST INFINITIVE	PRESENT PARTICIPLE	PAST PARTICIPLE
werden	geworden sein	werdend	geworden

	PRESENT	CONVERSATIONAL PAST	SIMPLE PAST	PAST PERFECT	FUTURE	FUTURE PERFECT
ich	werde	bin geworden	wurde	war geworden	werde werden	werde geworden sein
du	wirst	bist geworden	wurdest	warst geworden	wirst werden	wirst geworden sein
er/sie/es	wird	ist geworden	wurde	war geworden	wird werden	wird geworden sein
wir	werden	sind geworden	wurden	waren geworden	werden werden	werden geworden sein
ihr	werdet	seid geworden	wurdet	wart geworden	werdet werden	werdet geworden sein
sie/Sie	werden	sind geworden	wurden	waren geworden	werden werden	werden geworden sein

	PRESENT CONDITIONAL	PERFECT CONDITIONAL	PRESENT SUBJUNCTIVE	PRESENT PERFECT SUBJUNCTIVE	IMPERFECT SUBJUNCTIVE	PAST PERFECT SUBJUNCTIVE
ich	würde werden	würde geworden sein	werde (würde)	sei geworden	würde	wäre geworden
du	würdest werden	würdest geworden sein	werdest	seiest geworden	würdest	wärest geworden
er/sie/es	würde werden	würde geworden sein	werde	sei geworden	würde	wäre geworden
wir	würden werden	würden geworden sein	werden (würden)	seien geworden	würden	wären geworden
ihr	würdet werden	würdet geworden sein	werdet	seiet geworden	würdet	wäret geworden
sie/Sie	würden werden	würden geworden sein	werden (würden)	seien geworden	würden	wären geworden

Imperative: Werde!, Werden wir!, Werdet!, Werden Sie!

KÖNNEN *to be able to*

PRESENT INFINITIVE	PAST INFINITIVE	PRESENT PARTICIPLE	PAST PARTICIPLE
können	**gekonnt haben**	**könnend**	**gekonnt (können)***

*The model verbs **können, dürfen, müssen, sollen,** and **wollen** appear in the past in their infinitive forms when used with another verb, for example: **er muss es tun** (*he has to do it*) becomes **er hat es tun müssen** (*he had to do it*), with a double infinitive, in the past.

	PRESENT	CONVERSATIONAL PAST	SIMPLE PAST	PAST PERFECT	FUTURE	FUTURE PERFECT
ich	kann	habe gekonnt*	konnte	hatte gekonnt	werde können	werde gekonnt haben
du	kannst	hast gekonnt	konntest	hattest gekonnt	wirst können	wirst gekonnt haben
er/sie/es	kann	hat gekonnt	konnte	hatte gekonnt	wird können	wird gekonnt haben
wir	können	haben gekonnt	konnten	hatten gekonnt	werden können	werden gekonnt haben
ihr	könnt	habt gekonnt	konntet	hattet gekonnt	werdet können	werdet gekonnt haben
sie/Sie	können	haben gekonnt	konnten	hatten gekonnt	werden können	werden gekonnt haben

	PRESENT CONDITIONAL	PERFECT CONDITIONAL	PRESENT SUBJUNCTIVE	PRESENT PERFECT SUBJUNCTIVE	IMPERFECT SUBJUNCTIVE	PAST PERFECT SUBJUNCTIVE
ich	würde können	würde gekonnt haben	könne	habe (hätte) gekonnt	könnte	hätte gekonnt
du	würdest können	würdest gekonnt haben	könnest	habest gekonnt	könntest	hättest gekonnt
er/sie/es	würde können	würde gekonnt haben	könne	habe gekonnt	könnte	hätte gekonnt
wir	würden können	würden gekonnt haben	können (könnten)	haben (hätten) gekonnt	könnten	hätten gekonnt
ihr	würdet können	würdet gekonnt haben	könnet	habet gekonnt	könntet	hättet gekonnt
sie/Sie	werden können	würden gekonnt haben	können (könnten)	haben (hätten) gekonnt	könnten	hätten gekonnt

DÜRFEN *to be allowed to*

PRESENT INFINITIVE	PAST INFINITIVE	PRESENT PARTICIPLE	PAST PARTICIPLE
dürfen	gedurft haben	dürfend	gedurft (dürfen)*

*The modal verbs können, dürfen, müssen, sollen, and wollen appear in the past in their infinitive forms when used with another verb, for example: er muss es tun (*he has to do it*) becomes er hat es tun müssen (*he had to do it*), with a double infinitive, in the past.

	PRESENT	CONVERSATIONAL PAST	SIMPLE PAST	PAST PERFECT	FUTURE	FUTURE PERFECT
ich	darf	habe gedurft*	durfte	hatte gedurft	werde dürfen	werde gedurft haben
du	darfst	hast gedurft	durftest	hattest gedurft	wirst dürfen	wirst gedurft haben
er/sie/es	darf	hat gedurft	durfte	hatte gedurft	wird dürfen	wird gedurft haben
wir	dürfen	haben gedurft	durften	hatten gedurft	werden dürfen	werden gedurft haben
ihr	dürft	habt gedurft	durftet	hattet gedurft	werdet dürfen	werdet gedurft haben
sie/Sie	dürfen	haben gedurft	durften	hatten gedurft	werden dürfen	werden gedurft haben

	PRESENT CONDITIONAL	PERFECT CONDITIONAL	PRESENT SUBJUNCTIVE	PRESENT PERFECT SUBJUNCTIVE	IMPERFECT SUBJUNCTIVE	PAST PERFECT SUBJUNCTIVE
ich	würde dürfen	würde gedurft haben	dürfe	habe (hätte) gedurft	dürfte	hätte gedurft
du	würdest dürfen	würdest gedurft haben	dürfest	habest gedurft	dürftest	hättest gedurft
er/sie/es	würde dürfen	würde gedurft haben	dürfe	habe gedurft	dürfte	hätte gedurft
wir	würden dürfen	würden gedurft haben	dürfen (dürften)	haben (hätten) gedurft	dürften	hätten gedurft
ihr	würdet dürfen	würdet gedurft haben	dürfet	habet gedurft	dürftet	hättet gedurft
sie/Sie	würden dürfen	würden gedurft haben	dürfen (dürften)	haben (hätten) gedurft	dürften	hätten gedurft

MÜSSEN *to be obliged to, to have to*

PRESENT INFINITIVE	PAST INFINITIVE	PRESENT PARTICIPLE	PAST PARTICIPLE
müssen	gemusst haben	müssend	gemusst (müssen) *

The modal verbs **können, dürfen, müssen, sollen,** and **wollen** appear in the past in their infinitive forms when used with another verb, for example: **er muss es tun** (*he has to do it*) becomes **er hat es tun müssen** (*he had to do it*), with a double infinitive, in the past.

	PRESENT	CONVERSATIONAL PAST	SIMPLE PAST	PAST PERFECT	FUTURE	FUTURE PERFECT
ich	muss	habe gemusst*	musste	hatte gemusst	werde müssen	werde gemusst haben
du	musst	hast gemusst	musstest	hattest gemusst	wirst müssen	wirst gemusst haben
er/sie/es	muss	hat gemusst	musste	hatte gemusst	wird müssen	wird gemusst haben
wir	müssen	haben gemusst	mussten	hatten gemusst	werden müssen	werden gemusst haben
ihr	müsst	habt gemusst	musstet	hattet gemusst	werdet müssen	werdet gemusst haben
sie/Sie	müssen	haben gemusst	mussten	hatten gemusst	werden müssen	werden gemusst haben

	PRESENT CONDITIONAL	PERFECT CONDITIONAL	PRESENT SUBJUNCTIVE	PRESENT PERFECT SUBJUNCTIVE	IMPERFECT SUBJUNCTIVE	PAST PERFECT SUBJUNCTIVE
ich	würde müssen	würde gemusst haben	müsse	habe (hätte) gemusst	müsste	hätte gemusst
du	würdest müssen	würdest gemusst haben	müssest	habest gemusst	müsstest	hättest gemusst
er/sie/es	würde müssen	würde gemusst haben	müsse	habe gemusst	müsse	hätte gemusst
wir	würden müssen	würden gemusst haben	müssen (müssten)	haben (hätten) gemusst	müssten	hätten gemusst
ihr	würdet müssen	würdet gemusst haben	müsset	habet gemusst	müsstet	hättet gemusst
sie/Sie	würden müssen	würden gemusst haben	müssen (müssten)	haben (hätten) gemusst	müssten	hätten gemusst

WISSEN *to know*

PRESENT INFINITIVE	PAST INFINITIVE	PRESENT PARTICIPLE	PAST PARTICIPLE
wissen	gewusst haben	wissend	gewusst

	PRESENT	CONVERSATIONAL PAST	SIMPLE PAST	PAST PERFECT	FUTURE	FUTURE PERFECT
ich	weiß	habe gewusst	wusste	hatte gewusst	werde wissen	werde gewusst haben
du	weißt	hast gewusst	wusstest	hattest gewusst	wirst wissen	wirst gewusst haben
er/sie/es	weiß	hat gewusst	wusste	hatte gewusst	wird wissen	wird gewusst haben
wir	wissen	haben gewusst	wussten	hatten gewusst	werden wissen	werden gewusst haben
ihr	wisst	habt gewusst	wusstet	hattet gewusst	werdet wissen	werdet gewusst haben
sie/Sie	wissen	haben gewusst	wussten	hatten gewusst	werden wissen	werden gewusst haben

	PRESENT CONDITIONAL	PERFECT CONDITIONAL	PRESENT SUBJUNCTIVE	PRESENT PERFECT SUBJUNCTIVE	IMPERFECT SUBJUNCTIVE	PAST PERFECT SUBJUNCTIVE
ich	würde wissen	würde gewusst haben	wisse	habe (hätte) gewusst	wüsste	hätte gewusst
du	würdest wissen	würdest gewusst haben	wissest	habest gewusst	wüsstest	hättest gewusst
er/sie/es	würde wissen	würde gewusst haben	wisse	habe gewusst	wüsste	hätte gewusst
wir	würden wissen	würden gewusst haben	wissen (wüssten)	haben (hätten) gewusst	wüssten	hätten gewusst
ihr	würdet wissen	würdet gewusst haben	wisset	habet gewusst	wüsstet	hättet gewusst
sie/Sie	würden wissen	würden gewusst haben	wissen (wüssten)	haben (hätten) gewusst	wüssten	hätten gewusst

Imperative: Wisse!, Wissen wir!, Wisst!, Wissen Sie!

GEHEN *to go*

PRESENT INFINITIVE	PAST INFINITIVE	PRESENT PARTICIPLE	PAST PARTICIPLE
gehen	gegangen sein	gehend	gegangen

	PRESENT	CONVERSATIONAL PAST	SIMPLE PAST	PAST PERFECT	FUTURE	FUTURE PERFECT
ich	gehe	bin gegangen	ging	war gegangen	werde gehen	werde gegangen sein
du	gehst	bist gegangen	gingst	warst gegangen	wirst gehen	wirst gegangen sein
er/sie/es	geht	ist gegangen	ging	war gegangen	gehen	wird gegangen sein
wir	gehen	sind gegangen	gingen	waren gegangen	werden gehen	werden gegangen sein
ihr	geht	seid gegangen	gingt	wart gegangen	werdet gehen	werdet gegangen sein
sie/Sie	gehen	sind gegangen	gingen	waren gegangen	werden gehen	werden gegangen sein

	PRESENT CONDITIONAL	PERFECT CONDITIONAL	PRESENT SUBJUNCTIVE	PRESENT PERFECT SUBJUNCTIVE	IMPERFECT SUBJUNCTIVE	PAST PERFECT SUBJUNCTIVE
ich	würde gehen	würde gegangen sein	gehe (ginge)	sei gegangen	ginge	wäre gegangen
du	würdest gehen	würdest gegangen sein	gehest	seiest gegangen	gingest	wärest gegangen
er/sie/es	würde gehen	würde gegangen sein	gehe	sei gegangen	ginge	wäre gegangen
wir	würden gehen	würden gegangen sein	gehen (gingen)	seien gegangen	gingen	wären gegangen
ihr	würdet gehen	würdet gegangen sein	gehet	seid gegangen	ginget	wäret gegangen
sie/Sie	würden gehen	würden gegangen sein	gehen (gingen)	seien gegangen	gingen	wären gegangen

Imperative: Gehe!, Gehen wir!, Geht!, Gehen Sie!

KOMMEN *to come*

PRESENT INFINITIVE	PAST INFINITIVE	PRESENT PARTICIPLE	PAST PARTICIPLE
kommen	gekommen sein	kommend	gekommen

	PRESENT	CONVERSATIONAL PAST	SIMPLE PAST	PAST PERFECT	FUTURE	FUTURE PERFECT
ich	komme	bin gekommen	kam	war gekommen	werde kommen	werde gekommen sein
du	kommst	bist gekommen	kamst	warst gekommen	wirst kommen	wirst gekommen sein
er/sie/es	kommt	ist gekommen	kam	war gekommen	wird kommen	wird gekommen sein
wir	kommen	sind gekommen	kamen	waren gekommen	werden kommen	werden gekommen sein
ihr	kommt	seid gekommen	kamt	wart gekommen	werdet kommen	werdet gekommen sein
sie/Sie	kommen	sind gekommen	kamen	waren gekommen	werden kommen	werden gekommen sein

	PRESENT CONDITIONAL	PERFECT CONDITIONAL	PRESENT SUBJUNCTIVE	PRESENT PERFECT SUBJUNCTIVE	IMPERFECT SUBJUNCTIVE	PAST PERFECT SUBJUNCTIVE
ich	würde kommen	würde gekommen sein	(komme) käme	sei gekommen	käme	wäre gekommen
du	würdest kommen	würdest gekommen sein	kommest	seiest gekommen	kämest	wärest gekommen
er/sie/es	würde kommen	würde gekommen sein	komme	sei gekommen	käme	wäre gekommen
wir	würden kommen	würden gekommen sein	(kommen) kämen	seien gekommen	kämen	wären gekommen
ihr	würdet kommen	würdet gekommen sein	kommet	seid gekommen	kämet	wäret gekommen
sie/Sie	würden kommen	würden gekommen sein	(kommen) kämen	seien gekommen	kämen	wären gekommen

Imperative: Komm!, Kommen wir!, Kommt!, Kommen Sie!

37. OTHER IRREGULAR VERBS

When the present subjunctive form is in parentheses, it indicates that it is identical to the present indicative. Whenever this occurs, the imperfect or the past perfect subjunctive form is used.

beginnen *to begin*	
Present Participle	beginnend
Present Indicative	ich beginne, du beginnst, er beginnt, wir beginnen, ihr beginnt, Sie beginnen, sie beginnen
Present Subjunctive	(ich beginne), du beginnest, er beginne, wir beginnen, ihr beginnet, (Sie beginnen), (sie beginnen)
Simple Past	ich begann
Imperfect Subjunctive	ich begänne (begönne)
Past Participle	begonnen
Conversational Past	ich habe begonnen
Past Perfect Indicative	ich hatte begonnen
Past Perfect Subjunctive	ich hätte begonnen
Future	ich werde beginnen
Future Perfect	ich werde begonnen haben
Conditional	ich würde beginnen
Conditional Perfect	ich würde begonnen haben
Imperative	beginn! beginnen wir! beginnt! beginnen Sie!

bleiben *to remain*	
Present Participle	bleibend
Present Indicative	ich bleibe, du bleibst, er bleibt, wir bleiben, ihr bleibt, Sie bleiben, sie bleiben
Present Subjunctive	ich bleibe, du bleibest, er bleibe, wir bleiben, ihr bleibet, Sie bleiben, sie bleiben
Simple Past	ich blieb
Imperfect Subjunctive	ich bliebe
Past Participle	geblieben
Conversational Past	ich bin geblieben
Past Perfect Indicative	ich war geblieben
Present Perfect Subjunctive	ich sei geblieben
Past Perfect Subjunctive	ich wäre geblieben
Future	ich werde bleiben
Future Perfect	ich werde geblieben sein
Conditional	ich würde bleiben
Conditional Perfect	ich würde geblieben sein
Imperative	bleib! bleiben wir! bleibt! bleiben Sie!

bringen *to bring*

Present Participle	**bringend**
Present Indicative	**ich bringe, du bringst, er bringt, wir bringen, ihr bringt, Sie bringen, sie bringen**
Present Subjunctive	**(ich bringe), du bringest, er bringe, (wir bringen), ihr bringet, (Sie bringen, sie bringen)**
Simple Past	**ich brachte**
Imperfect Subjunctive	**ich brächte**
Past Participle	**gebracht**
Conversational Past	**ich habe gebracht**
Past Perfect Indicative	**ich hatte gebracht**
Present Perfect Subjunctive	**ich habe (hatte) gebracht**
Past Perfect Subjunctive	**ich hätte gebracht**
Future	**ich werde bringen**
Future Perfect	**ich werde gebracht haben**
Conditional	**ich würde bringen**
Conditional Perfect	**ich würde gebracht haben**
Imperative	**bring! bringen wir! bringt! bringen Sie!**

denken *to think*	
Present Participle	denkend
Present Indicative	ich denke, du denkst, er denkt, wir denken, ihr denkt, Sie denken, sie denken
Present Subjunctive	(ich denke), du denkest, er denke, (wir denken), ihr denket, (Sie denken, sie denken)
Simple Past	ich dachte
Imperfect Subjunctive	ich dächte
Past Participle	gedacht
Conversational Past	ich habe gedacht
Past Perfect Indicative	ich hatte gedacht
Present Perfect Subjunctive	(ich habe gedacht)
Past Perfect Subjunctive	ich hätte gedacht
Future	ich werde denken
Future Perfect	ich werde gedacht haben
Conditional	ich würde denken
Conditional Perfect	ich würde gedacht haben
Imperative	denke! (denk!) denken wir! denkt! denken Sie!

essen *to eat*	
Present Participle	essend
Present Indicative	ich esse, du isst, er isst, wir essen, ihr esst, Sie essen, sie essen
Present Subjunctive	(ich esse), du essest, er esse, (wir essen), ihr esset, (Sie essen, sie essen)
Simple Past	ich aß
Imperfect Subjunctive	ich äße
Past Participle	gegessen
Conversational Past	ich habe gegessen
Past Perfect Indicative	ich hatte gegessen
Present Perfect Subjunctive	ich (hatte) habe gegessen
Past Perfect Subjunctive	ich hätte gegessen
Future	ich werde essen
Future Perfect	ich werde gegessen haben
Conditional	ich würde essen
Conditional Perfect	ich würde gegessen haben
Imperative	iss! essen wir! esst! essen Sie!

fahren *to drive*	
Present Participle	**fahrend**
Present Indicative	**ich fahre, du fährst, er fährt, wir fahren, ihr fahrt, Sie fahren, sie fahren**
Present Subjunctive	**ich (fahre) führe, du fahrest, er fahre, (wir fahren), ihr fahret, (Sie fahren, sie fahren)**
Simple Past	**ich fuhr**
Imperfect Subjunctive	**ich führe**
Past Participle	**gefahren**
Conversational Past	**ich bin gefahren**
Past Perfect Indicative	**ich war gefahren**
Present Perfect Subjunctive	**ich sei gefahren**
Past Perfect Subjunctive	**ich wäre gefahren**
Future	**ich werde fahren**
Future Perfect	**ich werde gefahren sein**
Conditional	**ich würde fahren**
Conditional Perfect	**ich würde gefahren sein**
Imperative	**fahr! fahren wir! fahrt! fahren Sie!**

fallen *to fall*	
Present Participle	**fallend**
Present Indicative	**ich falle, du fällst, er fällt, wir fallen, ihr fallt, Sie fallen, sie fallen**
Present Subjunctive	**ich (falle) fiele, du fallest, er falle, (wir fallen), ihr fallet, (Sie fallen, sie fallen)**
Simple Past	**ich fiel**
Imperfect Subjunctive	**ich fiele**
Past Participle	**gefallen**
Conversational Past	**ich bin gefallen**
Past Perfect Indicative	**ich war gefallen**
Present Perfect Subjunctive	**ich sei gefallen**
Past Perfect Subjunctive	**ich wäre gefallen**
Future	**ich werde fallen**
Future Perfect	**ich werde gefallen sein**
Conditional	**ich würde fallen**
Conditional Perfect	**ich würde gefallen sein**
Imperative	**falle! fall! fallen wir! fallt! fallen Sie!**

finden *to find*	
Present Participle	**findend**
Present Indicative	**ich finde, du findest, er findet, wir finden, ihr findet, Sie finden, sie finden**
Present Subjunctive	**ich (finde) fände, du findest, er finde, (wir finden), ihr findet, (Sie finden, sie finden)**
Simple Past	**ich fand**
Imperfect Subjunctive	**ich fände**
Past Participle	**gefunden**
Conversational Past	**ich habe gefunden**
Past Perfect Indicative	**ich hatte gefunden**
Present Perfect Subjunctive	**ich habe gefunden**
Past Perfect Subjunctive	**ich hätte gefunden**
Future	**ich werde finden**
Future Perfect	**ich werde gefunden haben**
Conditional	**ich würde finden**
Conditional Perfect	**ich würde gefunden haben**
Imperative	**finde! finden wir! findet! finden Sie!**

fliegen *to fly*	
Present Participle	**fliegend**
Present Indicative	**ich fliege, du fliegst, er fliegt, wir fliegen, ihr fliegt, Sie fliegen, sie fliegen**
Present Subjunctive	**ich (fliege) flöge, du fliegest, er fliege, (wir fliegen), ihr flieget, Sie fliegen, (sie fliegen)**
Simple Past	**ich flog**
Imperfect Subjunctive	**ich flöge**
Past Participle	**geflogen**
Conversational Past	**ich bin geflogen**
Past Perfect Indicative	**ich war geflogen**
Present Perfect Subjunctive	**ich sei geflogen**
Past Perfect Subjunctive	**ich wäre geflogen**
Future	**ich werde fliegen**
Future Perfect	**ich werde geflogen sein**
Conditional	**ich würde fliegen**
Conditional Perfect	**ich würde geflogen sein**
Imperative	**fliege! fliegen wir! fliegt! fliegen Sie!**

heißen *to be called*	
Present Participle	**heißend**
Present Indicative	**ich heiße, du heißt, er heißt, wir heißen, ihr heißt, Sie heißen, sie heißen**
Present Subjunctive	**ich (heiße) heiße, du heißest, er heiße, (wir heißen), ihr heißet, (Sie heißen, sie heißen)**
Simple Past	**ich hieß**
Imperfect Subjunctive	**ich hieße**
Past Participle	**geheißen**
Conversational Past	**ich habe geheißen**
Past Perfect Indicative	**ich hatte geheißen**
Present Perfect Subjunctive	**ich (habe) hätte geheißen**
Past Perfect Subjunctive	**ich hätte geheißen**
Future	**ich werde heißen**
Future Perfect	**ich werde geheißen haben**
Conditional	**ich würde heißen**
Conditional Perfect	**ich würde geheißen haben**
Imperative	**heiße! heißen wir! heißt! heißen Sie!**

helfen *to help*	
Present Participle	helfend
Present Indicative	ich helfe, du hilfst, er hilft, wir helfen, ihr helft, Sie helfen, sie helfen
Present Subjunctive	(ich helfe), du helfest, er helfe, (wir helfen), ihr helfet, (Sie helfen, sie helfen)
Simple Past	ich half
Imperfect Subjunctive	ich hälfe, ich hülfe
Past Participle	geholfen
Conversational Past	ich habe geholfen
Past Perfect Indicative	ich hatte geholfen
Present Perfect Subjunctive	ich (habe) hätte geholfen
Past Perfect Subjunctive	ich hätte geholfen
Future	ich werde helfen
Future Perfect	ich werde geholfen haben
Conditional	ich würde helfen
Conditional Perfect	ich würde geholfen haben
Imperative	hilf! helfen wir! helft! helfen Sie!

kennen *to know*	
Present Participle	**kennend**
Present Indicative	**ich kenne, du kennst, er kennt, wir kennen, ihr kennt, Sie kennen, sie kennen**
Present Subjunctive	**ich (kenne) kennte, du kennest, er kenne, (wir kennen), ihr kennet, (Sie kennen, sie kennen)**
Simple Past	**ich kannte**
Imperfect Subjunctive	**ich kannte**
Past Participle	**gekannt**
Conversational Past	**ich habe gekannt**
Past Perfect Indicative	**ich hatte gekannt**
Present Perfect Subjunctive	**ich (habe) hätte gekannt**
Past Perfect Subjunctive	**ich hätte gekannt**
Future	**ich werde kennen**
Future Perfect	**ich werde gekannt haben**
Conditional	**ich würde kennen**
Conditional Perfect	**ich würde gekannt haben**
Imperative	**kenne! kennen wir! kennt! kennen Sie!**

laden *to load*	
Present Participle	ladend
Present Indicative	ich lade, du lädst, er lädt, wir laden, ihr ladet, Sie laden, sie laden
Present Subjunctive	ich (lade) lüde, du ladest, er lad, (wir laden), ihr ladet, (Sie laden, sie laden)
Simple Past	ich lud
Imperfect Subjunctive	ich lüde
Past Participle	geladen
Conversational Past	ich habe geladen
Past Perfect Indicative	ich hatte geladen
Present Perfect Subjunctive	ich (habe) hätte geladen
Past Perfect Subjunctive	ich hätte geladen
Future	ich werde laden
Future Perfect	ich werde geladen haben
Conditional	ich würde laden
Conditional Perfect	ich würde geladen haben
Imperative	lade! laden wir! ladet! laden Sie!

lassen *to let*

Present Participle	**lassend**
Present Indicative	**ich lasse, du lässt, er lässt, wir lassen, ihr lasst, Sie lassen, sie lassen**
Present Subjunctive	**ich (lasse) ließe, du lassest, er lasse, (wir lassen), ihr lasset, Sie lassen, (sie lassen)**
Simple Past	**ich ließ**
Imperfect Subjunctive	**ich ließe**
Past Participle	**gelassen**
Conversational Past	**ich habe gelassen**
Past Perfect Indicative	**ich hatte gelassen**
Present Perfect Subjunctive	**ich (habe) hätte gelassen**
Past Perfect Subjunctive	**ich hätte gelassen**
Future	**ich werde lassen**
Future Perfect	**ich werde gelassen haben**
Conditional	**ich würde lassen**
Conditional Perfect	**ich würde gelassen haben**
Imperative	**lass! lassen wir! lasst! lassen Sie!**

laufen *to run*	
Present Participle	**laufend**
Present Indicative	**ich laufe, du läufst, er läuft, wir laufen, ihr lauft, Sie laufen, sie laufen**
Present Subjunctive	**ich (laufe) liefe, du laufest, er laufe, (wir laufen), ihr laufet, Sie laufen, (sie laufen)**
Simple Past	**ich lief**
Imperfect Subjunctive	**ich liefe**
Past Participle	**gelaufen**
Conversational Past	**ich bin gelaufen**
Past Perfect Indicative	**ich war gelaufen**
Present Perfect Subjunctive	**ich sei gelaufen**
Past Perfect Subjunctive	**ich wäre gelaufen**
Future	**ich werde laufen**
Future Perfect	**ich werde gelaufen sein**
Conditional	**ich würde laufen**
Conditional Perfect	**ich würde gelaufen sein**
Imperative	**lauf! laufen wir! lauft! laufen Sie!**

leiden *to suffer, to endure*	
Present Participle	**leidend**
Present Indicative	**ich leide, du leidest, er leidet, wir leiden, ihr leidet, Sie leiden, sie leiden**
Present Subjunctive	**ich (leide) litte, du leidest, er leide, (wir leiden), ihr leidet, Sie leiden, (sie leiden)**
Simple Past	**ich litt**
Imperfect Subjunctive	**ich litte**
Past Participle	**gelitten**
Conversational Past	**ich habe gelitten**
Past Perfect Indicative	**ich hatte gelitten**
Present Perfect Subjunctive	**ich (habe) hätte gelitten**
Past Perfect Subjunctive	**ich hätte gelitten**
Future	**ich werde leiden**
Future Perfect	**ich werde gelitten haben**
Conditional	**ich würde leiden**
Conditional Perfect	**ich würde gelitten haben**
Imperative	**leide! leiden wir! leidet! leiden Sie!**

lesen *to read*	
Present Participle	**lesend**
Present Indicative	**ich lese, du liest, er liest, wir lesen, ihr lest, Sie lesen, sie lesen**
Present Subjunctive	**ich (lese) läse, du lesest, er lese, (wir lesen), ihr leset, (Sie lesen, sie lesen)**
Simple Past	**ich las**
Imperfect Subjunctive	**ich läse**
Past Participle	**gelesen**
Conversational Past	**ich habe gelesen**
Past Perfect Indicative	**ich hatte gelesen**
Present Perfect Subjunctive	**ich (habe) hätte gelesen**
Past Perfect Subjunctive	**ich hätte gelesen**
Future	**ich werde lesen**
Future Perfect	**ich werde gelesen haben**
Conditional	**ich würde lesen**
Conditional Perfect	**ich würde gelesen haben**
Imperative	**lies! lesen wir! lest! lesen Sie!**

liegen *to lie (recline)*	
Present Participle	**liegend**
Present Indicative	**ich liege, du liegst, er liegt, wir liegen, ihr liegt, Sie liegen, sie liegen**
Present Subjunctive	**ich (liege) läge, du liegest, er liege, (wir liegen), ihr lieget, (Sie liegen, sie liegen)**
Simple Past	**ich lag**
Imperfect Subjunctive	**ich läge**
Past Participle	**gelegen**
Conversational Past	**ich habe gelegen**
Past Perfect Indicative	**ich hatte gelegen**
Present Perfect Subjunctive	**ich (habe) hätte gelegen**
Past Perfect Subjunctive	**ich hätte gelegen**
Future	**ich werde liegen**
Future Perfect	**ich werde gelegen haben**
Conditional	**ich würde liegen**
Conditional Perfect	**ich würde gelegen haben**
Imperative	**liege! liegen wir! liegt! liegen Sie!**

lügen *to lie (say something untrue)*	
Present Participle	**lügend**
Present Indicative	**ich lüge, du lügst, er lügt, wir lügen, ihr lügt, Sie lügen, sie lügen**
Present Subjunctive	**ich lüge, du lügest, er lüge, wir lügen, ihr lüget, Sie lügen, sie lügen**
Simple Past	**ich log**
Imperfect Subjunctive	**ich löge**
Past Participle	**gelogen**
Conversational Past	**ich habe gelogen**
Past Perfect Indicative	**ich hatte gelogen**
Present Perfect Subjunctive	**ich (habe) hätte gelogen**
Past Perfect Subjunctive	**ich hätte gelogen**
Future	**ich werde lügen**
Future Perfect	**ich werde gelogen haben**
Conditional	**ich würde lügen**
Conditional Perfect	**ich würde gelogen haben**
Imperative	**lüge! lügen wir! lügt! lügen Sie!**

nehmen *to take*	
Present Participle	**nehmend**
Present Indicative	**ich nehme, du nimmst, er nimmt, wir nehmen, ihr nehmt, Sie nehmen, sie nehmen**
Present Subjunctive	**ich (nehme) nähme, du nehmest, er nehme, (wir nehmen), ihr nehmet, (Sie nehmen, sie nehmen)**
Simple Past	**ich nahm**
Imperfect Subjunctive	**ich nähme**
Past Participle	**genommen**
Conversational Past	**ich habe genommen**
Past Perfect Indicative	**ich hatte genommen**
Present Perfect Subjunctive	**ich (habe) hätte genommen**
Past Perfect Subjunctive	**ich hätte genommen**
Future	**ich werde nehmen**
Future Perfect	**ich werde genommen haben**
Conditional	**ich würde nehmen**
Conditional Perfect	**ich würde genommen haben**
Imperative	**nimm! nehmen wir! nehmt! nehmen Sie!**

nennen *to name*	
Present Participle	nennend
Present Indicative	ich nenne, du nennst, er nennt, wir nennen, ihr nennt, Sie nennen, sie nennen
Present Subjunctive	ich (nenne) nennte, du nennest, er nenne, (wir nennen), ihr nennet, (Sie nennen, sie nennen)
Simple Past	ich nannte
Imperfect Subjunctive	ich nennte
Past Participle	genannt
Conversational Past	ich habe genannt
Past Perfect Indicative	ich hatte genannt
Present Perfect Subjunctive	ich (habe) hätte genannt
Past Perfect Subjunctive	ich hätte genannt
Future	ich werde nennen
Future Perfect	ich werde genannt haben
Conditional	ich würde nennen
Conditional Perfect	ich würde genannt haben
Imperative	nenne! nennen wir! nennt! nennen Sie!

rufen *to call*	
Present Participle	**rufend**
Present Indicative	**ich rufe, du rufst, er ruft, wir rufen, ihr ruft, Sie rufen, sie rufen**
Present Subjunctive	**ich (rufe) riefe, du rufest, er rufe, (wir rufen), rufet, (Sie rufen, sie rufen)**
Simple Past	**ich rief**
Imperfect Subjunctive	**ich riefe**
Past Participle	**gerufen**
Conversational Past	**ich habe gerufen**
Past Perfect Indicative	**ich hatte gerufen**
Present Perfect Subjunctive	**ich (habe) hätte gerufen**
Past Perfect Subjunctive	**ich hätte gerufen**
Future	**ich werde rufen**
Future Perfect	**ich werde gerufen haben**
Conditional	**ich würde rufen**
Conditional Perfect	**ich würde gerufen haben**
Imperative	**ruf! rufen wir! ruft! rufen Sie!**

schaffen *to create*	
Present Participle	**schaffend**
Present Indicative	**ich schaffe, du schaffst, er schafft, wir schaffen, ihr schafft, Sie schaffen, sie schaffen**
Present Subjunctive	**ich (schaffe) schüfe, du schaffest, er schaffe, (wir schaffen), ihr schaffet, (Sie schaffen, sie schaffen)**
Simple Plan	**ich schuf**
Imperfect Subjunctive	**ich schüfe**
Past Participle	**geschaffen**
Conversational Past	**ich habe geschaffen**
Past Perfect Indicative	**ich hatte geschaffen**
Present Perfect Subjunctive	**ich (habe) hätte geschaffen**
Past Perfect Subjunctive	**ich hätte geschaffen**
Future	**ich werde schaffen**
Future Perfect	**ich werde geschaffen haben**
Conditional	**ich würde schaffen**
Conditional Perfect	**ich würde geschaffen haben**
Imperative	**schaffe! schaffen wir! schafft! schaffen Sie!**

schlafen *to sleep*	
Present Participle	**schlafend**
Present Indicative	**ich schlafe, du schläfst, er schläft, wir schlafen, ihr schlaft, sie schlafen**
Present Subjunctive	**ich (schlafe) schliefe, du schlafest, er schlafe, (wir schlafen), ihr schlafet, (Sie schlafen, sie schlafen)**
Simple Past	**ich schlief**
Imperfect Subjunctive	**ich schliefe**
Past Participle	**geschlafen**
Conversational Past	**ich habe geschlafen**
Past Perfect Indicative	**ich hatte geschlafen**
Present Perfect Subjunctive	**ich (habe) hätte geschlafen**
Past Perfect Subjunctive	**ich hätte geschlafen**
Future	**ich werde schlafen**
Future Perfect	**ich werde geschlafen haben**
Conditional	**ich würde schlafen**
Conditional Perfect	**ich würde geschlafen haben**
Imperative	**schlafe! schlafen wir! schlaft! schlafen Sie!**

schlagen *to beat, to strike*	
Present Participle	**schlagend**
Present Indicative	**ich schlage, du schlägst, er schlägt, wir schlagen, ihr schlagt, Sie schlagen, sie schlagen**
Present Subjunctive	**ich (schlage) schlüge, du schlagest, er schlage, (wir schlagen), ihr schlaget, (Sie schlagen, sie schlagen)**
Simple Past	**ich schlug**
Imperfect Subjunctive	**ich schlüge**
Past Participle	**geschlagen**
Conversational Past	**ich habe geschlagen**
Past Perfect Indicative	**ich hatte geschlagen**
Present Perfect Subjunctive	**ich (habe) hätte geschlagen**
Past Perfect Subjunctive	**ich hätte geschlagen**
Future	**ich werde schlagen**
Future Perfect	**ich werde geschlagen haben**
Conditional	**ich würde schlagen**
Conditional Perfect	**ich würde geschlagen haben**
Imperative	**schlage! (schlag!) schlagen wir! schlagt! schlagen Sie!**

schreiben *to write*	
Present Participle	**schreibend**
Present Indicative	**ich schreibe, du schreibst, er schreibt, wir schreiben, ihr schreibt, Sie schreiben, sie schreiben**
Present Subjunctive	**ich (schreibe) schriebe, du schreibest, er schreibe, (wir schreiben), ihr schreibet, (Sie schreiben, sie schreiben)**
Simple Past	**ich schrieb**
Imperfect Subjunctive	**ich schriebe**
Past Participle	**geschrieben**
Conversational Past	**ich habe geschrieben**
Past Perfect Indicative	**ich hatte geschrieben**
Present Perfect Subjunctive	**ich (habe) hätte geschrieben**
Past Perfect Subjunctive	**ich hätte geschrieben**
Future	**ich werde schreiben**
Future Perfect	**ich werde geschrieben haben**
Conditional	**ich würde schreiben**
Conditional Perfect	**ich würde geschrieben haben**
Imperative	**schreib! schreiben wir! schreibt! schreiben Sie!**

schwimmen *to swim*	
Present Participle	**schwimmend**
Present Indicative	**ich schwimme, du schwimmst, er schwimmt, wir schwimmen, ihr schwimmt, Sie schwimmen, sie schwimmen**
Present Subjunctive	**ich (schwimme) schwömme, du schwimmest, er schwimme, (wir schwimmen), ihr schwimmet, (Sie schwimmen, sie schwimmen)**
Simple Past	**ich schwamm**
Imperfect Subjunctive	**ich schwömme (schwämme)**
Past Participle	**geschwommen**
Conversational Past	**ich bin geschwommen**
Past Perfect Indicative	**ich war geschwommen**
Present Perfect Subjunctive	**ich sei geschwommen**
Past Perfect Subjunctive	**ich wäre geschwommen**
Future	**ich werde schwimmen**
Future Perfect	**ich werde geschwommen sein**
Conditional	**ich würde schwimmen**
Conditional Perfect	**ich würde geschwommen sein**
Imperative	**schwimm! schwimmen wir! schwimmt! schwimmen Sie!**

senden *to send (to broadcast)*	
Present Participle	sendend
Present Indicative	ich sende, du sendest, er sendet, wir senden, ihr sendet, Sie senden, sie senden
Present Subjunctive	ich (sende) sendete, du sendest, er sendet, (wir senden), ihr sendet, (Sie senden, sie senden)
Simple Past	ich sandte (ich sendete)
Imperfect Subjunctive	ich sendete
Past Participle	gesandt (gesendet)
Conversational Past	ich habe gesandt (gesendet)
Past Perfect Indicative	ich hatte gesandt (gesendet)
Present Perfect Subjunctive	ich (habe) hätte gesandt (gesendet)
Past Perfect Subjunctive	ich hätte gesandt (gesendet)
Future	ich werde senden
Future Perfect	ich werde gesandt (gesendet) haben
Conditional	ich würde senden
Conditional Perfect	ich würde gesandt (gesendet) haben
Imperative	sende! senden wir! sendet! senden Sie!

singen *to sing*

Present Participle	**singend**
Present Indicative	**ich singe, du singst, er singt, wir singen, ihr singt, Sie singen, sie singen**
Present Subjunctive	**ich (singe) sänge, du singest, er singe, (wir singen), ihr singet, (Sie singen, sie singen)**
Simple Past	**ich sang**
Imperfect Subjunctive	**ich sänge**
Past Participle	**gesungen**
Conversational Past	**ich habe gesungen**
Past Perfect Indicative	**ich hatte gesungen**
Present Perfect Subjunctive	**ich (habe) hatte gesungen**
Past Perfect Subjunctive	**ich hätte gesungen**
Future	**ich werde singen**
Future Perfect	**ich werde gesungen haben**
Conditional	**ich würde singen**
Conditional Perfect	**ich würde gesungen haben**
Imperative	**sing! singen wir! singt! singen Sie!**

sitzen *to sit*	
Present Participle	**sitzend**
Present Indicative	**ich sitze, du sitzt, er sitzt, wir sitzen, ihr sitzt, Sie sitzen, sie sitzen**
Present Subjunctive	**ich (sitze) sässe, du sitzest, er sitze, (wir sitzen), ihr sitzet, (Sie sitzen, sie sitzen)**
Simple Past	**ich sass**
Imperfect Subjunctive	**ich sässe**
Past Participle	**gesessen**
Conversational Past	**ich habe gesessen**
Past Perfect Indicative	**ich hatte gesessen**
Present Perfect Subjunctive	**ich (habe) hätte gesessen**
Past Perfect Subjunctive	**ich hätte gesessen**
Future	**ich werde sitzen**
Future Perfect	**ich werde gesessen haben**
Conditional	**ich würde sitzen**
Conditional Perfect	**ich würde gesessen haben**
Imperative	**sitz! sitzen wir! sitzt! sitzen Sie!**

stehen *to stand*	
Present Participle	**stehend**
Present Indicative	**ich stehe, du stehst, er steht, wir stehen, ihr steht, Sie stehen, sie stehen**
Present Subjunctive	**ich (stehe) stünde/stände du stehest, er stehe, (wir stehen), ihr stehet, (Sie stehen, sie stehen)**
Simple Past	**ich stand**
Imperfect Subjunctive	**ich stünde, ich stände**
Past Participle	**gestanden**
Conversational Past	**ich habe gestanden**
Past Perfect Indicative	**ich hatte gestanden**
Present Perfect Subjunctive	**ich (habe) hätte gestanden**
Past Perfect Subjunctive	**ich hätte gestanden**
Future	**ich werde stehen**
Future Perfect	**ich werde gestanden haben**
Conditional	**ich würde stehen**
Conditional Perfect	**ich würde gestanden haben**
Imperative	**steh! stehen wir! steht! stehen Sie!**

stehlen *to steal*	
Present Participle	stehlend
Present Indicative	ich stehle, du stiehlst, er stiehlt, wir stehlen, ihr stehlt, Sie stehlen, sie stehlen
Present Subjunctive	ich (stehle) stöhle/stähle, du stehlest, er stehle, (wir stehlen), ihr stehlet, (Sie stehlen, sie stehlen)
Simple Past	ich stahl
Imperfect Subjunctive	ich stöhle, ich stähle
Past Participle	gestohlen
Conversational Past	ich habe gestohlen
Past Perfect Indicative	ich hatte gestohlen
Present Perfect Subjunctive	ich (habe) hätte gestohlen
Past Perfect Subjunctive	ich hätte gestohlen
Future	ich werde stehlen
Future Perfect	ich werde gestohlen haben
Conditional	ich würde stehlen
Conditional Perfect	ich würde gestohlen haben
Imperative	stiehl! stehlen wir! stehlt! stehlen Sie!

springen *to jump*	
Present Participle	springend
Present Indicative	ich springe, du springst, er springt, wir springen, ihr springt, Sie springen, sie springen
Present Subjunctive	ich (springe) spränge, du springest, er springe, (wir springen), ihr springet, (Sie springen, sie springen)
Simple Past	ich sprang
Imperfect Subjunctive	ich spränge
Past Participle	gesprungen
Conversational Past	ich bin gesprungen
Past Perfect Indicative	ich war gesprungen
Present Perfect Subjunctive	ich sei gesprungen
Past Perfect Subjunctive	ich wäre gesprungen
Future	ich werde springen
Future Perfect	ich werde gesprungen sein
Conditional	ich würde springen
Conditional Perfect	ich würde gesprungen sein
Imperative	spring! springen wir! springt! springen Sie!

tragen *to carry*	
Present Participle	**tragend**
Present Indicative	**ich trage, du trägst, er trägt, wir tragen, ihr tragt, Sie tragen, sie tragen**
Present Subjunctive	**ich (trage) trüge, du tragest, er trage, (wir tragen), ihr traget, (Sie tragen, sie tragen)**
Simple Past	**ich trug**
Imperfect Subjunctive	**ich trüge**
Past Participle	**getragen**
Conversational Past	**ich (habe) hätte getragen**
Past Perfect Indicative	**ich hatte getragen**
Present Perfect Subjunctive	**ich habe getragen**
Past Perfect Subjunctive	**ich hätte getragen**
Future	**ich werde tragen**
Future Perfect	**ich werde getragen haben**
Conditional	**ich würde tragen**
Conditional Perfect	**ich würde getragen haben**
Imperative	**trag! tragen wir! tragt! tragen Sie!**

treffen *to meet*	
Present Participle	**treffend**
Present Indicative	**ich treffe, du triffst, er trifft, wir treffen, ihr trefft, Sie treffen, sie treffen**
Present Subjunctive	**ich (treffe) träfe, du treffest, er treffe, (wir treffen), ihr treffet, (Sie treffen, sie treffen)**
Simple Past	**ich traf**
Imperfect Subjunctive	**ich träfe**
Past Participle	**getroffen**
Conversational Past	**ich habe getroffen**
Past Perfect Indicative	**ich hätte getroffen**
Present Perfect Subjunctive	**ich (habe) hätte getroffen**
Past Perfect Subjunctive	**ich hätte getroffen**
Future	**ich werde treffen**
Future Perfect	**ich werde getroffen haben**
Conditional	**ich würde treffen**
Conditional Perfect	**ich würde getroffen haben**
Imperative	**triff! treffen wir! trefft! treffen Sie!**

trinken *to drink*

Present Participle	**trinkend**
Present Indicative	**ich trinke, du trinkst, er trinkt, wir trinken, ihr trinkt, Sie trinken, sie trinken**
Present Subjunctive	**ich (trinke) tränke, du trinkest, er trinke, (wir trinken), ihr trinket, (Sie trinken, sie trinken)**
Simple Past	**ich trank**
Imperfect Subjunctive	**ich tränke**
Past Participle	**getrunken**
Conversational Past	**ich habe getrunken**
Past Perfect Indicative	**ich hatte getrunken**
Present Perfect Subjunctive	**ich (habe) hätte getrunken**
Past Perfect Subjunctive	**ich hätte getrunken**
Future	**ich werde trinken**
Future Perfect	**ich werde getrunken haben**
Conditional	**ich würde trinken**
Conditional Perfect	**ich würde getrunken haben**
Imperative	**trink! trinken wir! trinkt! trinken Sie!**

tun *to do*	
Present Participle	**tuend**
Present Indicative	**ich tue, du tust, er tut, wir tun, ihr tut, Sie tun, sie tun**
Present Subjunctive	**ich (tue) täte, du tuest, er tue, (wir tun), ihr tuet, (Sie tun, sie tun)**
Simple Past	**ich tat**
Imperfect Subjunctive	**ich täte**
Past Participle	**getan**
Conversational Past	**ich habe getan**
Past Perfect Indicative	**ich hatte getan**
Present Perfect Subjunctive	**ich (habe) hätte getan**
Past Perfect Subjunctive	**ich hätte getan**
Future	**ich werde tun**
Future Perfect	**ich werde getan haben**
Conditional	**ich würde tun**
Conditional Perfect	**ich würde getan haben**
Imperative	**tue! tun wir! tut! tun Sie!**

vergessen *to forget*	
Present Participle	vergessend
Present Indicative	ich vergesse, du vergisst, er vergisst, wir vergessen, ihr vergesst, Sie vergessen, sie vergessen
Present Subjunctive	ich (vergesse) vergäße, du vergessest, er vergesse, (wir vergessen), ihr vergesset, (Sie vergessen, sie vergessen)
Simple Past	ich vergaß
Imperfect Subjunctive	ich vergäße
Past Participle	vergessen
Conversational Past	ich habe vergessen
Past Perfect Indicative	ich hatte vergessen
Present Perfect Subjunctive	ich (habe) hätte vergessen
Past Perfect Subjunctive	ich hätte vergessen
Future	ich werde vergessen
Future Perfect	ich werde vergessen haben
Conditional	ich würde vergessen
Conditional Perfect	ich würde vergessen haben
Imperative	vergiss! vergessen wir! vergesst! vergessen Sie!

verlieren *to lose*	
Present Participle	verlierend
Present Indicative	ich verliere, du verlierst, er verliert, wir verlieren, ihr verliert, Sie verlieren, sie verlieren
Present Subjunctive	ich (verliere) verlöre, du verlierest, er verliere, (wir verlieren), ihr verlieret, (Sie verlieren, sie verlieren)
Simple Past	ich verlor
Imperfect Subjunctive	ich verlöre
Past Participle	verloren
Conversational Past	ich habe verloren
Past Perfect Indicative	ich hatte verloren
Present Perfect Subjunctive	ich (habe) hätte verloren
Past Perfect Subjunctive	ich hätte verloren
Future	ich werde verlieren
Future Perfect	ich werde verloren haben
Conditional	ich würde verlieren
Conditional Perfect	ich würde verloren haben
Imperative	verlier(e)! verlieren wir! verliert! verlieren Sie!

The following is a list of German language websites and other informational websites that students of German may find interesting and useful.

www.livinglanguage.com	The Living Language site offers online courses, descriptions of supplemental learning material, resources for teachers and librarians, and much more
www.leo.org	A comprehensive online German dictionary
www.deutschland.de	Germany portal
www.schweiz.ch	Switzerland portal
www.oesterreich.at	Austria portal
www.dw-world.de	*Deutsche Welle,* broadcasting live news on the internet
www.spiegel.de	The German magazine *Der Spiegel,* featuring articles on politics and current events
www.stern.de	The German magazine *Der Stern,* featuring a variety of articles on entertainment and current affairs
www.tagesspiegel.de	The Berlin daily *Der Tagesspiegel* (published in Berlin)

www.zeit.de	The national weekly *Die Zeit* (published in Hamburg)
www.welt.de	The national daily *Die Welt* (published in Hamburg)
www.mz-web.de	The *Mitteldeutsche Zeitung* (published in Halle)
www.sueddeutsche.de	The daily *Die Süddeutsche* (published in Munich)
www.faz.net	The daily *Frankfurter Allgemeine Zeitung* (published in Frankfurt, Main)
www.bahn.de	German train travel
www.oebb.at	Austrian train travel
www.rail.ch	Swiss train travel
www.daskochrezept.de	Traditional German recipes
www.wohnung-heute.de	Real estate for German speaking countries